MW01079130

Life of David

Discipleship Lessons from 1 and 2 Samuel

and Bible Study Commentary for Personal Devotional Use, Small Groups or
Sunday School Classes, and Sermon Preparation for Pastors and Teachers

JesusWalk® Bible Study Series

by Dr. Ralph F. Wilson
Director, Joyful Heart Renewal Ministries

Additional books, and reprint licenses are available at:
www.jesuswalk.com/books/david.htm

Free Participant Guide handout sheets are available at:
www.jesuswalk.com/david/david-lesson-handouts.pdf

JesusWalk® Publications
Loomis, California

Paperback

ISBN-13: 978-0-9847340-6-1

ISBN-10: 0984734066

Library of Congress Control Number: 2012913441

Library of Congress subject headings:

    David, King of Israel

    Bible. O.T. Samuel, 1st

    Bible. O.T. Samuel, 2nd

    Bible. O.T. Kings, 1st

Suggested Classifications

    Library of Congress: BS580.D3

    Dewey Decimal System: 222.4

Published by JesusWalk® Publications, P.O. Box 565, Loomis, CA 95650-0565, USA.

JesusWalk is a registered trademark and Joyful Heart is a trademark of Joyful Heart Renewal Ministries.

Unless otherwise noted, all the Bible verses quoted are from the New International Version (International Bible Society, 1973, 1978), used by permission.

120806

This book is dedicated to:

My mother-in-law Ruth Costello, who encouraged me to write it;

To my wife, Jean, with whom I've had many discussions of David's life;

To the participants in the Wednesday Potluck Bible Study

at the First Baptist Church of Nevada City; and

To the men of my Tuesday Morning Denny's Bible Study

who worked together with me

to find the connections between David's story and our own.

Preface

Why do people love David's story?

First, **David's story is exciting**. David's encounter with Goliath is probably the best-known Bible account of all time. A shepherd boy trusts in Yahweh and defeats a huge, experienced warrior with only his faith, a sling, and a stone. There are "chance" encounters in caves and deserts, beautiful women and palace intrigue. There are last-minute escapes amidst pursuits by two kings – first Saul and then his own son Absalom.

James J. Tissot, "Festivities in Honor of King David" (1896-1902), gouache on board, The Jewish Museum, New York.

Ultimately, David prevails to conquer and administer a huge empire in the east Mediterranean. It's exhilarating!

Second, **David's story is inspiring**. This mighty warrior is both a committed believer and a prolific singer-songwriter, whose lyrics still inspire readers 3,000 years after they were first set down. His faith and love and Spirit-inspired insights fill nearly 75 songs that we have available. He has learned to trust Yahweh in the depths of depression and the extremes of danger. And he knows how to offer the high praises of God as he sees God in all his glory. David points us to his God.

Third, **David's story is human**. This lover of God has flaws that threaten to destroy his spirit and his family. In David, we watch a man who falls very low, but repents to take hold of God's grace and forgiveness, and is ultimately restored and redeemed. He points us to hope in God's mercy for ourselves.

Fourth, **David's story is manly**. Men in our day struggle with the notion that faith in God is primarily for women – that real men don't do church! David's life helps us see how a great warrior and leader of men works to integrate his faith into his own life and to allow his faith to direct the course of his career.

Fifth, **David's story is morally challenging**. He is guided by moral principles that find their root in Yahweh. He rules righteously, rather than selfishly. And he sets a standard for righteousness in government that challenges us today. He lives in a world far from our own – with palaces and harems as well as giants and fierce hand-to-hand combat. But underlying the differences are the moral guidelines that keep us steady.

Finally, **David's story is ongoing**. God chose him to be the ancestor and type of the Messiah, the Son of David and Son of God – Jesus of Nazareth. The foundational Davidic Covenant – one of the most important themes in the whole Bible – finds its fulfillment in Christ, who proclaimed that the Kingdom of God is at hand. To understand Jesus, you need to start with David.

I think you'll find this *Life of David* useful for a number of purposes. It was originally written for an e-mail Bible study in the JesusWalk® Bible Study Series. After each of the three or four discussion questions for each lesson, you'll find a URL which leads you to an online forum where others are grappling with the same questions. You're invited to participate.

This material is designed to aid your study of David's life, with a special emphasis on what we can learn as Jesus' disciples today. Twenty maps and charts help you understand David's family as well as the geography of his sojourns, escapes, battles, and conquests. historical background and geopolitical context will help you to understand David in his own world and grasp his internal complexity.

He is a sweet psalmist, a leader, and a lover. He's a mighty warrior, a prophet and judge, a king, and the priest of his people. And he is a great sinner. But he takes hold of God's amazing grace and emerges with his faith restored. David teaches us about ourselves.

Classes and small groups will find this a helpful curriculum guide to their study of 1 and 2 Samuel, with handouts as well as thorough preparation for the leader. Thought-provoking questions will prompt many insightful discussions. If you find some of the lessons too long for the time you have, feel free to break a lesson into two parts to digest it more thoroughly.

Preachers and teachers will find a great deal of their research done for them. The lessons are heavily footnoted for those who want to dig deeper into word definitions, but the footnotes are optional for the general student.

This isn't a verse-by-verse commentary, however. We're covering 43 chapters in 13 lessons – 1 Samuel 14 to 31, all of 2 Samuel, plus 1 Kings 1-2. As a result, we'll move more quickly over much of the narrative material, but slow down when it comes to key events and important spiritual lessons. The goal is to help you see the major themes and big picture of David's life, while still absorbing the important details.

I hope that you'll be encouraged and inspired as you study the life of David. I know I have been! My prayer is that while you grapple with this passage of Scripture, the Holy Spirit will work with the Word to make you more like Jesus, the *Son of* David.

Yours in Christ's service,
Dr. Ralph F. Wilson
August 6, 2012
Loomis, California

Table of Contents

References and Abbreviations

Anderson   Arnold A. Anderson, *2 Samuel* (Word Biblical Commentary; Word, 1989)

BDB   Francis Brown, S.R. Driver, and Charles A. Briggs, *A Hebrew and English Lexicon of the Old Testament* (Clarendon Press, 1907)

Baldwin   Joyce G. Baldwin, *1 & 2 Samuel: An Introduction and Commentary* (Tyndale Old Testament Commentaries; Inter-Varsity Press, 1988)

Bergen   Robert D. Bergen, *1, 2 Samuel* (New American Commentary; Broadman & Holman, 1996)

Bright   John Bright, *History of Israel* (Fourth edition; Westminster John Knox Press, 2000)

Davis   John J. Davis, *The Birth of a Kingdom: Studies in I-II Samuel and I Kings 1-11* (Baker, 1970)

DOTHB   Bill T. Arnold and H.G.M. Williamson (editors), *Dictionary of the Old Testament: Historical Books* (InterVarsity Press, 2005)

Holladay   William L. Holladay, *A Concise Hebrew and Aramaic Lexicon of the Old Testament*, based on the Lexical work of Ludwig Koehler and Walter Baumgartner (Grand Rapids: Eerdmans / Leiden: E. J. Brill, 1988)

ISBE   Geoffrey W. Bromiley (general editor), *The International Standard Bible Encyclopedia* (Eerdmans, 1979-1988; revised from the 1915 edition)

Jones   Gwilym H. Jones, *1 and 2 Kings* (The New Century Bible; Eerdmans / Marshall Morgan & Scott, 1984, volume 1)

KJV   King James Version

Klein   Ralph W. Klein, *1 Samuel* (Word Biblical Commentary; Word, 1983)

Macmillan   Yohanan Aharoni and Michael Avi-Yonah, *The Macmillan Bible Atlas*
Bible Atlas   (Macmillan, 1968)

NIV   New International Version

NRSV   New Revised Standard Version

Oxford Bible   Herbert G. May (editor), *Oxford Bible Atlas* (London: Oxford
Atlas   University Press, 1962)

Tsumura   David Toshio Tsumura, *The First Book of Samuel* (New International
                    Commentary on the Old Testament; Eerdmans, 2007)

TWOT   R. Laird Harris, Gleason L. Archer, Jr., and Bruce K. Waltke, (editors),
                    Theological Wordbook of the Old Testament (2 volumes, Moody Press,
                    1980)

Reprint Guidelines

Copying the Handouts. In some cases, small groups or Sunday school classes would like to use these notes to study this material. That's great. An appendix provides copies of handouts designed for classes and small groups. There is no charge whatsoever to print out as many copies of the handouts as you need for participants.

Free Participant Guide handout sheets are available at:

www.jesuswalk.com/david/david-lesson-handouts.pdf

All charts and notes are copyrighted and must bear the line:

"Copyright © 2012, Ralph F. Wilson. All rights reserved. Reprinted by permission."

You may not resell these notes to other groups or individuals outside your congregation. You may, however, charge people in your group enough to cover your copying costs.

Copying the book (or the majority of it) in your congregation or group, you are requested to purchase a reprint license for each book. A Reprint License, $2.50 for each copy is available for purchase at

www.jesuswalk.com/books/david.htm

Or you may send a check to:

Dr. Ralph F. Wilson
JesusWalk Publications
PO Box 565
Loomis, CA 95650, USA

The Scripture says,

"The laborer is worthy of his hire" (Luke 10:7) and "Anyone who receives instruction in the word must share all good things with his instructor." (Galatians 6:6)

However, if you are from a third world country or an area where it is difficult to transmit money, please make a small contribution instead to help the poor in your community.

Introduction to the Life of David

On any measure of Old Testament saints, David is in the first-tier, along with Abraham and Moses. The name "David" appears to be connected with the Hebrew verbal root *dwd*, "to love," so his name probably means "beloved."[1] He is an amazing, multi-faceted, multi-gifted person.

First, he was a musician, "the sweet psalmist of Israel" (2 Samuel 23:1). As a youth, he practiced the harp on the sheep fields of Bethlehem. As a young man he became a court musician for Israel's first King – Saul. But as he grew, he began to write down the inspired songs or psalms that he wrote, so that his own compositions fill nearly half of the Book of Psalms.

But more than just a prolific lyricist and musician, David was a worshipper. His music wasn't just popular love songs. It was worship. It comprised the intense emotions of struggle and the high freedom of praise and everything in between. Music gave voice to David's faith and his soul-felt prayers.

Most musicians I know are gentle, artsy people. But David was the opposite. He was a renowned warrior, the most famous warrior in the history of Israel. His courage to stand up to and defeat Goliath is legendary. Saul made him an officer in his army where he began to win battles – not by standing back and giving orders, but by leading his men into battle himself, defeating his foes by the strength of his arm – and his faith in God! When Saul became jealous and began pursuing David, he gathered a band of 400 men, then

Dante Gabriel Rosetti (1828-1882), "King David" (1858-1864), watercolor on paper, 279 x 127 mm, from "The Seed of David". Tate Gallery, London.

[1] David F. Payne, "David," ISBE 1:876.

600, whom he forged into the fearsome army of a fugitive warlord. Because of his own courage and prowess as a warrior, he attracted the best warriors in the land to join him. David was a warrior.

But there's more to him. David was a nation-builder. Before him, Saul functioned as a local monarch over a loosely organized group of tribes. Through his own diplomatic efforts, David was able to unite these tribes into one nation. He conquered Jerusalem and made it capital of his growing empire. He built a palace, then brought the ark to reside in his new capital. Once he had consolidated power, David began to subdue the neighboring kingdoms that had pressured Israel's borders. He turned them into his vassals – the Philistines, the Edomites, Moabites, and Ammorites. When he conquered Hadadezer king of Zobah, an Aramean overlord of kingdoms all the way east to the Euphrates River, David became king over an empire that extended from the Brook of Egypt in the Negev Desert east to the great river. David was a nation-builder.

Mythic Hero or Real Person?

When you realize the extent of David's influence as he "served God's purpose in his own generation" (Acts 13:36), it's amazing that some people have asserted that he didn't really exist at all, that he was merely a myth.

In the mid-twentieth century a group of "biblical minimalists" began to doubt publicly that David and Solomon and the United Monarchy ever existed. After all, they said, there were no archaeological inscriptions and no references in any ancient literature except the Bible. Minimalist Philip Davies went so far as to remark that he "suspects that the figure of King David is about as historical as King Arthur."[2]

This rather arrogant view, which is entirely dismissive of the Biblical record, rests on the weak assumption that all the available archaeological evidence has been excavated, though only a small amount has been unearthed to date. Fortunately, however, several archaeological inscriptions *have* surfaced that clearly point to the historicity of King David's reign:

1. An inscription from an Old Aramaic stela in Tell Dan (dated about 840 BC) refers to the "House of David" in the context of a king.

2. An inscription on the stela of Mesha King of Moab also refers to the "House of David" in about the same period.

---

[2] Philip R. Davies, "'House of David' Built on Sand: The Sins of the Biblical Maximizers," *Biblical Archaeological Review*, 20, number 4 (1994), p. 55.

3. An inscription at Karnak by Pharaoh Shoshenq I records a victory over Rehoboam and Jeroboam in 926/925 BC referring to a place name in the Negev or south Judean area as the "heights of David," an inscription carved within 50 years of David's own lifetime.[3]

Was David a real person? Yes indeed!

Dating of David's Reign

When did David live and reign? The absolute date of David's reign is based primarily on counting backwards from a fixed event, specifically the Battle of Qarqar in 853 BC, in which Israel's King Ahab took part, as recorded on the Kurkh stela.[4] Dating is complex when you get into it. K.A. Kitchen determines the date for David's 40-year reign from about 1010 to 970 BC.[5] The primary scripture with relative dates of David's life is as follows:

> "David was thirty years old when he became king, and he reigned forty years. In Hebron he reigned over Judah seven years and six months, and in Jerusalem he reigned over all Israel and Judah thirty-three years." (2 Samuel 5:4-5; cf. 1 Kings 2:11)

While it's difficult to pinpoint relative dates for events in David's life, Appendix 4 gives approximate dates and ages at various points in his life.

Composition and Authorship of 1 and 2 Samuel and 1 Kings

Our primary source material for the study of David's life is found in 1 and 2 Samuel and the first chapter of 1 Kings, with some supplementary information in 1 Chronicles.

First and Second Samuel are actually part of one book in the Hebrew Bible, along with 1 and 2 Kings. It wasn't until the Greek Septuagint translation in the second century BC that these books were divided, perhaps so they would fit on standard-length scrolls. In the Septuagint, these four books are known as *Basileiōn A,B,C,D*, the four books of the kingdoms.

Authorship is obscure. Obviously, the editors drew upon a number of contemporary sources, since some are mentioned, such as, the Book of Jashar (2 Samuel 1:18), and the books of the annals of Solomon and the kings of Israel and Judah (1 Kings 11:41; 14:19; 14:29), which have not been preserved. Scholars identify several probable source documents that are woven into the narrative, such as the History of David's Rise (1

---

[3] Kitchen, *Reliability of the OT*, pp. 90-93.

[4] Baldwin, *1 and 2 Samuel*, p. 19.

[5] K.A. Kitchen, "Chronology," DOTHB, 183-184. K.A. Kitchen, *On the Reliability of the Old Testament* (Eerdmans, 2003), pp. 82-83. So John N. Oswalt, "Chronology of the OT," ISBE 1:673-685.

Samuel 16 – 2 Samuel 5:10 or 7:29) and the Succession Narrative (2 Samuel 9-20 and 1 Kings 1-2).

The composition of these books was widely debated in the twentieth century, but it is also obscure. Currently, their composition is seen as the work of one or more Deuteronomistic editors, perhaps first in the time of Josiah and then again during the exile.

Our text of 1 and 2 Samuel is derived primarily from three sources: the Masoretic Hebrew text, the Greek Septuagint translation, and Samuel manuscripts found among the Dead Sea Scrolls at Qumran. Of these, the Masoretic Hebrew text doesn't seem to have fared as well in transmission as the other two sources, though differences are minor.

Composition and Authorship of 1 and 2 Chronicles

First Chronicles adds quite a bit of material not included in 2 Samuel about David's involvement in preparing for building the temple, as well as in restructuring Levitical worship.

1 and 2 Chronicles were probably written sometime after the return from exile, as early as 527 BC and perhaps up to a century later. The purpose of Chronicles seems to be to help the returnees, most of whom had been born in exile, to gain a better understanding of who they are as the nation of Israel, a grasp of the David Covenant, and instructions concerning worship in the newly-constructed temple. We don't know much about the author or group of authors who composed Chronicles, except that they were probably Levitical scribes or priests. I refer to the author simply as "the Chronicler."[6]

Who Were the Philistines?

Before we get into the text itself, we need to examine the Philistines, Israel's neighbors to the west, with whom there is constant conflict during this period.

The Philistines apparently immigrated from the Aegean area in the early to mid-twelfth century BC. They settled primarily along the southwestern coastal strip of Canaan, the name "Palestine" deriving from the name "Philistine." The borders of Philistia are the Mediterranean on the west, the Brook of Egypt on the South, the low foothills of the Shepelah on the east, and the Yarkon River in the North, though at times they gained a foothold farther east into Israelite territory. They seem to have been a

---

[6] Rodney K. Duke, "Chronicles, Books of," DOTHB, pp. 161-181; Martin J. Selman, *1 Chronicles: An Introduction and Commentary* (Tyndale Old Testament Commentaries; Inter-Varsity Press, 1994), pp. 19-75.

loose confederation of five city-states: Ashdod, Ashkelon, Ekron, Gaza, and Gath (Joshua 13:3b). For the most part these city-states waged war singly, but on occasion they gathered together to wage a common battle, such as the Battle of Gilboa against the Israelites, in which Saul and Jonathan were killed (1 Samuel 28:1; 29:1-11).[7]

Of these cities, all but Gath have been positively identified in archaeological digs. Gath is probably to be identified with Tell es-Safi.[8]

Now that we've examined some of the introductory issues, let's turn to the events that ushered David onto the stage of history.

---

[7] Carl S. Ehrlich, "Philistines," DOTHB, pp. 782-792; William S. LaSor, "Philistines," ISBE 2:841-846.
[8] Steven M. Ortiz, "Gath," DOTHB, pp. 305-309.

1. Samuel Anoints David as King (1 Samuel 15-16)

We begin David's story not with Jesse his father, but with Saul, Israel's first king. Samuel the prophet had anointed Saul (1 Samuel 10:1) and the Holy Spirit had come upon him (10:6, 10). He ruled from his home town of Gibeah and helped deliver Israel from the threat of the Philistine attacks.

Saul's First Disobedience (13:8-14)

While Saul was a reasonably effective military leader, it became clear that his love for the Lord wasn't strong, nor was he very careful about obedience to God's direction through the prophet Samuel. The prophet had told him to wait as long as seven days for Samuel to offer a sacrifice to the Lord, before the army went into battle with the Philistines (13:8-13). But the prophet didn't come within that time – and Saul's troops were beginning to go home – so Saul offered the sacrifice himself. Just then Samuel appeared and told him,

Elizabeth Jane Gardner Bouguereau (American painter, 1837-1922), "The Shepherd David" (1895), oil on canvas, 60.5 x 40.4 inches, National Museum of Women in the Arts, Washington DC.

> "You acted foolishly. You have not kept the command the LORD your God gave you; if you had, he would have established your kingdom over Israel for all time. But now your kingdom will not endure; the LORD has sought out a man after his own heart and appointed him leader of his people, because you have not kept the LORD's command." (13:13-14)

Saul's Second Disobedience (1 Samuel 15:1-21)

The second time Saul disobeys the command of the Lord concerned the Amalekites, an arch enemy of Israel. This was a tribe that had attacked the children of Israel in the wilderness as they were escaping from Egypt under Moses (Exodus 8:7-16). Saul was told to attack the Amalekites and "totally destroy[1] everything that belongs to them," including their cattle (15:2-3). But Saul fails to obey fully. He preserves all the Amalekites' cattle!

The word of the Lord comes to Samuel at night:

> "I am grieved that I have made Saul king, because he has turned away from me and has not carried out my instructions." (1 Samuel 15:11a)

God isn't just looking at Saul's disobedient actions. He also sees Saul's heart that prompts this kind of disobedience – and is grieved!

Samuel goes to meet Saul at Gilgal, after he has returned from the battle with the Amalekites. Saul greets him with the words, "The LORD bless you! I have carried out the LORD's instructions." But Samuel replies, "What then is this bleating of sheep in my ears? What is this lowing of cattle that I hear?" (15:13-14).

Saul now begins to excuse himself. "The soldiers brought the cattle," he says, then adds "... to sacrifice them to the Lord, of course."

To Obey Is Better than Sacrifice (15:22-23)

Now Samuel pronounces a terrible judgment from the Lord, one from which we can learn much!

> "Does the LORD delight in burnt offerings and sacrifices
> as much as in obeying the voice of the LORD?
> To obey is better than sacrifice,
> and to heed is better than the fat of rams.
> For rebellion is like the sin of divination,
> and arrogance like the evil of idolatry.

---

[1] "Totally destroy" here and in 15:8, 9, 15, 18, 20, and 21 is the Hebrew word *hāram*. The basic meaning is the exclusion of an object from the use or abuse of man and its irrevocable surrender to God. The word is related to an Arabic root meaning "to prohibit, especially to ordinary use." The word "harem," meaning the special quarters for Muslim wives, comes from it. It is related also to an Ethiopic root, meaning "to forbid, prohibit, lay under a curse." Surrendering something to God meant devoting it exclusively to the service of God or putting it under a ban for utter destruction. Usually *hāram* means a ban for utter destruction, the compulsory dedication of something which impedes or resists God's work, which is considered to be accursed before God (Leonard J. Wood, *hāram*, TWOT #744a).

Because you have rejected the word of the LORD,
he has rejected you as king." (15:22-23)

Let's look carefully at the words in this passage.

Delight (*hēpes*).[2] So often we're not interested in really pleasing the Lord, but in just getting by, and perhaps obeying the letter (rather than the spirit) of the law. Those who love the Lord seek to delight and please him. Those who merely give intellectual assent to him don't really care. God looks at the heart (as we see in 16:7b).

Obedience (*shāma '*).[3] Obedience is a reliable sign of actual love for God. Jesus said, "If you love me, you will obey what I command" (John 14:15). It's pretty simple actually.

Voice of the LORD.[4] God can speak in many ways, for example, through prophets, through Scripture, and through pastors. In this case, Samuel had specifically prefaced his command: "Listen now to the message from the LORD" (15:1). We are responsible to obey what God says to us – in any form.

Rebellion[5] is doing what we decide to do rather than what God tells us. We excuse ourselves by our difficult circumstances, as did Saul. We may fool ourselves, but God is not amused. Obedience is doing what God tells us to do. Rebellion is doing it our way.

The sin of divination, witchcraft.[6] Notice carefully that the text doesn't say that rebellion *is* witchcraft! It says that rebellion is *like* witchcraft. I think the NRSV catches the proper sense: "For rebellion is no less a sin than divination." It is just as bad as witchcraft. Baldwin notes:

---

[2] *Hēpes* is the noun, "delight, pleasure." The basic meaning of the verb is to feel great favor towards something, "to experience emotional delight." In the case of the verb *hāpēs*, the object solicits favor by its own intrinsic qualities. The subject is easily attracted to it because it is desirable. Other parallel stems don't connote the degree of emotional involvement as this verb stem (Leon J. Wood, *hāpēs*, TWOT #712b).

[3] "Obeying" (15:22a) and "to obey" (15:22b) is *shāma '*, "hear, listen to, obey." *Shāma '* has the basic meaning "to hear." This is extended in various ways, generally involving an effective hearing or listening: 1) "listen to," "pay attention," 2) "obey" (with words such as "commandment" etc.), 3) "answer prayer," "hear," 4) "understand" and 5) "hear critically," "examine (in court)." The derived stems have appropriately modified meanings (Hermann J. Austel, *shāma '*, TWOT #2412).

[4] "Voice" is *kôl*, "voice, sound, noise…. *Kôl* primarily signifies a sound produced by the vocal cords, actual or figurative (*Kwl*, TWOT #1998a).

[5] "Rebellion" is the noun *merî*, from the verb *mārâ* "be rebellious against, disobedient towards." In the Hiphil stem the verb has the meaning, "to provoke (by defiance)" (Victor P. Hamilton, *mārâ*, TWOT #1242a).

[6] "Divination" (NIV, NRSV), "witchcraft" (KJV) is *qesem*, "Divination, witchcraft, sorcery, fortunetelling, omen, lot, oracle, decision." The exact meaning of this variety of occultism is unknown. Shaking or flinging down arrows, consulting seraphim, and hepatoscopy (looking at the liver) may be subcategories of *qesem* (Robert L. Alden, *qāsam*, TWOT #2044a).

"Obstinate resistance to God exalts self-will to the place of authority, which belongs only to God. That is why it is as bad as divination (by evil spirits), and tantamount to idolatry, for another god, self, has usurped his place."[7]

Arrogance, stubbornness.[8] Rebellion goes hand in hand with arrogance against God. We think we know better than God, so we do it our way instead of his – often with tragic results.

God has appointed Saul king to reign over Israel on God's behalf. God is the great suzerain; Saul is his vassal king. But by his rebellion, self will, and arrogance, Saul has disqualified himself to reign for God. He will be replaced!

Dear friend, have you rebelled against God's word and against the commands of Jesus? How long will you remain in rebellion? Jesus took your sin of rebellion on himself when he died on the cross. But you must repent of this sin if you want Jesus to take it away.

What follows is the first discussion question of this lesson series. Think deeply about the questions. If you go to the trouble of writing down your answers, it will help you form your answer carefully and thoughtfully. Then click on the web address (URL) following the question to post your answer on an online forum and read others' answers. Grasping spiritual lessons at the heart-level is the whole point of studying the Life of David. Do it!

Q1. (1 Samuel 15:22-23). What is rebellion? In what way is rebellion as bad as witchcraft or occult practices? What does rebellion have to do with arrogance? What can we do when we find rebellion against God in our hearts? What happens if we do nothing?
http://www.joyfulheart.com/forums/index.php?showtopic=1157

Samuel Leaves Saul (15:34-35)

At Saul's begging, Samuel doesn't shun Saul publicly, but appears alongside the king so he won't lose face. However, this is the last time the two are together. This chapter closes on a sad note:

---

[7] Baldwin, *1 and 2 Samuel*, p. 115.

[8] "Arrogance" (NIV), "stubbornness" (NRSV, KJV), "insubordination" (NASB) is the verb *pāṣar*, "push, press" (TWOT #1801), "urge someone strongly" (Holladay 295).

"³⁴ Then Samuel left for Ramah, but Saul went up to his home in Gibeah of Saul. ³⁵ Until the day Samuel died, he did not go to see Saul again, though Samuel **mourned** for him. And the LORD was **grieved** that he had made Saul king over Israel." (15:34-35)

Samuel "mourned" (NIV, KJV), "grieved" (NRSV) for Saul (15:35a; 16:1). The Lord "was grieved/sorry" (NIV, NRSV), "repented" (KJV) that he had appointed Saul (15:35b). Both words are the same in Hebrew: 'ābal, "mourn, lament." The word is also used to describe mourning rites for the dead.[9]

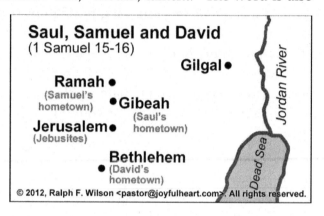

The lesson of this chapter is that we are to seek to please the Lord. That is what it means to love the Lord with all your heart, soul, mind, and strength.

> "Be imitators of God, therefore, as dearly loved children.... Live as children of light ... and find out what pleases the Lord." (Ephesians 5:1, 8b, 10)

Samuel Is Sent to Bethlehem (16:1-2)

Samuel loves Saul, and sees Saul's failure as his own failure. But God won't let him mope about the pain of the past. God gives Samuel a new mission.

> "The LORD said to Samuel, 'How long will you mourn for Saul, since I have rejected[10] him as king over Israel? Fill your horn with oil and be on your way; I am sending you to Jesse of Bethlehem. I have chosen one of his sons to be king.'" (16:1)

As Samuel gets ready for his trip, he takes a hollowed out ram's horn,[11] fills it with olive oil,[12] and plugs it so the oil won't splash out on his journey. Previously, Samuel

---

[9] J. Barton Payne, TWOT #6.

[10] "Rejected" is mā'as, "reject, despise." God rejects men who do not listen to him (Hosea 9:17). However, he will never reject them totally, for that would break his covenant (Leviticus 26:44) (Walter C. Kaiser, TWOT #1139).

[11] "Horn" is qeren, "Our word primarily denotes the horn(s) of various animals -- ram, wild oxen" (Leonard J. Copes, TWOT #2072a).

[12] "Oil" is shemen, "oil," generally olive oil, whether pure or prepared for various uses such as perfume or ointment. A synonym is yishār, which also means "olive oil." Shemen is the general word for olive oil in its various uses, while yishār refers to the fresh product. It is regularly associated with 'new wine' and 'grain' in reference to the produce of the land. Shemen played an important symbolic function in various

had used oil from a flask or vial[13] to anoint Saul king (10:1), after which the Holy Spirit came upon him (10:6, 9-10) and the Lord changed him into a different man (10:6). This mission is a similar king-making assignment.

Samuel tells the Lord, anointing a new king while the reigning king is still alive is dangerous – as if God didn't know. In the New Testament, Ananias expressed his fear to the Lord concerning his mission to commission Saul of Tarsus in Damascus (Acts 9), but God knew the danger. Saul had his fears, too, but rather than talking to the Lord about it, he had improvised – and disobeyed (13:7-14). In this case, God instructs Samuel to make a sacred sacrifice the reason for his visit (16:2b).

Notice God's words to Samuel: "I have chosen one of [Jesse's] sons to be king" (16:1d). "Chosen" (NIV), "provided for" (NRSV, KJV) is *rā'eh*, "see, look at, inspect." The word has several connotations, one of which is "to provide," usually of God's provision, such as God providing the lamb for Abraham on Mt. Moriah (Genesis 22:8, 14). As in English, to "see to" something is to "provide" it.[14] We worry about the failures of the past, but our God is our Provider, Yahweh Yireh (Jehovah Jireh) – from this same Hebrew root word: *rā'eh*. God has already provided for our needs and our future; we just need to go forward fearlessly following his direction.

Finding the King God Has Provided (16:3-11)

God tells Samuel to go to Bethlehem.

> "Invite Jesse to the sacrifice, and I will show you what to do. You are to anoint for me the one I indicate." (16:3)

"Indicate" (NIV), "name" (NRSV, KJV) is *'āmar*. The root idea of this extremely common word is "to say," rather than "to name." Wouldn't it be nice if God would say everything ahead of time, complete with names, times, and places? Certainly, God can do this – and occasionally does. But that isn't usually the way he works. He takes us one step at a time – probably so we don't run on ahead of him and improvise on our own! And that is how he led Samuel on this occasion. Samuel is told the father's name is Jesse. But the son is yet to be revealed.

---

consecration ceremonies. Thus kings and priests were anointed with oil, symbolizing the rich blessing of God (Hermann J. Austel, TWOT #2410c).

[13] "Flask" (NIV), "vial" (NRSV, KJV) is *pak*.

[14] Robert D. Culver, *rā'eh*, TWOT #2095.

Samuel has Jesse bring forward all his sons. When Samuel sees the firstborn, Eliab, he is sure he sees kingly material in this handsome man. But the Lord rebukes him inwardly – certainly not aloud!

> "⁶ When they came, he looked on Eliab and thought, 'Surely the LORD's anointed is now before the LORD.'
> ⁷ But the LORD said to Samuel, 'Do not look on his appearance or on the height of his stature, because I have rejected him; for the LORD does not see as mortals see; they look on the outward appearance, but the LORD looks on the heart.¹⁵'" (16:6-7)

This scene sounds like us. We're so used to judging by means of our physical sight and our social experience that it's easy to get it wrong when it comes to spiritual things. We need spiritual sight and discernment so we can see the heart. Samuel has natural instincts, but is mature enough to listen to the Holy Spirit and hear God's voice, to base his actions on what he hears from God.

Samuel goes through all the sons without God giving him the internal go-ahead. "Is there another son?" he asks. "Oh, the youngest," says Jesse, "but I didn't think he was important enough to bring to the feast."

Yet David, the youngest and least important in the family, is the one God has chosen.

Q2. (1 Samuel 16:3-12) How does this story teach us the importance of listening carefully to God's voice? What is our instinctive way of discerning? How is God teaching us to discern? How do we learn to listen to the Spirit?
http://www.joyfulheart.com/forums/index.php?showtopic=1158

A Handsome Young Man (16:12a)

Here's one of the few physical descriptions we have of David.

---

¹⁵ "Heart" is the noun *lēbāb*, "heart, understanding, mind" Concrete meanings of *lēb* referred to the internal organ and to analogous physical locations. However, in its abstract meanings, 'heart' became the richest biblical term for the totality of man's inner or immaterial nature. In biblical literature it is the most frequently used term for man's immaterial personality functions as well as the most inclusive term for them since, in the Bible, virtually every immaterial function of man is attributed to the "heart" (Andrew Bowling, TWOT #1071a).

"He was ruddy, with a fine appearance[16] and handsome features. [17]" (16:12a)

We're not really sure what "ruddy"[18] refers to. It may have referred to his red-tinted hair, or his reddish-brown or bronze complexion.[19]

David is a good-looking young man, which, I'm sure, makes it easier for him to lead and for people to follow. He *looks* like a hero – God made him that way. It's ironic, however, since God had just rebuked Samuel for looking on the outward appearance, for thinking he can "tell a book by its cover." But David's soul is beautiful, too – he is a man who loves the Lord and is "a man after God's own heart" (Acts 13:22; 1 Samuel 13:14).

David is depicted with red hair by Edward Burne-Jones, detail from 'David and Goliath' (1872), Vyner Memorial Window, Christ Church, Oxford, Lady Chapel, designed by Burne-Jones and made by Morris Co.

Anointing and the Holy Spirit (16:12b-13)

"[12b] Then the LORD said, 'Rise[20] and anoint him; he is the one.' [13] Then Samuel took the horn of oil, and anointed him in the presence of his brothers; and the spirit of the LORD came mightily upon David from that day forward." (16:12b-13)

Old Samuel has been sitting, waiting. But now, when the boy appears, God says to Samuel's spirit, "This is the one!" So Samuel gets up and pours oil on the boy's head anointing him. "Anoint" is *māshah*, from which we get the English word "Messiah" (*māshîah*) or "anointed one."[21] Anointing was known elsewhere in the ancient Near East

[16] "Fine appearance" (NIV), "beautiful eyes" (NRSV, NASB), "beautiful countenance" (KJV) uses two words: *yāpeh*, "fair, beautiful" + *ʿayin*, "eye" or "look, appearance." Holladay 271, meanings 1 and 2. Esthetically, *yāpeh* denotes "beauty as to outward appearance," used to describe women (Sarah, Rachel, Tamar, and Abishag) as well as men (Joseph and Absalom) (Paul R. Gilchrist, *yāpeh*, TWOT #890a).

[17] "Handsome features" (NIV), "handsome" (NRSV), "goodly to look at" (KJV) also consists of two words, *ṭôb*, "good" + *roʾî*, "looking, appearance" (Robert D. Culver, TWOT #2095f). While *ṭôb* means generally, "good," esthetic or sensual goodness may be denoted. It describes the beauty, or desirability of women. English idiom prefers "handsome" when the term describes men. (Andrew Bowling, *ṭôb*, TWOT #793a).

[18] "Ruddy" is *ʾadmônî*, "red, ruddy," from the same root (*ʾdm*) as Adam and Edom. (Leonard J. Coppes, TWOT #26h).

[19] Baldwin (*1 and 2 Samuel*, p. 122) speculates that, "ruddy implied light-skinned by comparison with his compatriots."

[20] "Rise/arise" is *qûm*, "rise, arise, stand." Our root refers essentially to the physical action "rising up" (Leonard J. Coppes, TWOT #1999).

[21] *Māshah* could refer in everyday usage to such acts as rubbing (*māshah*) a shield with oil (Isaiah 21:5), painting a house (Jeremiah 22:14), or applying oil to the body (Amos 6:6). Here it refers to ceremonial

among the Hittites and Egyptians,[22] and perhaps in the city-states of Canaan, but apparently not Assyria and Babylon.[23] Fleming says,

> "The effect of anointing was not just symbolic. Anointing oil was a pungent and durable perfume. Its fragrance persisted and its oil produced a permanent stain upon clothes."[24]

The anointing is significant politically. It designates David as the king-to-be and thus is dangerous for both Samuel and David. David is anointed twice more for political purposes by the men of Judah (2 Samuel 2:4a) and later by the elders of Israel (2 Samuel 5:3). But Samuel's anointing is much more significant spiritually than any political anointing! The narrator records:

> "From that day on the Spirit of the LORD came upon David in power." (16:13)

God's Spirit comes upon David. The phrase, "came in power" (NIV), "came mightily" (NRSV, NASB) uses the verb sālah, "rush,"[25] "be strong, effective, powerful."[26]

True, we see similar wording at Saul's anointing, where Samuel tells him that the Spirit will come upon him with power (10:6). But the simultaneous anointing and coming of the Holy Spirit upon David becomes the paradigm for the gift of the Holy Spirit in the New Testament. For example:

> "The Spirit of the Lord is on me, because he has anointed me...." (Luke 4:18)

> "But you will receive power when the Holy Spirit comes on you; and you will be my witnesses in Jerusalem, and in all Judea and Samaria, and to the ends of the earth." (Acts 1:8)

> "God anointed Jesus of Nazareth with the Holy Spirit and power...." (Acts 10:38)

> "He anointed us, set his seal of ownership on us, and put his Spirit in our hearts as a deposit, guaranteeing what is to come." (2 Corinthians 1:21b-22)

Indeed, twice the term "anointing" is substituted for "Holy Spirit" (1 John 2:20, 27).

---

induction into leadership offices, an action that involved the pouring of oil from a horn upon the head of an individual (Victor P. Hamilton, TWOT #1225).

[22] "In Egyptian culture it was the custom to anoint vassal kings, i.e., minor kings who owed allegiance to the great king of Egypt; in this light we may see the king of Israel as not a king in his own right, but a vassal of Yahweh, who is envisaged as the true king of Israel" (D.F. Payne, *I and II Samuel*, (Daily Study Bible; Westminster, 1982), p. 50, cited in Bergen, *1 and 2 Samuel*, p. 127).

[23] Franz Hesse, *chriō*, TDNT 9:497.

[24] Daniel E. Fleming, "Anointing," DOTHB 33.

[25] *Sālah*, TWOT #1916.

[26] *Sālah*, Holladay 306.

In some Christian circles, the term "an anointing" refers to a powerful ability to speak or minister. But, dear friends, whether we feel it or not, the Holy Spirit has come upon all Christian believers to give us power. According to our faith, so be it unto us.

When the Holy Spirit comes in power upon David it empowers him. The young man had been a harp-player and songwriter. Now he becomes an anointed, prophetic songwriter and the "sweet singer of Israel" (2 Samuel 23:1). The boy who has courageously defended his flock against the lion and the bear, now becomes the mighty warrior who defends his country against giants and Philistines (17:37). The young man who has shepherded his father's flock to find green pastures and still waters (Psalm 23:2), now becomes the shepherd[27] of a nation as its king – all by the powerful Holy Spirit who has come upon him.

> "I took you from the pasture and from following the flock to be ruler over my people Israel." (2 Samuel 7:8)

Q3. (1 Samuel 1:13) What is the significance of Samuel anointing David? What is the significance of the Holy Spirit coming upon David? How does this explain his success? How is the Holy Spirit upon us vital for our own success as disciples?
http://www.joyfulheart.com/forums/index.php?showtopic=1159

The Holy Spirit Comes upon David and Leaves Saul (16:14)

The Spirit who comes powerfully upon David is the same Spirit who simultaneously leaves Saul.

> "Now the Spirit of the LORD had departed from Saul, and an evil spirit from the LORD tormented him." (16:14)

This verse raises two questions:

1. How can the Holy Spirit leave a person? And

2. How can a good God send an evil spirit to a person?

---

[27] The term "shepherd" was widely used metaphorically throughout the ancient Near East to describe the office of king (e.g., Isaiah 44:28; Jeremiah 6:3; 49:19).

Both of these questions trouble our theology. I don't have any quick answers, only possible explanations.

First, the Holy Spirit leaving Saul has nothing to do with his salvation, as it might under the New Covenant. In the Old Testament, the Spirit comes to empower a person to do a task for God. In the New Testament, on the other hand, the presence of the Spirit is both empowering *and* the essential element of salvation, the agent of regeneration so that we might truly be born anew. We do know that after his sin, David refused to take the Holy Spirit's presence for granted. He prays in Psalm 51, the great penitential psalm,

> "Do not cast me from your presence
> or take your Holy Spirit from me." (Psalm 51:11)

In the same way that the Holy Spirit had left Saul, supernatural strength had left Samson during the period of the Judges. Delilah says,

> "'The Philistines are upon you, Samson!' When he awoke from his sleep, he thought, 'I will go out as at other times, and shake myself free.' But he did not know that the LORD had left him." (Judges 16:20)

For the Holy Spirit's power to leave us because of our persistent sin and disobedience is a sobering matter indeed. Let us strive not to grieve the Holy Spirit (Ephesians 4:30).

Second, we wonder how God can send an evil spirit, since James tell us: "God cannot be tempted by evil, nor does he tempt anyone" (James 1:13).

This is difficult. We cannot entirely avoid the difficulty, though we must realize the Bible teaches that both good and trouble can come from God (Job 2:10a, NIV), both prosperity and disaster (Isaiah 45:7).

Observe that that the term "evil spirit," which is used in the Gospels to designate a demon, doesn't necessarily refer to an "evil spirit" in this context. "Evil" is *ra ʿ*, an adjective that can have a wide range of meaning, ranging from misery to moral evil. Here it should be seen in the sense of "injurious."[28] Bergen comments:

> "It is possible – and perhaps preferable – to interpret the text not to mean that the Lord sent a morally corrupt demon, but rather another sort of supernatural being – an angel of judgment (cf. 2 Kings 19:35) – against Saul that causes him to experience constant misery."[29]

---

[28] Baldwin, *1 and 2 Samuel*, p. 122.
[29] Bergen, *1 and 2 Samuel*, p. 182.

Paul says that God judges rebellion by giving people fully over to their sin and its fruits (Romans 1:24-26). As we'll see in succeeding chapters, the torment Saul experiences seems to include fear and paranoia that prompt violent and irrational actions.[30]

David Plays for Saul (16:14-23)

King Saul's servants prescribe music to help calm him when these fearful spells come upon him. One servant recalls David's musical ability:

> "I have seen a son of Jesse of Bethlehem who knows how to play the harp. He is a brave man[31] and a warrior.[32] He speaks well[33] and is a fine-looking man.[34] And the LORD is with him." (16:18)

Here's a fine musician described in heroic terms. Plus, "the Lord is with him." How could Saul resist that kind of recommendation!

David plays the *kinnôr*, "a musical instrument having strings and a wooden frame," commonly associated in the Bible with joy and gladness.[35] The harp is an ancient instrument. The first illustration we have of the harp is from 3300-3000 BC in a rock etching at Megiddo.[36] The Canaanite version of this had two arms

Detail of Jewish *kinnor* player is found in a bas-relief in the palace of Assurbanipal (705-681 BC) at Nineveh, portraying the fall of the Judean city of Lachish.

with a box-shaped body. It was also the main instrument in the second temple orchestra.[37] The fundamental difference between a lyre and a harp is that in a harp, the

[30] "Torment" (NIV, NRSV), "trouble" (KJV) is *bāʿat*, "to be overtaken by sudden terror, to terrify" (Elmer A. Martens, TWOT #265). J. Hoftijzer sees this as "an experience of extreme fear and incapacitation" (cited by Bergen, 1 and 2 Samuel, p. 182, fn. 36).

[31] "Brave man" (NIV), "man of valor" (NRSV), "mighty valiant man" (KJV) is two words: *gibbôr hayil* – *gibbôr*, "mighty, strong, valiant, mighty man," the heroes or champions among the armed forces (John N. Oswalt, *gibbôr*, TWOT #310b) and *hayil*, "might, strength, power; able, valiant, virtuous, valor; army, host, forces; riches, substance, wealth; etc." (Carl Philip Weber, *hayil*, TWOT #624a).

[32] "Warrior" (NIV, NRSV), is two words, literally, "man of war" (KJV). The second word is *milhāmâ*, "battle, war," from *lāham*, "to fight, do battle" (TWOT #1104c). This seems to be an exaggeration or statement of strength and potential, since at this point, David hadn't fought in any war.

[33] "Speaks well" (NIV), "prudent in speech" (NRSV), "prudent in matters" (KJV) is two words, literally, "discern (*bîn*) between words/things/matters (*dābār*)."

[34] "Fine-looking man" (NIV), "man of good presence" (NRSV), "comely person" (KJV) uses the word "man" with *tōʾar*, "shape, form, beautiful, comely, fair, favored, goodly, resemble, visage" (Ronald F. Youngblood, TWOT #2491a).

[35] Tremper Longman III, *How to Read the Psalms* (InterVarsity Press, 1998), pp. 97-98.

[36] Michael Levy, "The Ancient Biblical Lyres." http://ancientlyre.com/?section=historical_details

[37] Foxvog and Kilmer, Daniel A. Foxvog and Ann D. Kilmer, "Music," ISBE 3:440-442, John N. Oswalt, *knr*, TWOT #1004a.

strings enter directly into the hollow body of the instrument, whereas on a lyre, the strings pass over a bridge, which transmits the vibrations of the strings to the body of the instrument, just as is the case with a modern guitar.

Saul summons David from the sheep fields to become a court musician and general equipment-bearer when he isn't singing.[38] His music does seem to help – for a while.

> "Whenever the spirit from God came upon Saul, David would take his harp and play. Then relief would come to Saul; he would feel better, and the evil spirit would leave him." (16:23)

What is the shepherd singer doing in the house of the king? What does God have in mind? As the story unfolds, it seems that God wants David in Saul's court to be exposed to the nuts and bolts of governing, to learn the art of leadership from that nation's leaders. It is a kind of apprenticeship for the future king of Israel.

It also may have been a time for writing songs. In the sheep fields David doesn't have the opportunity to write down the lyrics to his songs. In the court, David has that ability. Eventually, the collection of his songs fill nearly half the Psalter.

Q4. (1 Samuel 16:14-23) From Saul's perspective, why is David summoned to court? From God's perspective, what seem to be the reasons for this service in Saul's court? What things tend to prevent us from learning from God in the midst of the circumstances in which we find ourselves? What might make us more teachable?
http://www.joyfulheart.com/forums/index.php?showtopic=1163

Discipleship Lessons

As disciples who are eager to learn from the Lord, this passage contains several lessons for us:

1. **Obedience.** We learn a negative lesson from Saul – the importance of careful obedience to the commands of the Lord. As we grow as disciples, we must out-

---

[38] "Armor-bearer" is two words: *nāśā'*, "bear, carry" and *kelî*, a general word, referring to the equipment, containers, tools, etc., appropriate to a given service or occupation. Depending on the context it can be translated, "armor, bag, carriage, furniture, instrument, jewels, sacks, stuff, thing, tools, vessel, weapons" (John N. Oswalt, TWOT #982g). Here the word doesn't seem to refer to a specific military role, but a court attendant who carried the king's possessions wherever he wanted to go.

grow our tendency to self-will and rebellion. Otherwise we'll be of little use to the Lord we seek to serve.

2. **Listening**. From Samuel we learn the importance of listening carefully to the voice of the Spirit. As a prophet, God speaks to Samuel – as God can speak to each Christian believer who has received the Holy Spirit of God – you and me. Samuel has some preconceived judgments, but he is mature enough not to act on them. He waits for God to make clear his will.

3. **The Holy Spirit**. The activity of the Holy Spirit is central to this passage and to much of David's life. The Holy Spirit speaks, directs, empowers, and inspires prophetic song. Being responsive to the Holy Spirit is the key to success as a king or a prophet – or in any venture God calls us to.

4. **God's Arrangements**. Finally, we see how God uses "chance" opportunities to work out his will. Sometimes, we find ourselves in places we didn't choose and may not like very well. The appropriate question is not: "Why, Lord?" but rather "What do you want me to learn here?" God sees the beginning from the end, and will work out his purposes for us if we will be patient and open to him in every circumstance. God is forming disciples. Will you let him form you?

Prayer

Father, sometimes I'm so impatient! Forgive me. Help me to listen. Help me to obey, even if I don't understand what in the world you are doing. Fill me with your precious Holy Spirit and help me not to grieve Him. I yield myself to you to do your work in and through me in my present circumstances. I trust you, Lord! In Jesus' name, I pray. Amen.

Key Verses

"Does the LORD delight in burnt offerings and sacrifices
as much as in obeying the voice of the LORD?
To obey is better than sacrifice,
and to heed is better than the fat of rams.
[23] For rebellion is like the sin of divination,
and arrogance like the evil of idolatry." (1 Samuel 15:22-23a)

"The LORD does not look at the things man looks at.
Man looks at the outward appearance,
but the LORD looks at the heart." (1 Samuel 16:7b)

"So Samuel took the horn of oil and anointed him in the presence of his brothers, and from that day on the Spirit of the LORD came upon David in power." (1 Samuel 16:13)

2. David and Goliath: Bold Faith (1 Samuel 17)

The account of David and Goliath is the stuff of legend, the story of a young hero standing against established power, with inadequate resources, but with great courage – and winning! It has entered the vocabulary of our culture as the weak Davids of our day "speak truth to power" – and succeed, occasionally.

The Valley of Elah (17:1-3)

But David didn't know this when it all began. All he knew was that his brothers were fighting the Philistines. The Philistines, a sea people that had settled along the coastal plain, had sent their combined armies inland to a city of Judah, Socoh, into the Valley of Elah, threatening the Israelite tribes

James J. Tissot, 'David Slings the Stone' (1896-1902), gouache on board, The Jewish Museum, New York.

in the hill country of Judah. Saul called up the army and took a position that would prevent the Philistines from moving further inland.

> "¹ Now the Philistines gathered their forces for war and assembled at Socoh in Judah. They pitched camp at Ephes Dammim,¹ between Socoh² and Azekah. ² Saul and the Israelites assembled and camped in the Valley of Elah and drew up their battle line to meet the Philistines. ³ The Philistines occupied one hill and the Israelites another, with the valley between them." (17:1-3)

¹ The location of Ephes-Dammin isn't known with any certainty.
² Sucoh is identified with Khirbet Abbad, 14 miles west of Bethlehem. Two to three miles northwest was Azekah, Tell ez-Zakariyeh.

The valley of Elah is a triangle-shaped flat valley, located on the western edge of the Judean low hills or Shepelah. Elah is named after the terebinth tree (*Pistacia palaestina*). Only in the rainy season does water flow in the creek bed, Wadi

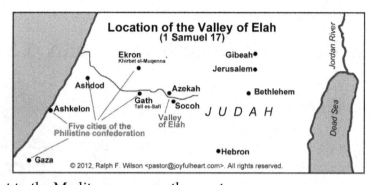

es-Sant, from the hills to the east to the Mediterranean on the west.

The coastal Philistines were constantly trying to encroach on Israelite territory in the Shepelah, the low hills to the east of their territory. The Valley of Elah was strategically important as a corridor from the coastal Philistine cities up to the center of the land of

Judah and its cities such as Bethlehem and Hebron. The Israelites must hold this potential attack route in order to protect the rest of Judah.

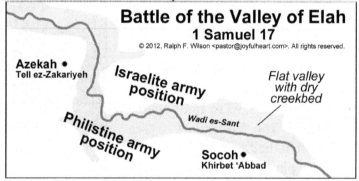

But now the Israelite and Philistine armies are at a stalemate. The Israelites are encamped across the hills on the north side of the valley to prevent the Philistines from moving up the valley farther into Israelite territory. The Philistines are encamped across the hills on the south side of the valley. Only a dry creek bed separates the two armies.

Goliath, the Philistine Champion (17:4-11)

Neither army is moving from its position. But twice a day, the boredom is broken by a huge man of war who taunts the Israelites.

> "⁴ A champion named Goliath, who was from Gath, came out of the Philistine camp. He was over nine feet tall. ⁵ He had a bronze helmet on his head and wore a coat of scale armor of bronze weighing five thousand shekels; ⁶ on his legs he wore bronze greaves, and a bronze javelin was slung on his back. ⁷ His spear shaft was like a weaver's rod, and its iron point weighed six hundred shekels. His shield bearer went ahead of him." (17:4-7)

The word translated "champion" is two words, literally, "man in between.[3]" The champion is "a man who steps out to fight between two battle lines" in single combat.[4] Goliath's challenge terrifies the Israelites.

> "Choose a man and have him come down to me. If he is able to fight and kill me, we will become your subjects; but if I overcome him and kill him, you will become our subjects and serve us." (17:8b-9)

The boast is probably more psychological warfare than a genuine offer from the Philistine generals for single combat to settle the battle.

But whether real or not, this giant intimidates the Israelite soldiers, none of whom would have been much taller than five feet plus a few inches.

No Israelite could see himself beating this monster. He was huge – "Over nine feet" literally "six cubits and a span"[5] – about 9 feet, 9 inches. He was probably the descendant of a clan of giants that had previously been observed in the area, perhaps the Rephaim or Anakim.[6]

His state-of-the-art weapons were massive. He wore a helmet, scale armor,[7] and protection for his legs – greaves. His spear was huge, and an assistant, the armor-bearer, carried his shield. The weapon slung on Goliath's back is more difficult to identify. The "javelin" (NIV, NRSV), "target" (KJV), *kîdôn*, is traditionally rendered, "dart, javelin."[8] More recently, based on the word's use in the War Scroll from Qumran, Molin has suggested that this is a scimitar, "a sword-like weapon for close action, with a handle, a straight piece, and a semi-circular blade, with a cutting edge on the outer side of the blade.[9] But the *kîdôn* seems to be differentiated from Goliath's sword (*ḥereb*) in 17:45.

David Supplies Food for His Brothers (17:12-24)

Our narrator is introducing the characters in the story. First, the protagonist: Goliath, then young David. David isn't in the army, but shepherding his father's sheep.

---

[3] *Bēnayim* is the dual form of *bên*, "between, among," here, "space between two armies" (BDB 108, 2).

[4] Roland De Vaux, *The Bible and the Ancient Near East* (Doubleday, 1971), pp. 124-125, cited by Tsumura, *1 Samuel*, p. 440.

[5] A cubit is the distance from the elbow to the fingertips, usually figured at 18 inches. A span is the distance from thumb to little finger when one's hand is splayed open as far as possible, usually figured at about 9 inches.

[6] Deuteronomy 2:20-21; 2 Samuel 21:20-22; Numbers 13:22, 28; Joshua 15:13-14.

[7] "Scale armor" (NIV), "coat of mail" (NRSV, KJV) is *qaśqeśet*, "scale" of a fish, thus here of "scale armor," known in Egypt and Mesopotamia (*Qaśqeśet*, BDB 903).

[8] *Kîdôn*, BDB 475.

[9] "Tsumura, *1 Samuel*, p. 443, who cites G. Molin, "What is a kidon?" JSS 1 (1956) 337; Klein, *1 Samuel*, p. 176.

However, he goes back and forth to make sure his brothers have food. The Israelite army is provisioned by family members supporting their own sons. David also relays news of his brothers to Jesse their father.

David Asks about Goliath's Defiance (17:25-30)

Just about the time David arrives, Goliath appears between the battle lines for one of his twice-daily taunts. David is appalled when he hears Goliath's rants, and asks some of the soldiers to tell him what's going on. It seems that King Saul has offered a huge reward to the warrior who slays Goliath, as well as marriage to the king's own daughter – but there have been no takers. David asks:

> "What will be done for the man who kills this Philistine and removes this disgrace from Israel? Who is this uncircumcised Philistine that he should defy the armies of the living God?" (17:26)

Soon, word gets around that there's a young man who isn't afraid of Goliath. When his oldest brother Eliab hears of it, he is furious:

> "Why have you come down here? And with whom did you leave those few sheep in the desert? I know how conceited you are and how wicked your heart is; you came down only to watch the battle." (17:28)

David's answer sounds so authentic, so characteristic of family arguments:

> "Now what have I done? Can't I even speak?" (17:29)

Eliab is embarrassed by David's naive comments because they reflect on his own lack of courage! But David isn't submitting to his brother's attempt to silence him. He asserts his right to speak his own opinion. Maybe he is the youngest, but he isn't afraid of his older brother!

Q1. (1 Samuel 17:26-30) Why is David so upset about Goliath's taunt? Why is Eliab, David's brother, so upset with David? What does this teach us about David's faith? What does it teach us about Eliab's character?

http://www.joyfulheart.com/forums/index.php?showtopic=1160

Saul Sends for David (17:31-33)

But now Saul hears about this brash young man – and is intrigued. He sends for him.

> "³² David said to Saul, 'Let no one lose heart on account of this Philistine; your servant will go and fight him.'
>
> ³³ Saul replied, 'You are not able to go out against this Philistine and fight him; you are only a boy, and he has been a fighting man from his youth.'" (17:32-33)

Saul, an accomplished warrior himself, tries to give David a reality check. But David doesn't accept it. As David explains his confidence, notice that this isn't just braggadocio, but faith in God.

> "'³⁴ Your servant has been keeping his father's sheep. When a lion or a bear came and carried off a sheep from the flock, ³⁵ I went after it, struck it and rescued the sheep from its mouth. When it turned on me, I seized it by its hair, struck it and killed it.
>
> ³⁶ Your servant has killed both the lion and the bear; this uncircumcised Philistine will be like one of them, because he has defied the armies of the living God. ³⁷ The LORD who delivered me from the paw of the lion and the paw of the bear will deliver me from the hand of this Philistine.'
>
> Saul said to David, 'Go, and the LORD be with you.'" (17:34-37)

Saul is convinced. Somehow, as David tells his story, a cinder of faith in Saul's heart springs to flame. He believes the boy!

A Combat-Tested Shepherd

Consider David's experience. He has been a "mere" shepherd, but he has done mortal combat with both lions and bears. He is fearless! When his flock is attacked, he doesn't take the easy way out. He chases after the predator, confronts it, kills it, and rescues the sheep from its jaws.

The Asiatic or Persian Lion (*Felis leo persica*) is now extinct in Palestine, the last sighting being in the 13th century AD. The only ones left in the wild are a few in the Gir Forest Sanctuary of northwestern India. But in biblical times they were abundant in Israel – and dangerous! Males reach a weight of 350 to 420 pounds (160 to 190 kg); the females get to 240 to 260 pounds (110 to 120 kg).

The Syrian Brown Bear (*Ursus arctos syriacus*) is also extinct in Palestine, but is in the trans-Caucasian region of the former Soviet Union, and in Iran, Iraq, and Turkey. While the Syrian Brown Bear is one of the smaller subspecies of brown bears, it isn't small! Its head and body length is up to 8 feet (2.4 meters). Shoulder height is 35 to 43 inches (89-

109 cm). Males weigh 220 to 660 pounds (100 to 300 kg), while females are about two-thirds the size of males.

King Saul is impressed. How many of his own soldiers would challenge a lion or bear? Few! So he gives David his blessing: "Go, and the LORD be with you" (17: 37b). David has inspired spiritual faith in the king. David has pointed him toward the power of Yahweh.

King Saul's Calculation

King Saul is convinced by David. But surely he is weighing the probabilities. At present, Goliath is demoralizing the Israelite troops. If this continues, they'll begin to desert in greater numbers. Something has to happen. If David is struck down by Goliath – as is certainly likely – the worst that would happen would be that the Philistines would wage an attack. Their psychological advantage is minor – the victory of a giant over a boy.

Saul isn't staking the entire battle on David's success. Goliath's challenge of a contest between representatives is only a taunt, a boast. But if David wins – and Saul believes that David has a chance of doing just that – the psychological advantage over the Philistines will be huge. It will be a shock that might very well determine the outcome of the ensuing battle.

Q2. (1 Samuel 17:34-37) What does David's explanation to Saul of his combat experience say about David's faith? How lethal is David as a warrior? Why do you think Saul allows him to go out to battle Goliath? Does Saul have faith? If so, what is the source of it?
http://www.joyfulheart.com/forums/index.php?showtopic=1161

David's Sling (17:38-39)

Saul proceeds to outfit David with his own armor. But since Saul stands head and shoulders above the average Israelite (10:23), his armor doesn't fit David. David tries it on, but can't move freely. He's not used to armor. This is the source of the saying, "trying to fight in someone else's armor." The armor would destroy David's chief advantage over the giant Philistine, his agility. Instead, David chooses his own weapons.

"[David] took his staff in his hand, chose five smooth stones from the stream, put them in the pouch of his shepherd's bag and, with his sling in his hand, approached the Philistine." (17:40)

Sling stones from the battle of Lachish, Judah (701 BC). British Museum.

The sling is an ancient weapon but very simple, and cheap enough for a shepherd boy to make and practice with while his sheep are grazing. David would have found a sling effective from a distance to deter animals that threatened his flock.

The sling is a projectile weapon, used to throw a blunt projectile with amazing speed. The length of the sling extends the leverage of the human arm, and the speed of the swing allows stones to be thrown at several times the force of throwing them by hand.

Slingers in the siege of Lachish, Judah (701 BC), bas-relief from the wall of Sennacherib's palace in Nineveh. British Museum, London.

The sling probably goes back to the Neolithic peoples around the Mediterranean. But since slings are biodegradable, archaeologists don't often recover them. Slingers were utilized by armies with deadly effect. The oldest actual sling we've found comes from the tomb of Egyptian pharaoh Tutankhamen, who died about 1325 BC. But to find sling stones or bullets is rather common.

At the base of the city wall of Lachish in Judah, hundreds of sling stones have been recovered from a 701 BC siege by the Assyrian king Sennacherib. These are limestone, round, from 1-3/4 to 2-1/3 inches (4.5 to 6 cm) in diameter.[10] These aren't just pebbles, but vary from the size of a golf ball to a bit less than a tennis ball. Imagine being struck in the forehead with a stone the size of a golf ball or tennis ball slung at close range at a speed of 100 miles per hour!

The young warrior David doesn't take Saul's sword. Rather, he takes his shepherd's staff for close combat and his sling for longer range attack. On his way he stops at the stream-bed of Wadi es-Sant, to select five smooth sling-stones, which he deposits in the pouch at his waist.

---

[10] The Israel Museum, Jerusalem, permanent collection.

David and Goliath Trade Boasts (17:41-47)

Goliath, however, is angry that they would send a mere lad against him – without even any armor! It is an affront to his prowess as a warrior! He sees David's staff and bellows an insult – "Am I a dog, that you come at me with sticks?" (17:43a). Insults ("trash talk") was common practice for soldiers trying to demoralize their opponents prior to close combat.

> "The Philistine cursed David by his gods. 'Come here,' he said, 'and I'll give your flesh to the birds of the air and the beasts of the field!'" (17:43b-44)

But David is undeterred. The young boy calls out to the grizzled giant the defiant challenge of Yahweh. Goliath boasts in his own prowess, but David boasts in Yahweh Almighty! The giant's vision is to destroy the boy. But look at the boy's vision: to defeat the entire Philistine army and display to the whole world the glory of Yahweh.

> "[45] You come against me with sword and spear and javelin, but I come against you in the name of the LORD Almighty, the God of the armies of Israel, whom you have defied. [46] This day the LORD will hand you over to me, and I'll strike you down and cut off your head. Today I will give the carcasses of the Philistine army to the birds of the air and the beasts of the earth, and the whole world will know that there is a God in Israel. [47] All those gathered here will know that it is not by sword or spear that the LORD saves; for the battle is the LORD's, and he will give all of you into our hands." (17:45-47)

"Name" (shēm) in verse 45 is used in a special sense, something like our power of attorney, where one person can act with the legal authority of another. To come "in the name of Yahweh Almighty," means to come with Yahweh's presence, power, authority, and divine appointment.[11] Goliath curses David by his (unnamed) gods, but David makes it clear that he is coming with Yahweh's power and authority. This is not just a military battle, it is a theological battle to demonstrate publicly Yahweh's superiority over other gods, that "the whole world will know that there is a God in Israel."

The Battle is the Lord's (17:45-47)

The spiritual heart of this lesson is found in verse 47:

> "All those gathered here will know that it is not by sword or spear that the LORD saves; for the battle is the LORD's, and he will give all of you into our hands." (17:47)

So often we trust in our own strength. Or, just as bad, feel powerless and defeated because we don't have any strength. On this occasion, David articulates a basic principle

---

[11] Gerald F. Hawthorne, "Name," ISBE 3:480-483.

of faith – God will act on our behalf when we trust in him and are obedient to his voice. This same principle is reiterated time after time throughout scripture:

Jonathan: "Nothing can hinder the LORD from saving,
whether by many or by few." (1 Samuel 14:6b)

To Jehoshaphat: "Do not be afraid or discouraged because of this vast army.
For the battle is not yours, but God's." (2 Chronicles 20:15)

Hezekiah: "With him is only the arm of flesh,
but with us is the LORD our God to help us
and to fight our battles." (2 Chronicles 32:8)

"No king is saved by the size of his army;
no warrior escapes by his great strength.
A horse is a vain hope for deliverance;
despite all its great strength it cannot save.
But the eyes of the LORD are on those who fear him,
on those whose hope is in his unfailing love....
We wait in hope for the LORD;
he is our help and our shield." (Psalm 33:16-18, 20)

"I do not trust in my bow,
my sword does not bring me victory;
but you give us victory over our enemies,
you put our adversaries to shame.
In God we make our boast all day long,
and we will praise your name forever." (Psalm 44:6-8)

"There is no wisdom, no insight,
no plan that can succeed against the LORD.
The horse is made ready for the day of battle,
but victory rests with the LORD." (Proverbs 21:30-31)

"Yet I will show love to the house of Judah;
and I will save them
– not by bow, sword or battle,
or by horses and horsemen,
but by the LORD their God." (Hosea 1:7)

"'Not by might nor by power,
but by my Spirit,' says the LORD Almighty." (Zechariah 4:6)

"If God is for us, who can be against us?
... No, in all these things we are more than conquerors
through him who loved us." (Romans 8:31, 37)

"You, dear children, are from God and have overcome them,
because the one who is in you
is greater than the one who is in the world." (1 John 4:4)

Q3. (1 Samuel 17:47) Why do we so often forget that "the battle is the Lord's"? What does that phrase actually mean? How can we avoid the arrogance of pulling God into our battles ("God is on my side"), rather than engaging in His battles ("I am on God's side")?
http://www.joyfulheart.com/forums/index.php?showtopic=1162

David's Deadly Sling (17:48-54)

The words have been said. Now it's time for action. Everything happens quickly at this point.

"⁴⁸ As the Philistine moved closer to attack him, David ran quickly toward the battle line to meet him.

⁴⁹ Reaching into his bag and taking out a stone, he slung it and struck the Philistine on the forehead. The stone sank into his forehead, and he fell face down on the ground. ⁵⁰ So David triumphed over the Philistine with a sling and a stone; without a sword in his hand he struck down the Philistine and killed him.

⁵¹ David ran and stood over him. He took hold of the Philistine's sword and drew it from the scabbard. After he killed him, he cut off his head with the sword." (17:48-51a)

David keeps the sword and other weapons (17:54) – to the victor goes the spoils. He later recovers the sword from the tabernacle at Nob when he is fleeing from Saul (21:9).

Goliath's death has a devastating effect on the Philistine army's morale. One moment they imagine the giant making quick work of the boy challenger. The next moment, their champion is lying on the ground and the boy is cutting off his head. The momentum has shifted in a moment. They flee for their lives!

Saul Inquires about David's Family (17:55-58)

Saul doesn't seem to know who either David or his father are and makes inquiries. We can imagine the next scene: David stands before Saul with Goliath's dripping head at his side:

"⁵⁷ As soon as David returned from killing the Philistine, Abner took him and brought him before Saul, with David still holding the Philistine's head. ⁵⁸ 'Whose son are you, young man?' Saul asked him. David said, 'I am the son of your servant Jesse of Bethlehem.'" (17:57-58)

What's wrong here? Hasn't Saul met David earlier when he played the harp to quiet Saul's evil moods? Wasn't he an armor-bearer? (16:21) I think two things are going on.

1. **Sources**. The historical books of the Bible were compiled from a number of independent sources into a single document that once extended from 1 Samuel through 2 Kings. From a stylistic viewpoint, the detailed story of David and Goliath is obviously a masterpiece of storytelling that was inserted in its entirety at this point. The editor doesn't try to harmonize each source with every other. You're seeing the "seams" that remained when 1 Samuel was put together.

2. **Relative importance**. Though David is the center of *our* interest, when he is brought into to Saul's court he is merely a servant to be called when the king is in a bad mood. It's unlikely that Saul conversed with him; he is only a court musician, that's all. And being an armor-bearer for a king isn't like being the caddy for a pro golfer. All it means is that David is one of the carriers when the king decides to go somewhere. He is a minor court functionary. So it's not surprising that neither Saul nor Abner, Saul's general, remember his name or his family.

Disciple Lessons from David and Goliath

1. **Faith vs. fear**. We need to be motivated primarily by our faith, not hindered from action by our fears.

2. **God's glory** is more important than our own victory. David is concerned for God's reputation, not his own.

3. **The battle is the Lord's**. So often we think we're alone in what we're facing. But if we're living for God, he is present no matter what is going on in our lives. And if the cause affects his kingdom and his glory, it is *His* battle, not ours at all.

4. **Importance of preparation**. Even though we rely on the Spirit, we are not so foolish as to make no preparation. As St. Augustine once said, "Pray as though everything depended on God. Work as though everything depended on you." Faith and preparation are not mutually exclusive.

Prayer

Father, give us bold faith like the young David. So often we are motivated by our fears rather than by our faith. Forgive us for thinking so selfishly. Give us a broad vision for your purposes and your kingdom, and then make us warriors for you! In Jesus' name. Amen.

Key Verses

"Your servant has killed both the lion and the bear; this uncircumcised Philistine will be like one of them, because he has defied the armies of the living God. The LORD who delivered me from the paw of the lion and the paw of the bear will deliver me from the hand of this Philistine." (1 Samuel 17:36-37)

"You come against me with sword and spear and javelin, but I come against you in the name of the LORD Almighty, the God of the armies of Israel, whom you have defied." (1 Samuel 17:45)

"All those gathered here will know that it is not by sword or spear that the LORD saves; for the battle is the LORD's, and he will give all of you into our hands." (1 Samuel 17:47)

3. Jonathan's Friendship, Saul's Jealousy (1 Samuel 18-20)

While still holding the dripping head of Goliath, David appears before Saul, who asks about his family. In the king's tent at that time is Saul's son and heir, Jonathan. He is probably a decade older than David, but there is an instant bond between the two.

David's Bond with Jonathan (18:1)

> "After David had finished talking with Saul, Jonathan became one in spirit with David, and he loved him as himself." (18:1)

What is the nature of this bond? The text uses two words to describe it.

"Became one" (NIV), **"was bound"** (NRSV), **"was knit"** (KJV) is *qāshar*. The root idea is "tie up, bind," metaphorically, "to be allied with." It can even carry the idea, "to conspire, form a conspiracy, make a plot," which characterizes Jonathan's and David's later plan to help David escape from King Saul.[1] The KJV translates the clause quite literally: "The soul of Jonathan was knit with the soul of David," using the Hebrew noun *nepesh*, "life, soul, person," from the verb, *nāpash*, "breathe."[2] The breath or essence of David's life is bound to Jonathan.

"Loved" is *'āhab*, a general word that can describe a whole range of affection, from love between human beings to a love for food, love for God's commandments,

James J. Tissot, detail of 'Friendship of David and Jonathan' (1896-1902) gouache on board, Jewish Museum, New York. David is on the left, Jonathan on the right.

---

[1] *Qāshar*, Holladay, 327; "bind, league together, conspire" (BDB 905).

[2] Bruce K. Waltke, *nāpash*, TWOT #1395a. "In numerous passages reference is made to the inclination or disinclination of the soul. It is frequently used in connection with 'love.'"

or even a love for evil. The word can describe the love of a parent for a child, a husband for a wife, a woman for a man, Ruth for Naomi, etc. It is the word used in the classic text, "Love your neighbor as yourself" (Leviticus 19:18).[3] Later, in his eulogy at Jonathan's death, David says,

> "I grieve for you, Jonathan my brother;
> you were very dear to me.
> Your love (ʾahabâ) for me was wonderful,
> more wonderful than that of women." (2 Samuel 1:26)

The modern homosexual movement has portrayed David and Jonathan as homosexual lovers, but there is no evidence whatsoever of a sexual element to their relationship. Clearly, David is heterosexual. This is just an example of people trying use the Bible to justify what the Bible clearly condemns.[4] In addition, this interpretation ignores deep bonds of masculine friendship in this culture that are quite non-sexual in nature.

Covenant with Jonathan (18:2-4)

From then on, David is attached to Saul's court.

> "[2] From that day Saul kept David with him and did not let him return to his father's house. [3] And Jonathan made a covenant with David because he loved him as himself.
> [4] Jonathan took off the robe he was wearing and gave it to David, along with his tunic, and even his sword, his bow and his belt." (18:2-4)

We see in this passage the idea of "covenant" – the same word used to describe the covenant between Yahweh and the people of Israel at Mount Sinai. While that covenant was like a suzerain-vassal treaty, "covenant" (berît) here is more personal, an "alliance of friendship" between individuals.[5] The word is used several times in these chapters (18:3; 20:8, 16, 18) where the nature of this covenant is developed further. This covenant underlies David's actions years later towards Jonathan's son Mephibosheth (2 Samuel 9).

Notice that this covenant is sealed by gifts of a robe, tunic, sword, bow, and belt from Jonathan to David. We have the same idea in the use of a ring in our wedding service. The 1559 *Book of Common Prayer* reads:

---

[3] Robert L. Alden, ʾāhab, TWOT #29.
[4] Leviticus 18:22; 20:13; Romans 1:26-27; 1 Corinthians 6:9-11; 1 Timothy 1:8-10; Genesis 19; Jude 7. Though the Bible condemns the sin, we are called to love people who struggle with same-sex attractions. The ministry of Exodus International (www.exodusinternational.org) helps homosexuals work through some of these issues.
[5] Elmer B. Smick, berît, TWOT #282a.

"Forasmuch as (groom) and (bride) have consented together in holy wedlock, and have witnessed the same before God, and this company, and thereto have given and pledged, their troth to other, and have declared the same by giving and receiving of a ring, and by joining of hands, I pronounce that they be man and wife together."[6]

The covenant is confirmed by receiving a gift in the same way that a small monetary deposit seals a business transaction in our day.

High Rank in the Army (18:5)

David's military prowess is not lost on Saul. He rises rapidly to leadership in Saul's army.

"Whatever Saul sent him to do, David did it so successfully that Saul gave him a high rank[7] in the army. This pleased all the people, and Saul's officers as well." (18:5)

I think it's fascinating to see that Saul's officers were pleased by David's advancement in rank. You'd expect officers to be jealous of David's rapid promotion and feel threatened. But they are not. They recognize that David has earned his position – and they are pleased to see his achievement recognized. This is evidence of David's personal charisma that attracted people to him – which we'll see when David begins to build his own army after fleeing from Saul (22:2).

David's Glory and Saul's Jealousy (18:6-9)

The narrator has fast-forwarded to David's rise in the army, but now he comes back to David's triumphant return after killing Goliath. David becomes very popular with the people – especially the women!

"[6] When the men were returning home after David had killed the Philistine, the women came out from all the towns of Israel to meet King Saul with singing and dancing, with joyful songs and with tambourines and lutes. [7] As they danced, they sang:

'Saul has slain his thousands,
and David his tens of thousands.'

[8] Saul was very angry; this refrain galled[8] him. 'They have credited David with tens of thousands,' he thought, 'but me with only thousands. What more can he get but the kingdom?' [9] And from that time on Saul kept a jealous eye on David." (18:6-9)

---

[6] "The Form of Solemnization of Matrimony," *The Book of Common Prayer* (1559). I modernized the spelling
[7] "Gave him a high rank" (NIV), "set him over" (NRSV, KJV) is *śûm*, "put, place, set, appoint, make," here, "the placing is into an authority position" (Gary G. Cohen, *śûm*, TWOT #2243).

Many people become jealous and paranoid when someone else's success puts them in a lesser light. This jealousy and fear – and mental instability – motivate many of Saul's later actions.

But the song of the women, "Saul has slain his thousands, and David his tens of thousands," had become part of the popular culture. Even the Philistine kings had heard of it (21:11; 29:5). It must have been a constant bitter reminder to Saul of his own failures and rejection as king.

Saul Tries to Kill David (18:10-12)

David returns to his former duty as court musician – but this time Saul is well-aware of who he is – and his huge popularity among the people.

> "[10] The next day an evil spirit from God came forcefully[9] upon Saul. He was prophesying[10] in his house, while David was playing the harp, as he usually did. Saul had a spear in his hand [11] and he hurled it, saying to himself, 'I'll pin David to the wall.' But David eluded him twice. [12] Saul was afraid of David, because the LORD was with David but had left Saul." (18:10-12)

During a particularly violent episode, Saul throws a spear at David – not once, but twice! Note the dual motives in verse 12: (1) fear and (2) jealousy. Saul is out of control!

Saul's Plan for David to Fall in Battle (18:13-16)

Saul can't stand to have David around, so he promotes him to be a general and sends him away.

> "So he sent David away from him and gave him command over a thousand men, and David led the troops in their campaigns." (18:13)

Apparently, Saul's intentions are two-fold: (1) to get David away from him and out of his court, and (2) to put him in a dangerous place so that he will be killed, as we'll see in verses 17b and 21. But Saul's plan backfires.

---

[8] "Galled" (NIV), "was angry" (NRSV), "was wroth" (KJV) is ḥārâ, "burn, be kindled," of anger (BDB 354, 1a).

[9] The phrase "came forcefully upon" (NIV), "rushed upon" (NRSV), "came upon" (KJV) is ṣālah, which is used to describe the Holy Spirit coming upon David in Lesson 1.

[10] The text says that Saul was "prophesying" (NIV, KJV) or "raved" (NRSV) under the influence of an evil spirit. Usually prophecy is viewed positively in the Bible, but it is not uncommon for people to prophesy under the power of an evil spirit (1 Kings 18:29; 22:19; Zechariah 13:2-4; Matthew 7:15-16, 22; 1 Corinthians 12:3; 1 John 4:2-3; Acts 16:16.). That is what was happening to Saul.

"[14] In everything he did he had great success, because the LORD was with him. [15] When Saul saw how successful he was, he was afraid of him. [16] But all Israel and Judah loved David, because he led them in their campaigns." (18:14-16)

Rather than being killed in battle, David proves to be both a powerful warrior and a leader of men. The ability to have others follow you when their lives are at risk is not just a matter of authority. Men won't long follow someone they believe to be a stupid leader who will get them killed. But the men find that they trust David. He leads them to victory. He has consistent success,[11] which brings him even greater publicity and adulation among the people. Notice the reason for David's success: "because the LORD was with him" (18:14).

Q1. (1 Samuel 18:13-16). Why does Saul send David into battle? What is the result? To what does the narrator attribute David's success?
http://www.joyfulheart.com/forums/index.php?showtopic=1164

Saul's Older Daughter, Merab (18:17-18)

But Saul doesn't give up trying to kill David.

"Saul said to David, 'Here is my older daughter Merab. I will give her to you in marriage; only serve me bravely and fight the battles of the LORD.' For Saul said to himself, 'I will not raise a hand against him. Let the Philistines do that!'" (18:17)

Saul is shrewd and deceitful. Notice that Saul's current offer of his daughter in marriage is not the reward promised to the one who slew Goliath (17:25), but rather has strings attached. David must continue fighting, and thus increase the chances that he will be killed in battle. David's answer shows wisdom, humility, and realism. "My family isn't worthy of such an honor," he replies. He can't afford a bridal gift fit for the king's daughter, so Saul marries his older daughter to someone else.

---

[11] "Have success" (NIV, NRSV), "behave wisely" (KJV) in verses 14 and 15 is *śākal*, which can mean both "to be wise, understand," and "to prosper, have success" (Louis Goldberg, TWOT #2263; Holladay 352, 4). It has this meaning elsewhere also (1 Kings 2:3; Jeremiah 10:21; 2 Kings 18:7).

Saul's Treachery Regarding His Daughter Michal (18:20-22)

When Saul hears that his younger daughter is in love (*ʾāhab*) with David, he sees another opportunity to get David killed.

> "'I will give her to him,' he thought, 'so that she may be a snare to him and so that the hand of the Philistines may be against him.'" (18:21a)

Saul appeals to both David's macho pride and his military prowess – and succeeds. He passes the word that the bride price is not financial, but military success. Saul says to David, "Now you have a second opportunity to become my son-in-law."

> "'Say to David, 'The king wants no other price for the bride than a hundred Philistine foreskins, to take revenge on his enemies.' Saul's plan was to have David fall by the hands of the Philistines." (18:25)

Saul is more subtle now, and conveys his words and motivations through his attendants rather than directly.

The opportunity to marry the king's daughter – especially if he is able to pay the bride price by his own efforts – pleases David who takes him up on his offer. Instead of 100 Philistines, David and his men double the amount. They kill 200 Philistines, circumcise the corpses, and deliver the foreskins to Saul. By marrying Michal, David is now son-in-law to the king.

Q2. (1 Samuel 18:18-22) Which of the following is David's chief motive for marrying Michal, in your opinion? Argue for the motivation that makes the most sense to you: (1) pride in his military prowess, (2) obedience to Saul's desires, (3) love or desire for Michal, or (4) enjoyment in killing Philistines.
http://www.joyfulheart.com/forums/index.php?showtopic=1165

In spite of the fact that David is fighting successful battles for Israel and securing the kingdom for Saul, the king is intensely jealous of David.

> "When Saul realized that the LORD was with David ... Saul became still more afraid of him, and he remained his enemy the rest of his days." (18:28-29)

This is sad, because David is Saul's most loyal subject. Even later, when he gets two perfect opportunities to kill Saul, David refuses to take his life (24:7; 26:9-11).

Saul Tries to Kill David (19:1-17)

Now Saul becomes open about his desire to get rid of David.

"Saul told his son Jonathan and all the attendants to kill David. But Jonathan was very fond[12] of David" (19:1).

Jonathan warns David, and then succeeds in talking his father out of this madness.

"Let not the king do wrong to his servant David; he has not wronged you, and what he has done has benefited you greatly.... Why then would you do wrong to an innocent man like David by killing him for no reason?" (19:4-5)

Saul is convinced and swears an oath:

"As surely as the LORD lives, David will not be put to death" (19:6).

This is not his last oath to spare David. He vows this twice more – and again reneges on his promise (24:16-20; 26:21). One of the character flaws that makes Saul unworthy to be king is his unwillingness to honor his own solemn promises.

Soon we see a repeat of Saul throwing his spear to try to kill David while he plays the harp (17:9-10). This time David realizes that Saul will not be deterred from killing him, so he flees the palace.

That night at home, David's wife Michal encourages David to leave in the middle of the night by escaping out a window. As a ruse, Michal says that David is ill and puts a life size object[13] in David's bed to deceive the men sent to kill David. Then she claims that David had threatened her if she didn't aid his escape.

At this point Michal seems to be on David's side, as her future in the kingdom is tied up with David's. She lies about David threatening her in order to protect herself. Her loyalty isn't really to David, it appears, but to her own best interests.

---

[12] "Was fond of" (NIV), "took great delight in" (NRSV, cf. KJV) is *hāpēs*, "to experience emotional delight." The basic meaning is to feel great favor towards something. Leon J. Wood, TWOT #712.

[13] "Idol" (NIV, NRSV), "image" (KJV) is *terāphîm*, "idols, images," here, "a large, anthropomorphic idol."[13] Here it must have been something in the shape of a man under the covers to simulate David's presence in the bed. Or is it possibly a scarecrow type of straw man covered with a blanket to deceive Saul's men? This would require teraphim to be used differently here than it is used elsewhere in the Old Testament. But what was Michal doing with a teraphim, an object of idol worship that had been condemned earlier by Samuel? "For rebellion is like the sin of divination, and arrogance like the evil of idolatry (*terāphîm*)" (15:23a). Michal's access to a teraphim says something about her spiritual condition. Michal trusted in the teraphim; David trusted in the Lord.

David Flees to Samuel (19:18-24)

Looking for a place of refuge, David flees to elderly Samuel in Ramah, about an hour's walk from Saul's capital in Gibeah. Baldwin observes, "Far from being a lone figure, Samuel presided over a center where prophets engaged in worship."[14] But even there, Saul sends men to capture David. What happens to these men – and what later happens to Saul himself – is amusing.

> "[20] But when they saw a group of prophets prophesying, with Samuel standing there as their leader, the Spirit of God came upon Saul's men and they also prophesied. [21] Saul was told about it, and he sent more men, and they prophesied too. Saul sent men a third time, and they also prophesied.... Saul went to Naioth[15] at Ramah. But the Spirit of God came even upon him, and he walked along prophesying until he came to Naioth. [24] He stripped off his robes and also prophesied in Samuel's presence. He lay that way all that day and night. This is why people say, 'Is Saul also among the prophets?'" (1 Samuel 19:20-21, 23-24)

Something similar had happened to Saul when he had first been anointed king (10:10).

It's not useful – or faithful to the text – to understand this in Freudian terms as some kind of mass hysteria. Clearly, this is some kind of involuntary possession by the Holy Spirit that moves people from their intent to kill David to speaking the things of God. Occasionally, we see this today when people are "slain" by the Spirit and for a few minutes seem to lose their connection with their normal state. Elsewhere, we see the Holy Spirit coming upon Moses' elders (Numbers 11:25-26) and the disciples on the Day of Pentecost (Acts 2), resulting in prophecy. You don't have to "understand" everything the Holy Spirit does so you can label it. Jesus described the activity of the Spirit as mysterious: "The wind blows wherever it pleases. You hear its sound, but you cannot tell where it comes from or where it is going" (John 3:8). The Holy Spirit is not under our control; we are under His.

It's sad to realize that for Saul, nothing is sacred – that's the implication of Saul seeking to kill David in the very sanctuary of Israel's prophet Samuel. Saul's fear and need to control have pushed him to total rebellion against God, even though he realizes that God has anointed David to be king.

Q3. (1 Samuel 19:18-24) What does it tell us about Saul's faith that he pursues David even when he has sought the sanctuary of the prophet Samuel? Why do people

[14] Baldwin, *1 and 2 Samuel*, p. 133.

[15] Naioth means literally, "dwellings/habitations," and may refer to a religious compound within Ramah (Bergen, *1 and 2 Samuel*, p. 210). Klein sees "camps" or "huts" as the best translation (*1 Samuel*, p. 198).

prophesy when the Holy Spirit comes upon them? What is the relationship between this incident and the Day of Pentecost (Acts 2)?
http://www.joyfulheart.com/forums/index.php?showtopic=1166

David and Jonathan (20:1-23)

David concludes that he isn't safe even with the prophet Samuel. He arranges a secret meeting with Saul's son, Jonathan. Consider how much trust this must have taken on David's part. If Jonathan betrays David to his father Saul, he can become king himself. Still, Jonathan has made a covenant with David and keeps it.

David decides to test Saul's intentions. When David fails to appear at the monthly New Moon festival (Numbers 10:10) when he customarily dined at the king's table, Jonathan will make excuses for David and then judge Saul's reaction. "If he loses his temper, you can be sure that he is determined to harm me" (20:7b).

You can see language indicating binding oaths several times in this passage:

"You have brought him into a covenant with you before the LORD" (20:8a)

"By the LORD, the God of Israel...." (20:12a)

"May the LORD deal with me, be it ever so severely...." (20:13a)

"So Jonathan made a covenant with the house of David, saying, 'May the LORD call David's enemies to account.' And Jonathan had David reaffirm his oath out of love for him, because he loved him as he loved himself." (20:16-17)

Jonathan and David need to be able to trust one another. David must trust that Jonathan won't betray him to Saul. Jonathan must trust David that his family will not be killed when David eventually assumes the throne. Upon ascending the throne, a king would usually kill all his potential rivals in order to secure his kingship. David promises not to do this with regard to Jonathan or to his descendants.

Finally, they develop a plan so that Jonathan can communicate Saul's intentions to David secretly – a taste of spy-craft from 1000 BC. If Jonathan tells his archery assistant to look for arrows in one area, it means that there is no danger from Saul, but if he tells him the arrows are farther away, it means that David must flee.

David Is Absent from the New Moon Festival (20:24-34)

At the New Moon festival, Saul ignores David's absence the first day, but on the second day, he questions it and, as planned, Jonathan makes excuses for David. This triggers Saul's anger, and he calls Jonathan the "son of a perverse and rebellious woman," an insult meaning, "perverse rebel."[16] Again, Saul explains to Jonathan that David is a threat to his throne.

When Jonathan defends David, Saul hurls the nearby spear at his own son! The man is out of control, willing to kill his own son for associating with David. At least Saul's intentions are clear: "Jonathan knew that his father intended to kill David" (20:33b).

Jonathan and David Weep Together (20:35-42)

The next morning, as planned, Jonathan gives David the signal that Saul indeed intends to kill him. Then Jonathan sends his young assistant back to the palace and David comes out of hiding. He formally honors Jonathan, the king's son, by prostrating himself before him three times.

> "Then they kissed each other and wept together – but David wept the most. Jonathan said to David, 'Go in peace, for we have sworn friendship with each other in the name of the LORD, saying, "The LORD is witness between you and me, and between your descendants and my descendants forever."'" (20:41-42)

David is risking his life by trusting Jonathan, who is his rival for the throne. Jonathan is risking his life by helping his father's chief enemy escape, knowing that it may keep him from becoming king. They make an enduring covenant between the "house of David" and the "house of Jonathan" that will affect their descendants also.

> "Then Jonathan said to David, 'Go in peace, since both of us have sworn in the name of the LORD, saying, 'The LORD shall be **between**[17] me and you, and **between** my descendants and your descendants, forever.'" (20:42, NRSV)

"Sworn" means that they have taken solemn oaths before the Lord. "Peace" recalls that they have sworn not to cause harm to each other. Notice the phrase using the word "between" in verse 23:

> "And about the matter you and I discussed – remember, the LORD is [witness] **between** you and me forever." (20:23)

This recalls the familiar Mizpah saying 800 years earlier on the occasion of Jacob's parting from his uncle Laban:

---

[16] Baldwin, p. 136.

[17] *Bayin*, preposition, "between" is used four times in the Hebrew text of this sentence.

"May the LORD keep watch **between** you and me when we are away from each other. If you mistreat my daughters or if you take any wives besides my daughters, even though no one is with us, remember that **God is a witness between** you and me." (Genesis 31:49-50)

You will recall that there was no longer any trust between Jacob and Laban. Yet they parted with the assurance that the Lord was a witness to their agreement with each other. Of course, when David and Jonathan part, there is great trust between them – and great risk for both of them. Their last words recall that the Lord will be watching that each of them fulfills his part of the covenant.

Q4. (1 Samuel 20:35-42) What is the nature of the covenant between David and Jonathan? What does David receive? What does Jonathan receive? Who benefits the most from this covenant? Is it self-serving – or not? What is the significance that God is witness to the covenant?
http://www.joyfulheart.com/forums/index.php?showtopic=1167

It's touching to imagine their parting. The NIV translates verse 41, "Then they kissed each other and wept together – but David wept the most," suggesting that they were in competition with each other, but that doesn't make sense. *The Message* captures the scene better:[18]

"They kissed one another and wept, friend over friend, David weeping especially hard." (20:41, *The Message*)

David is leaving the honor and relative stability of the king's palace and his own military command. What faces him now is the life of a fugitive, always looking over his shoulder, pursued relentlessly by the most powerful man in the kingdom, intent on his death. And David is leaving his closest, dearest friend, Jonathan, who is risking his own future by being loyal to David. It is almost too much to bear. One chapter of his life is

---

[18] Tsumura (*1 Samuel*, p. 524) catches the sense better with, "until David cried louder," that is, until David's emotions overflowed completely, "until David made (his voice) great/magnified."

closing forever and another chapter – a dark and foreboding chapter – is opening. David is weeping as Jonathan turns to go back to the city while David walks into exile alone.

Disciple Lessons

What are the lessons for disciples here? The text contrasts the evil, conniving, fear-filled jealousy of Saul with the purity of selfless love. I think we can learn several things:

1. **Male friendships**. There can be deep, tender friendships between men without a hint of sexual attraction. This is a lesson that needs to be heard by our culture. Men don't need to be afraid of or apologetic for their love for other men.
2. **Fear and jealousy**, if we let them have a place in our lives, are evil and can be extremely destructive to those around us.
3. **Covenants or promises** between people can endure. God, who is witness to our promises, calls us to a high standard in keeping them.
4. **Enemies**. Living a righteous life doesn't make us immune to others seeing themselves as our enemies. We are responsible for our own lives, but we can't be responsible for others' reactions to us. Our motives may be pure, but that doesn't keep others from hating us. It happens to the best of us – perhaps *especially* to the best.

Prayer

Father, it's sad for us to see Saul's hatred and jealousy. Some of us have felt great pain in our relationships, and have had to flee because of the dysfunction in our families. O Lord, help us not to allow our pain to turn us into bitter people ourselves. By your grace, give us friends with whom we can experience the kind of covenant of trust that David and Jonathan experienced. When we don't have best friends like this, we certainly miss them. Lord, in all of our conflicts and struggles, we trust in you – that you are working out our lives according to your own purposes. In Jesus' name, we pray. Amen.

Key Verses

"After David had finished talking with Saul, Jonathan became one in spirit with David, and he loved him as himself." (1 Samuel 18:1)

"When the men were returning home after David had killed the Philistine, the women came out from all the towns of Israel to meet King Saul with singing and dancing, with joyful songs and with tambourines and lutes. As they danced, they sang: 'Saul has slain his thousands, and David his tens of thousands.'" (1 Samuel 18:6-7)

"Saul was afraid of David, because the LORD was with David but had left Saul." (1 Samuel 18:12)

"Jonathan said to David, 'Go in peace, for we have sworn friendship with each other in the name of the LORD, saying, "The LORD is witness between you and me, and between your descendants and my descendants forever."'" (1 Samuel 20:42)

4. David Flees from Saul (1 Samuel 21-23)

Put yourself in David's sandals for a moment. The king whom David honors seeks to kill him. Saul will stop at nothing – even at sacred boundaries! When David seeks sanctuary with Israel's revered prophet Samuel, Saul no longer fears God. Except for God's intervention, Saul would have killed David in Samuel's very home (19:18-24).

James J. Tissot, "David in the Wilderness of Ziph" (1896-1902) gouache on board, Jewish Museum, New York.

Jonathan, his dearest friend, can no longer associate with him. In fact, David's very presence puts others is danger – as we'll soon see (22:6-19).

David is on his own, a fugitive, running for his life. Yes, God will be with him during this time – abundantly – but David is just learning to walk with the Lord. David is desperate and without resources to make an escape.

David Visits the Tabernacle at Nob (21:1)

The first leg of David's flight is to the tabernacle of the Lord at Nob, probably about two miles from his hideout with Samuel.

Since Joshua and for 300 years, Shiloh[1] had been the location of the tabernacle (Joshua 18:1). Here, the boy Samuel had been raised under Eli the high priest. But when the ark was lost and Eli's sons were killed (1 Samuel 4-7), Shiloh was abandoned and apparently destroyed (Psalm 78:60; Jeremiah 7:4, 12-15; 26:6).

[1] Shiloh has been identified with the present Khirbet Seilun.

The tabernacle, the center of Yahweh worship, has moved to Nob[2] – even though the ark is no longer within it. Nob is "the town of the priests" (22:19) where the Bread of the Presence (showbread) is put before the Lord weekly (21:6), as prescribed in the Torah (Leviticus 24:5-9). The high priest's ephod is also here containing the Urim and Thummim used to inquire of the Lord (1 Samuel 21:9).

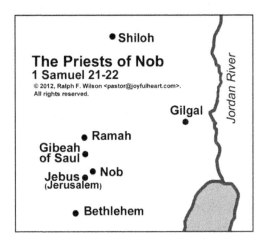

The high priest may well have been aware of Saul's attempt to capture David at nearby Naioth, so he is afraid when he sees David by himself. If Ahimelech knowingly assists a fugitive, Saul is likely to kill him, so David makes up a story about a sudden secret mission that the king has sent him on in order to protect the priest. Is this deliberate deception? Perhaps, but David may be referring to the mission that King Yahweh is sending him on as the anointed of the Lord.[3] (For a more thorough discussion, see Appendix 6. Considering David's Deceit.)

David Is Given Holy Bread (21:3-6)

David requests food. The only food Ahimelech has to give him is some consecrated showbread, some loaves of the Bread of the Presence, that had been before the Lord in the tabernacle the previous week. It is holy, and normally only eaten by the priests themselves (Leviticus 24:5-9). Ahimelech does his due diligence to protect the holiness of the bread by asking David if his men are ritually clean – specifically, if they have had sex that would make them ritually unclean until evening (Leviticus 15:16-18; Exodus 19:15; 1 Corinthians 7:5). David assures him that he and his men are ritually clean and Ahimelech gives him some bread.

Jesus cites this incident when he is questioned about eating grain on the Sabbath.

"'Have you never read what David did when he and his companions were hungry and in need? In the days of Abiathar the high priest,[4] he entered the house of God and ate

---

[2] We're not exactly sure where Nob is, though it may be just north of Jerusalem (Isaiah 10:28-32), perhaps at Bahurim or the Mount of Olives, or further north near Tell Shuafat.

[3] Bergen (*1 and 2 Samuel*, p. 221) cites several scriptures to show the likelihood that David is referring to King Yahweh (1 Samuel 8:7; 12:12), as he does in the Psalms (5:2; 20:9; 24:7-10; 29:10; 68:24; 145:1).

[4] Abiathar was Ahimelech's son, who may have served as high priest alongside his father. He is more famous than his father, since he served David as priest. That's probably why Jesus refers to him here.

the consecrated bread, which is lawful only for priests to eat. And he also gave some to his companions.' Then he said to them, 'The Sabbath was made for man, not man for the Sabbath. So the Son of Man is Lord even of the Sabbath.'" (Mark 2:25-28)

The Pharisees had criticized his disciples for plucking some grain heads to munch on as they walked through a wheat field – in itself entirely legal in Jesus' day. But because this took place on the Sabbath, the Pharisees were classifying this as "harvesting," which was "work." Jesus cites this incident as if to say to the legalistic Pharisees: The Bible itself gives examples of flexibility in interpreting the rules. If the great David was allowed to eat of the holy bread, how much more the Son of Man!

The Sword of Goliath – and Dark Foreshadowing (21:7-9)

David asks Ahimelech if there are any weapons available. It turns out that the sword of Goliath is "wrapped in a cloth behind the ephod" – perhaps to preserve it in Yahweh's presence as a token of God's great victory over the Philistines that day. He gives it to David.

But David's presence has not gone undetected. The narrator records:

"Now one of Saul's servants was there that day, detained before the LORD; he was Doeg the Edomite, Saul's head shepherd." (21:7)

Doeg, one of Saul's servants is there, "detained before the LORD," perhaps for some punishment or penance – we're not sure.[5] Doeg is not an Israelite, but probably a captive from Saul's campaign against Edom (14:47). Later, Doeg reports this incident to Saul, with dire consequences (22:6-19)!

David Feigns Insanity before Achish of Gath (21:10-15)

David doesn't linger at Nob. He flees west to one of the main Philistine cities for protection. It wasn't uncommon for a fugitive to seek refuge with his pursuer's enemy, so David appeals for asylum from Achish, king of Gath.[6]

Indeed, Achish grants David asylum. All is well until members of Achish's court begin to recall who David really is – an arch enemy of the Philistines, the man who in his youth had killed Gath's own champion, Goliath (17:4).

---

[5] Berger, 1 and 2 Samuel, p. 223; Baldwin, 1 and 2 Samuel, p. 138.

[6] The location of Gath has been greatly debated. While five different sites have been suggested, "current excavations at Tell es-Safi and the geopolitical context of Gath in the Biblical narrative make Tell es-Safi the probably site of the ancient city, and this identification retains widespread support among most archaeologists and biblical scholars" (Steven M. Ortiz, "Gath," DOTHB 305).

> "Isn't this David, the king of the land? Isn't he the one they sing about in their dances:
> 'Saul has slain his thousands,
> and David his tens of thousands'?" (21:11)

At this point, David realizes that he is in grave danger! But he is resourceful:

> "He pretended to be insane in their presence; and while he was in their hands he acted like a madman, making marks on the doors of the gate and letting saliva run down his beard" (21:13)

David's ruse works! (See Appendix 6. Considering David's Deceit.) Achish concludes that he must be insane rather than a threat. I love Achish's retort to his courtiers' insistent requests to bring David before the king for questioning:

> "Am I so short of madmen that you have to bring this fellow here to carry on like this in front of me? Must this man come into my house?'" (21:15)

Achish is happy to be rid of him – and David is happy to escape with his life. He travels a few miles east to Adullam.

David Gathers 400 Men at the Cave of Adullam (22:1-4)

Adullam (which means "refuge") was a Canaanite city, east of Gath, west of Bethlehem. Close by was a hill that was fortified and known for its caves, some of them quite large.[7]

By now, Saul is beginning to threaten anyone related to David – including his family in Bethlehem. Saul is crazy with rage and they fear for their lives. So when they hear that David has found a place to hide, they go to join him. For example, David's brothers and sisters and their children join David at Adullam. Three of David's nephews, the sons of his sister Zeruiah, turn out to be outstanding warriors in their own right – Joab, Abishai, and Asahel. Since David is one of the youngest sons of his father, these nephews may by fairly close to his age.

The family members are not alone in seeking refuge with David.

> "All those who were in distress[8] or in debt[9] or discontented[10] gathered around him, and he became their leader. About four hundred men were with him." (22:2)

---

[7] Aid-el-ma (Hurvat Adulam) is probably the location of Adullam, about 2-1/2 miles (4 km) south of the Valley of Elah, and about 20 miles (32 km) west from Bethlehem. At this place is a hill some 450 feet (140 meters) high pierced with numerous caverns, some of them large enough to hold 200 or 300 men (William S. LaSor, "Adullam," ISBE 1:98).

[8] "Distress" is *māṣôq*, "straitness, straits, stress," from *ṣûq*, "constrain, bring into straits, press upon," similar to the Arabic for "be narrow, be tight" (BDB 848).

[9] "Debt" is *nāshâ*, "lend on interest or usury, be a creditor" (TWOT #1424).

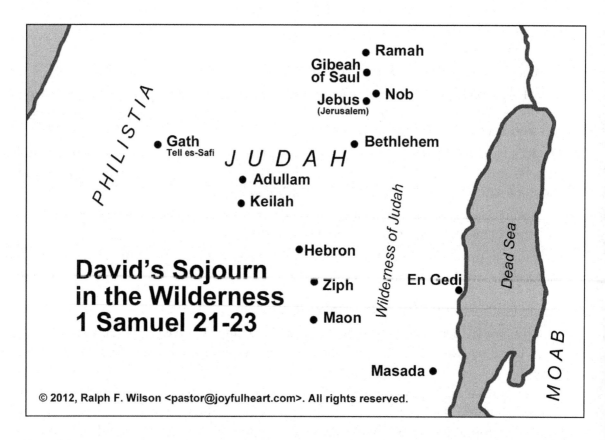

David begins to attract others whom Saul is pursuing – those who owe money being hounded for repayment, rebels who want to overthrow Saul, and probably a few bandits who are wanted for various crimes. Many have a price on their head. Can you imagine trying to unite and lead such a motley crew? Whatever leadership skills David has developed so far are tested and honed here!

But the number doesn't stop at 400; it continues to grow to about 600 men (23:13; 25:13), with even more joining him at Ziklag (1 Chronicles 12:1-20). The Chronicler says:

---

[10] "Discontented" is *mārâ*, "bitter, bitterness" (BDB 606).

James J. Tissot, 'David's Valiant Men' (1896-1902) gouache on board, Jewish Museum, New York

"Day after day men came to help David, until he had a great army, like the army of God." (1 Chronicles 12:22)

David has become a powerful warlord with his own private army[11] – and the responsibility to feed them and their families!

Q1. (1 Samuel 22:2) Why were David's men attracted to him? What did they have in common? Why kind of men were these? What difficulties do you think David probably had in leading them?

http://www.joyfulheart.com/forums/index.php?showtopic=1168

---

[11] Old Testament historian John Bright (*A History of Israel* (Fourth edition; Westminster John Knox Press, 2000), p. 193.) probably overstates it when he says: "For some time David pursued a precarious existence as a bandit chief, playing both ends against the middle, striking the Philistines as opportunity offered, dodging continually to escape the clutches of Saul, and meanwhile supporting himself by extracting 'protection' from wealthy citizens who could afford it (1 Samuel 25:7-8, 15-16)."

David's Mighty Men (2 Samuel 23:8-39 = 1 Chronicles 11:10-47)

Here is where we ought to mention some of the legendary warriors who become part of David's band – the Three and the Thirty! Towards the end of 2 Samuel the narrator names and recounts some of the exploits of these mighty men, but we'll examine them here instead of in Lesson 13. You can almost hear the whispered stories of their exploits as told around flickering campfires.

The Three (2 Samuel 23:8-12)

1. Josheb-Basshebeth, a Tahkemonite, chief of the Three. "He raised his spear against eight hundred men, whom he killed in one encounter" (2 Samuel 23:8).
2. Eleazar son of Dodai the Ahohite. "The men of Israel retreated, but he stood his ground and struck down the Philistines till his hand grew tired and froze to the sword" (2 Samuel 23:9-10).
3. Shammah son of Agee the Hararite. "Israel's troops fled from [the Philistines], but Shammah took his stand in the middle of the field. He defended it and struck the Philistines down" (2 Samuel 23:11-12).

Leaders (2 Samuel 23:18-23)

- Abishai the brother of Joab son of Zeruiah was chief of the Three. "He raised his spear against three hundred men, whom he killed" (2 Samuel 23:18). As mentioned above, Joab and Abishai are David's nephews.
- Benaiah son of Jehoiada from Kabzeel, in charge of his bodyguard. "He struck down two of Moab's best men. He also went down into a pit on a snowy day and killed a lion. And he struck down a huge Egyptian ... and killed him with his own spear." (2 Samuel 23:20-21)

The Thirty (2 Samuel 23:24-39)

Here's the list:

1. Asahel the brother of Joab
2. Elhanan son of Dodo from Bethlehem
3. Shammah the Harodite
4. Elika the Harodite
5. Helez the Paltite
6. Ira son of Ikkesh from Tekoa
7. Abiezer from Anathoth
8. Mebunnai the Hushathite
9. Zalmon the Ahohite
10. Maharai the Netophathite
11. Heled son of Baanah the Netophathite
12. Ithai son of Ribai from Gibeah in Benjamin
13. Benaiah the Pirathonite
14. Hiddai from the ravines of Gaash

15. Abi-Albon the Arbathite
16. Azmaveth the Barhumite
17. Eliahba the Shaalbonite,
18. The sons of Jashan,
19. Jonathan son of Shammah the Hararite
20. Ahiam son of Sharar the Hararite
21. Eliphelet son of Ahasbai the Maacathite
22. Eliam son of Ahithophel the Gilonite
23. Hezro the Carmelite
24. Paarai the Arbite
25. Igal son of Nathan from Zobah the son of Hagri
26. Zelek the Ammonite
27. Naharai the Beerothite, the armor-bearer of Joab son of Zeruiah,
28. Ira the Ithrite
29. Gareb the Ithrite
30. Uriah the Hittite

These men forge a bond with David in difficult times by their bravery and endurance. When David becomes king, they receive high places in the army.

The last-named mighty warrior is Uriah the Hittite, who is killed at David's command as the cover-up for David's affair with his wife, Bathsheba, while he is away at war (2 Samuel 11). So much for loyalty!

Part of this warrior lore is a story from the time that David was in the stronghold[1] at the cave of Adullam. David had spoken aloud of his wish for "a drink of water from the well near the gate of Bethlehem." He never imagined that any would take him seriously. But the Three, at great risk to their lives, broke through Philistine lines, got the water, and brought it back. When David realized what they had done,

> "He refused to drink it; instead, he poured it out before the LORD. 'Far be it from me, O LORD, to do this!' he said. 'Is it not the blood of men who went at the risk of their lives?'" (2 Samuel 23:16b-17)

It is the stuff of legend!

David Flees to the Wilderness of Judah (1 Samuel 22:3-5)

After a look at David's mighty men in 2 Samuel 23, we go back to the sequence in 1 Samuel again.

---

[1] The "stronghold" in 2 Samuel 23:14 is probably different than the one referred to in 1 Samuel 22:4, since the area seems to be nearer to Bethlehem than a location in the Judean wilderness. "Stronghold" (NIV, NRSV), "hold" (KJV) is a generic word, not a place name. *Meṣûdâ* means "fastness, stronghold" (BDB 845). 1 Samuel 22:4-5; 24:22; 2 Samuel 5:17; 23:14; 1 Chronicles 11:16. Jerusalem is referred to as "the fortress of Zion" in 2 Samuel 5:7.

The caves at Adullam are still vulnerable to Saul's army. So David and his army find another stronghold,[2] perhaps in the wilderness of Judah. While in that region, David goes to Moab, east of the Dead Sea, and leaves his aging parents in the care of the king of Moab.

The prophet Gad is apparently part of David's band at this time – probably one of the ways David is able to hear God's voice when he inquires of the Lord. Gad tells him: "'Do not stay in the stronghold. Go into the land of Judah.' So David left and went to the forest of Hereth."[3] God is watching out for David.

Saul Questions the Benjamites' Loyalty (22:6-10)

Though Saul knows where David is, he can't seem to capture him. He is paranoid and accuses his tribesmen, the Benjamites, of conspiracy – of keeping him in the dark about Jonathan's covenant with David.

This accusation prompts Doeg the Edomite to tell Saul – belatedly – that he had seen David getting help from the high priest Ahimelech (21:1-9). Doeg says:

> "Ahimelech inquired of the LORD for him; he also gave him provisions and the sword of Goliath the Philistine." (22:10)

Saul Destroys the Priests of Nob (22:11-19)

Saul now suspects all the priests of conspiring with his enemy David – even though they didn't know anything about David's flight at the time. He summons Ahimelech the high priest, who protests his innocence. Saul doesn't believe him and orders his guards to kill all the priests. They are unwilling "to raise a hand to strike the priests of the LORD" (22:17b). So Saul orders Doeg the Edomite – who isn't a true Israelite or believer in Yahweh – to kill them. The narrator reports the sad story:

> "So Doeg the Edomite turned and struck them down. That day he killed eighty-five men who wore the linen ephod. He also put to the sword Nob, the town of the priests, with its men and women, its children and infants, and its cattle, donkeys and sheep." (22:18-19)

Saul utterly annihilates all the priests and their entire town! He is so out of control that he will kill Yahweh's own consecrated servants!

---

[2] The location of "the stronghold" (NIV, NRSV), "the hold" (KJV) isn't clear. The Hebrew word is *meṣûdâ*. There is no consensus among scholars regarding the location. It is probably not the cave of Adullam. It could be a location in Moab, or perhaps Masada. We just don't know.

[3] The exact location of the Forest of Hereth eludes us. For details, see William S. LaSor, "Hereth, Forest of," ISBE 2:687.

This mass murder severely damages Saul's ability to lead. He has lost any moral high ground among his people. And he loses his ability to seek God's will through the Urim and Thummim, which the priests possess. Now Saul has to make decisions blind. Since he can no longer inquire of the Lord, he ultimately turns to sorcery, the witch of Endor (1 Samuel 28).

Abiathar the Priest Flees to David (22:20-23)

But one priest escapes the slaughter.

> "Abiathar, a son of Ahimelech son of Ahitub, escaped and fled to join David.... Now Abiathar son of Ahimelech had brought the ephod down with him when he fled to David at Keilah." (22:20)

When David learns about Saul's slaughter, he is heartsick and feels that it is his fault. He invites the high priest's son, Abiathar,[4] to stay with him for his own safety. But there is another important benefit of Abiathar's presence – the ephod.

The ephod is part of the high priest's garments that include the Urim and Thummim, apparently lots used to determine God's will when David inquires of Yahweh.[5] David now has the ability to seek God's will about key decisions. In addition, both David and the prophet Gad possess a prophetic gift to hear from God (2 Samuel 23:1-2). David is led by the Lord, while Saul acts in the dark. Out of tragedy, God brings light.

Inquiring of the Lord regarding Keilah (23:1-12)

Immediately, David needs to inquire of the Lord. Philistine raiders are attacking the walled Judean city of Keilah,[6] just south of the Cave of Adullam, and stealing their crops right at harvest time.

> "2 [David] inquired of the LORD, saying, 'Shall I go and attack these Philistines?' The LORD answered him, 'Go, attack the Philistines and save Keilah.' 3 But David's men said to him, 'Here in Judah we are afraid. How much more, then, if we go to Keilah against the Philistine forces!' 4 Once again David inquired of the LORD, and the LORD answered him, 'Go down to Keilah, for I am going to give the Philistines into your hand.'" (23:2-4)

[4] See Appendix 1. Genealogy of the Priesthood.
  www.jesuswalk.com/david/genealogy_of_the_priesthood_in_davids_time.htm
[5] See Ralph F. Wilson, "Inquiring of the Lord," *Paraclete*, Fall 1986, pp. 23-26.
  www.joyfulheart.com/scholar/inquire.htm
[6] Keilah is the modern Khirbet Qîlā, about 8 miles northwest of Hebron.

"Inquire" is *shā'al*, "ask, inquire," in particular, asking God for guidance.[7] Notice that in this instance, the answers David receives are "yes" or "no." This probably represents the use of the Urim and Thummim. These seem to be a pair of lots that can answer: yes, no, and maybe. Though we don't know for sure, you can easily imagine a pair of lots, each marked with "yes" on one side and "no" on the other. If, when the lots are cast, they both come up the same, the answer is clear. But if they come up with different answers, then the answer is not clear.

The Lord confirms to David that he should attack the marauding Philistines at Keilah and he does so successfully, saving the town.

David's men stay at Keilah for a time, but David realizes that he is vulnerable there. Saul can lay siege to the city and capture him. So he inquires of the Lord again and receives the answer that the citizens of Keilah will indeed surrender him to Saul rather than resist Saul's siege. David moves on.

> "So David and his men, about six hundred in number, left Keilah and kept moving from place to place. When Saul was told that David had escaped from Keilah, he did not go there." (23:13)

Being able to consult the Lord is vital to David's security so that he can remain in God's will.

Q2. (1 Samuel 22:20-23:12) What did Abiathar and the ephod have to do with "inquiring of the Lord?" Why did David inquire of the Lord? What huge advantage does the person have who seeks God's will before acting? How can you find God's will at key points in your life?

http://www.joyfulheart.com/forums/index.php?showtopic=1169

Hiding in the Wilderness of Ziph (23:14a)

> "David stayed in the desert strongholds and in the hills of the Desert of Ziph. Day after day Saul searched for him, but God did not give David into his hands." (23:14a)

David has sought refuge with the prophet Samuel and the king of Gath. He has hidden in caves and cities, but he isn't safe anywhere. Saul's spies are everywhere,

---

[7] R. Laird Harris, *shā'al*, TWOT #2303.

reporting on his every movement. And so David turns to the Judean desert for his own survival.

When we think of desert, the endless sands of the Sahara may come to mind, but this doesn't describe the kind of desert you find in Judah. Arid, rocky, and rugged are better descriptors. The desert is a dry place, where water is not easily found. It is barren and can be terrifying, lonely, with a solitude that can be frightening.

If you were to draw an east-west cross-section of Judah through Hebron, on the west you find the coastal plain where the Philistines live. Then, going east, you come to the lower hills, the Shepelah, where Judean towns are being threatened by Philistine encroachment. Then you come to the hill country, a north-south ridge upon which you find major Judean cities such as Hebron and Jerusalem. Farther east – between the ridge and the Dead Sea – is the Judean desert, extending to an escarpment which drops precipitously down to the Dead Sea and the Jordan Valley. It is cut by many rocky, dry wadis and steep canyons.

The Judean desert receives only four inches of rain a year due to the rain shadow effect of the ridge of mountains. When the wilderness does receive rain, however, the desert blossoms – for a short time. But somehow, amidst the scrub, sheep and goats can be grazed and find sustenance in the desert.

In the Judean wilderness, David can find safety. It is rugged country where a guerilla force might sustain itself, but an regular army couldn't last long. Its rocky formations provide tremendous protection against attack. Indeed, in some of his psalms, David draws a parallel between God's protection and these wilderness fortresses:

> "Turn your ear to me,
> come quickly to my rescue;
> be my **rock of refuge**, a strong **fortress** to save me.
> Since you are my **rock** and my **fortress**,
> for the sake of your name lead and guide me.
> Free me from the **trap** that is set for me,
> for you are my **refuge**." (Psalm 31:2-4)

Here's another psalm from this period that recalls some of the high rocks in which David and his band hide from Saul:

> I love you, O LORD, my strength.
> The LORD is my **rock**, my **fortress** and my deliverer;
> my God is my **rock**, in whom I **take refuge**.
> He is my shield and the horn of my salvation, my **stronghold**.
> I call to the LORD, who is worthy of praise,

and I am saved from my enemies....
With your help I can advance against a troop;
with my God I can scale a wall....
He makes my feet like the feet of a deer;
he enables me to stand on the heights. (Psalm 18:1-3, 29, 33)

While the Judean Desert is the term for the whole area, our text refers more precisely to the Desert of Ziph (23:25) and the Desert of Maon (23:25). These would be the wilderness areas to the east of the cities named. Ziph is probably to be identified with Tell Ziph, about 5 miles southeast of Hebron, while Maon is the modern Khirbet Ma'în, about 4-1/2 miles south of Ziph.

I can hardly imagine how a band of 600 men and their families could survive in the Judean wilderness. They suffer often from hunger and thirst. Psalm 63 is "a psalm of David when he was in the desert of Judah." You can see hints here and there of his struggle.

"¹ O God, you are my God, earnestly I seek you;
my soul **thirsts** for you, my **body longs** for you,
in a dry and weary land where there is no water....
⁴ I will praise you as long as I live,
and in your name I will lift up my hands.
⁵ My soul will be satisfied as with the **richest of foods**;
with singing lips my mouth will praise you.
⁶ On my bed I remember you;
I think of you through the watches of the night.
⁷ Because you are my help,
I sing in the shadow of your wings.
⁸ My soul clings to you;
your right hand upholds me." (Psalm 63:1, 4-8)

Some scholars have suggested that David made living forcing wealthy men like Nabal to pay "protection money,"[8] but this speculation isn't supported by the Scripture. Such a policy certainly wouldn't have endeared him to his Judean tribe members – who later anoint him as king.[9] Some families may have gone home – if they were able – during this period. No doubt David did receive help from sympathetic people. We just don't know how David's men all survived; probably some didn't.

---

[8] Klein (*1 Samuel*, p. 246) says, that David asked for provisions "as payment for the protection he had provided Nabal's shepherds."

[9] Baldwin (*1 and 2 Samuel*, p. 147) believes that David limited himself to extorting only the rich in Judah who oppressed the poor. Even Nabal's servants didn't like him (25:17).

Jonathan Encourages David at Horesh (23:14-18)

Fear has driven David into the desert: "Day after day Saul searched for him," (23:14a). To say that David was afraid is not the same as to suggest that he was not courageous. Fear and courage coexist.

But God even cares about our anxieties! In this case, God sends Jonathan to encourage David. He is at Horesh, an unknown area in the desert east of Ziph.[10] Saul is after him, and Jonathan – perhaps travelling with his father's army – comes to find him. David's men let him pass because of David's affection for the king's son – and because of the covenant of peace David has with Jonathan. The narrator records that Jonathan "helped him find strength in God" (23:16). Observe Jonathan's words:

> "Don't be afraid. My father Saul will not lay a hand on you. You will be king over Israel, and I will be second to you. Even my father Saul knows this." (23:17)

They renew their covenant before Yahweh before Jonathan returns home.

Q3. (1 Samuel 23:14-18) Why does Jonathan visit David in the wilderness? What risk is there for David? What risk is there for Jonathan? What do you think it meant to David? Have you ever received a visit from a friend when you needed it most?
http://www.joyfulheart.com/forums/index.php?showtopic=1170

Saul Nearly Captures David in the Judean Wilderness (23:19-28)

But our popular hero is not loved by all – even the inhabitants of Ziph from his own tribe of Judah. They send a delegation to Saul's capital to report David's exact location – "in the strongholds at Horesh, on the hill of Hakilah, south of Jeshimon" (23:19).[11]

David then moves a few miles south to the desert of Maon. Saul is hot on David's trail in a deadly game of cat and mouse.

---

[10] "Horesh" (NIV, NRSV), "wood" (KJV) is *ḥōresh*, which may mean "wood" or "wooded height" (BDB 362), though some associate it with Khirbet Khoreisa, about 2 miles south of Ziph (Klein, *1 Samuel*, p. 231).

[11] We don't know the location referred to. Jeshimon is a more general word referring to the barren eastern part of the Judean mountains stretching toward the Dead Sea. "This desolate region of waterless land and soft chalky hills with numerous caves has been throughout history a refuge for fugitives, outlaws, and those who withdrew from society" (J. Franklin Prewitt, "Jeshimon," ISBE 2:1032-1033).

"Saul was going along one side of the mountain, and David and his men were on the other side, hurrying to get away from Saul." (23:26)

But just as they are about to capture David, a messenger reports to Saul about a Philistine raid. He is forced to break off his pursuit to defend his country against the Philistines. The Lord's timing is exquisite.

Now David travels to the "strongholds of En Gedi," the impenetrable rock formations overlooking the oasis of En Gedi (23:29). We'll discuss more about his time in En Gedi in Lesson 5.

Historical Ascriptions of the Psalms of David

David is closely identified with worship music in the Bible (Amos 6:5). He sang to calm his sheep on the hillsides and for King Saul in his palace (1 Samuel 16:14-23; 18:10-11), accompanying himself on a lyre or harp. He is called "the sweet psalmist of Israel" (2 Samuel 23:1), with 73 psalms attributed to him – nearly half of the Book of Psalms. Several of these contain ascriptions that tell us on what occasion he wrote the psalm. Here are some of them, placed in approximately chronological order.

1 Samuel 19:11	**Psalm 59**. "When Saul had sent men to watch David's house in order to kill him."
21:12-15	**Psalm 56**. "When the Philistines had seized him in Gath."
21:13-15	**Psalm 34**. "When he pretended to be insane before Abimelech, who drove him away, and he left." A beautiful acrostic psalm.
22:9-10	**Psalm 52**. "When Doeg the Edomite had gone to Saul and told him, 'David has gone to the house of Ahimelech.'"
22:1	**Psalm 57**. "When he had fled from Saul into the cave."
22:1	**Psalm 142**. "When he was in the cave."
22:5; 23:14-16, 23f	**Psalm 63**. "When he was in the Desert of Judah."
23:19	**Psalm 54**. "When the Ziphites had gone to Saul and said, 'Is not David hiding among us?'"
Chapter 22	**Psalm 18**. "He sang to the LORD the words of this song when the LORD delivered him from the hand of all his enemies and from the hand of Saul."
2 Samuel 8:13-14	**Psalm 60**. "When he fought Aram Naharaim and Aram Zobah, and when Joab returned and struck down twelve thousand Edomites in the Valley of Salt."

| 12:13 | **Psalm 51.** "When the prophet Nathan came to him after David had committed adultery with Bathsheba." |
| Chapter 15 | **Psalm 3.** "When he fled from his son Absalom." |

Q4. (Psalms 18, 34, 54, 56, 58, 59, 142) In these ascriptions to these psalms, how many celebrate happy occasions? How many arise from struggles? What does this tell you about David's relationship with God? What does this tell you about his faith during trials? Which is your favorite among these psalms? Why?
http://www.joyfulheart.com/forums/index.php?showtopic=1171

Lessons for Disciples

What do we learn from these chapters that we can apply to our own lives? Several things.

1. **Provision.** God provides for his servants, even in times of desperate need, as David found bread and a sword in the house of the Lord.

2. **God's fashioning.** Every great person has times of seeming failure, as well as times of success and adulation. Don't judge too soon that God has forgotten you. He is molding you into a finely-crafted instrument that he can use in his work.

3. **Leaders.** Leaders tend to attract followers when they are struggling as well as when they're on top, as David gathered a band of mighty men in the wilderness. Look for a person that people are following and you'll find a leader.

4. **Learning.** Times of struggle are often when you learn the most and do your best work. Don't discount the difficulties you face in your wilderness as wasted time.

5. **Guidance.** The ability to seek God's will is a very precious gift. David had this in the presence of the Urim and the Thummim, the company of a prophet, and his own prophetic gift. You can find God's will if you seek him with all your heart, since, if you're a Christian, you possess the Holy Spirit of God who connects you with the very mind of Christ (1 Corinthians 2:10-16).

6. **Betrayal.** Even people you have helped may well betray you, as the residents of Keilah and Ziph will betray David. You will meet disappointment. But don't

despair! You have an unshakable Rock, the Lord your God. He will never leave you or forsake you (Hebrews 13:5)!

7. **Praise**. We are to praise God in all circumstances (1 Thessalonians 5:16-18), as David did in many of his Wilderness-era psalms. Our joy is in the Lord himself, not in whether everything is going well or not.

Wilderness times are terribly difficult. They strip us down to the essentials and test us to the very core so that we know what is really important. Several times in the Bible we see God using the desert to refine his people. The Israelites spent 40 years in the desert. Jesus spent 40 days. The Apostle Paul spent 3 years. David's time is one of refining and connecting firmly to the Rock of Israel.

Have you been through a wilderness experience? Are you going through one right now? God has not forsaken you. He loves you like he loved David. He is with you in the wilderness, and he is using this time to mold you into a new person. Embrace Him. This time will pass. But when you come out of your wilderness, you'll be better prepared for the future God will unfold before you. God is working out his plan in you.

Prayer

Lord, you know what we're going through, what we've been through. It seems so very hard! But we are confident that you are the God of the wilderness as well as the God of prosperous times. We can count on you. You will be to us a Refuge, a Fortress, a Shade by day and Shield by night. Thank you, O Lord. Give us strength! In Jesus' name, we pray. Amen.

Key Verses

"David left Gath and escaped to the cave of Adullam. When his brothers and his father's household heard about it, they went down to him there. All those who were in distress or in debt or discontented gathered around him, and he became their leader. About four hundred men were with him." (1 Samuel 22:1-2)

"Once again David inquired of the LORD, and the LORD answered him, 'Go down to Keilah, for I am going to give the Philistines into your hand.' ... (Now Abiathar son of Ahimelech had brought the ephod down with him when he fled to David at Keilah.)" (1 Samuel 23:4, 6)

"David stayed in the desert strongholds and in the hills of the Desert of Ziph. Day after day Saul searched for him, but God did not give David into his hands." (1 Samuel 23:14)

5. David Spares the Lord's Anointed (1 Samuel 24-28)

David has two opportunities to kill King Saul, and both times he refuses to kill his arch enemy or allow his men to do so. Why? These accounts reveal something we need to learn about anger, pride, revenge, humility, and submission to the Lord's will. It contains some profound lessons taught against the background of the violence of the Late Bronze Age.

James J. Tissot, "David and Saul in the Cave" (1896-1902), gouache on board, The Jewish Museum, New York.

This is a long and complex lesson. If you're teaching it, you might want to divide it into two lessons.

David Hides in the Wilderness of En Gedi (24:1-2)

Chapter 23 closed with Saul coming very close to capturing David, only to be called away to defend Israelite cities against the marauding Philistines. Now Saul is back with an army 3,000 strong.

He has learned from his spies that David is hiding out in the Judean Desert in the rocky fortresses above the oasis of En Gedi or *'Ein Gedi* on the west bank of the Dead Sea. David's men are in a rock formation known then as the Crags of the Wild Goats,[1] a natural stronghold, honeycombed with caves, that is easy to defend against attackers.

The name "Ein Gedi" means "spring of the goat," referring to the wild goats that populate this rugged area. Ein Gedi and its year-round stream is one of four major springs in this otherwise parched eastern portion of the Judean Desert. The area includes

---

[1] We're not sure of the exact location of the "Crags of the Wild Goats," except that it is a rock outcropping near the Dead Sea.

a steep cliff or escarpment that falls more than 2,000 feet (625 meters) from the plateau of the desert (at about 650 feet, or 200 meters, *above* sea level) to the Dead Sea (at 1,388 feet, or 423 meters, *below* sea level).

David Spares Saul's Life in the Cave (24:3-7)

> "[Saul] came to the sheep pens along the way; a cave was there, and Saul went in to relieve himself.[2] David and his men were far back in the cave. [4] The men said, 'This is the day the LORD spoke of when he said to you, "I will give your enemy into your hands for you to deal with as you wish.""" (24:3-4a)

We have no record of such a prophecy prior to this, though it was obviously known to David's men.

David's band is completely silent as David stealthy creeps up to where Saul is probably now resting in the privacy and cool of the cave. Saul's 3,000 men are outside; he is vulnerable.

> "Then David crept up unnoticed and cut off a corner of Saul's robe." (24:4b)

David's action has considerable significance. Taking a portion of the royal robe could have been interpreted in that time as a transfer of power from Saul to David. In addition, David's action may have rendered Saul's robe – Saul's visible sign of kingship – non-compliant with requirements of the law by removing tassels from its corner (Numbers 14:38-39; Deuteronomy 22:12). That's why David is "conscience-stricken," since by voiding Saul's claim to kingship in this way, he is moving against "the Lord's anointed." He has to explain this to his men, who are bent on killing Saul when they have this chance. Many of them are under Saul's death sentence, just like David is. The temptation to kill Saul is almost overpowering.

> "[6] [David] said to his men, 'The LORD forbid that I should do such a thing to my master, the LORD's anointed, or lift my hand against him; for he is the anointed of the LORD.' [7] With these words David rebuked his men and did not allow them to attack Saul. And Saul left the cave and went his way." (24:6-7)

If David had indeed killed Saul in the cave, he and his 600 men would have had to face Saul's troops outside the cave. But these troops would have been leaderless – and many of them realized the validity of David's claim to the throne. Probably David himself had led some of these troops when he had been one of Saul's generals.

---

[2] This is a Hebrew idiom, literally it is "to cover his feet." It refers to the Israelite practice of disposing of human excrement in a sanitary manner through covering it over with dirt (Deuteronomy 23:13; Bergen *1&2 Samuel*, p. 238, fn. 113).

Could David have gotten away with killing Saul and claiming the throne? Probably. But David's refusal to attack Saul isn't based on strategic or even moral grounds. It is based on the profound respect that David has for Yahweh – the fear of the Lord. God, David reasons, has put Saul into the kingship. For David, rebellion against Saul is tantamount to rebellion against the Lord himself who has anointed Saul.

David Asserts His Loyalty to Saul (24:8-15)

David waits to confront Saul until the king and his bodyguards are some distance away. Then he prostrates himself before the king. He waves a piece of the king's robe, and indicates that he could have killed Saul except for his own conviction:

"I will not lift my hand against my master, because he is the LORD's anointed." (24:10)

David is not silent. He publicly accuses Saul of wronging him by trying to kill an innocent man, and calls upon Yahweh's justice to prevail.

"May the LORD judge between you and me. And may the LORD avenge the wrongs you have done to me, but my hand will not touch you. As the old saying goes,

'From evildoers come evil deeds,'
so my hand will not touch you." (24:12-13)

The point of the proverb he quotes is that, if David were an evil doer, Saul would have been long dead. David continues with heavy sarcasm:

"Against whom has the king of Israel come out? Whom are you pursuing? A dead dog? A flea?" (24:14)

The phrase "a dead dog" denotes self-abasement or self-disparagement, as in 2 Samuel 9:8 – an object of insignificance.[3] The flea, too, is an image of insignificance, in the same way that a mustard seed is figurative of tininess.[4] David says something similar in 26:20 when he takes Saul's spear and water jug while he is sleeping. His point is that Saul is squandering vast national resources fielding an army of 3,000 men to hunt down someone who is no threat to him or to the kingdom – a loyal citizen. David closes his case with an appeal to God's bar of justice.

"May the LORD be our judge and decide between us. May he consider my cause and uphold it; may he vindicate me by delivering me from your hand." (24:15)

---

[3] Tsumura (1 Samuel, p. 571) cites McCarter to the effect that "dog," "dead dog," and "stray dog" are also found with this meaning in Akkadian and in the Lachish letters.

[4] Par'ōsh, BDB 829.

Q1. (1 Samuel 24:1-15) Why doesn't David kill Saul when he has the chance? What motive do David and his men have for killing a king who is trying to kill them? What is David's rationale for sparing Saul? What does this tell us about David's character? About his faith? What does it say about David's leadership ability that he is able to dissuade his men from killing Saul?
http://www.joyfulheart.com/forums/index.php?showtopic=1172

This principle of "lifting one's hand against the Lord's anointed" extends beyond an anointed king to any of God's servants. God warns Abimelech king of Gerar not to harm Abraham (Genesis 20:7). He warns Laban not to harm Jacob (Genesis 31:24). The psalmist refers to these warnings:

> "Do not touch my anointed ones;
> do my prophets no harm." (Psalm 105:15; cf. 1 Chronicles 16:22)

Jesus taught his disciples:

> "He who receives you receives me,
> and he who receives me receives the one who sent me.
> Anyone who receives a prophet because he is a prophet
> will receive a prophet's reward,
> and anyone who receives a righteous man because he is a righteous man
> will receive a righteous man's reward.
> And if anyone gives even a cup of cold water to one of these little ones
> because he is my disciple,
> I tell you the truth, he will certainly not lose his reward." (Matthew 10:40-42)

> "He who listens to you listens to me;
> he who rejects you rejects me;
> but he who rejects me rejects him who sent me." (Luke 10:16)

This doesn't mean that Jesus' disciples and servants today can't be called to account. Paul taught both respect for the leader's office *and* accountability:

> "The elders who direct the affairs of the church well are worthy of double honor, especially those whose work is preaching and teaching.... Do not entertain an accusation against an elder unless it is brought by two or three witnesses. Those who sin are to be rebuked publicly, so that the others may take warning." (1 Timothy 5:17, 19-20)

Paul also quotes the law:

> "Do not speak evil about the ruler of your people" (Acts 23:5b, quoting Exodus 22:28)

I've seen how horribly Christians sometimes speak about their pastors. I've heard of the way people sometimes cruelly treat men and women of God. It is shameful!

Dear friends, we need to have a fear of the Lord in relation to God-appointed leaders. Just like David refused to lift his hand against the Lord's anointed, we need to show respect for the office – even if the people who fill the office are imperfect.

Q2. (1 Samuel 24:12) How do we apply the principle of not lifting a hand against the Lord's anointed in our day? What provisions are there in 1 Timothy 5:19-20 for calling leaders to account. What do you think God will do to those who slander, persecute, and martyr his appointed leaders?
http://www.joyfulheart.com/forums/index.php?showtopic=1173

Saul Repents (24:16-22)

Saul's response is both humble and emotional. He weeps aloud. He acknowledges the righteousness of David's position and calls on Yahweh to reward David for his mercy to Saul. Then he publicly acknowledges that David will be his successor:

> "I know that you will surely be king and that the kingdom of Israel will be established in your hands." (24:20)

Finally, he asks David to swear before Yahweh that when David becomes king he will not "cut off my descendants or wipe out my name from my father's family" (24:21). David had already sworn in his covenant with Jonathan to protect Jonathan's offspring (20:15, 42). Now he voluntarily extends this promise to cover all of Saul's descendants. He gives his solemn oath. This is why he does not kill Ish-Bosheth, Saul's remaining son who reigns over Israel after Saul's death (2 Samuel 4:11-12).

> "Then Saul returned home, but David and his men went up to the stronghold." (25:22b)

The stronghold here probably refers to the Crag of the Wild Goats where David and his men had been hiding for protection. David doesn't trust Saul's words enough to return with him. Saul has broken his promises too often for David to trust him now (19:6). People can say many kind things, but their actions show their true heart.

The Death of Samuel (25:1a)

"Now Samuel died, and all Israel assembled and mourned for him; and they buried him at his home in Ramah." (25:1a)

Samuel's death marks the end of an era for Israel. He is the last of the judges, and is no longer present to be Saul's conscience. This report also sets the reader up for Saul's seeking of Samuel's spirit through a spiritist medium in 28:7-25.

Nabal the Carmelite (25:1b-3)

David still doesn't return home; he knows that Saul's heart is false. Instead, he moves his band to the western side of the Judean desert near Maon. Now the narrator gives us a quick pen sketch of Nabal who lives nearby.

"His name was Nabal and his wife's name was Abigail. She was an intelligent and beautiful woman, but her husband, a Calebite,[5] was surly and mean in his dealings." (25:3)

Nabal is fabulously wealthy, with 1,000 goats and 3,000 sheep. The narrator tells us that Nabal is shearing, a time traditionally celebrated by feasting with plenty to spare.[6]

David's Request for Provisions Is Rudely Rejected (25:4-13)

David sends a delegation of 10 young men to ask Nabal politely for some provisions. They are to remind him how David's men hadn't stolen any his sheep, even when they had the opportunity.

"When your shepherds were with us, we did not mistreat them, and the whole time they were at Carmel nothing of theirs was missing." (25:7)

Later, David recalls aloud how faithful he had been to Nabal – "all my watching over this fellow's property in the desert so that nothing of his was missing" (25:21). David has acted righteously, not unrighteously. He has only asked the wealthy sheep baron for whatever provisions he can spare.

"Therefore be favorable toward my young men, since we come at a festive time. Please give your servants and your son David whatever you can find for them." (25:8)

[5] Caleb, one of the faithful spies of Canaan under Moses (Numbers 13-14). During the Conquest, he conquered the walled city of Hebron and was given territory around it (Joshua 14-15; 21:12). David's later marriage into this Calebite family probably gave him greater political strength when it came time for the elders of Judah to anoint him king in Hebron (2 Samuel 5:1-3; so Klein, *1 Samuel*, p. 248).
[6] Baldwin, *1 and 2 Samuel*, p. 147.

But Nabal answers rudely, suggesting that David is nothing but a runaway slave, probably a smear at David for having left Saul. Nabal knows who David is, all right, but chooses to insult him instead of giving him what he asks. It is a mistake.

When David hears of Nabal's insult, he is livid. "Put on your swords!" he angrily commands his men, and he takes 400 of his men to slaughter Nabal and plunder all that he has.

Abigail's Wise and Humble Response (25:14- 35)

Fortunately, Nabal's beautiful wife Abigail hears about Nabal's foolish insults ("Nabal" means fool) – and immediately takes action. She prepares a great deal of food as fast as she can and loads it on donkeys to take to David.

- 200 loaves of bread
- 2 skins of wine
- 5 dressed sheep
- 5 seahs of roasted grain
- 100 cakes of raisins
- 200 cakes of pressed figs

David has sworn vengeance: "May God deal with David, be it ever so severely, if by morning I leave alive one male of all who belong to him!" (25:23) – a foolish oath!

When Abigail sees David, she prostrates herself at his feet and makes abject apologies for her husband's foolish insults. Then she appeals to David's reputation as a righteous man before Yahweh:

> "Now since **the LORD has kept you**, my master, **from bloodshed and from avenging yourself with your own hands**, as surely as the LORD lives and as you live, may your enemies and all who intend to harm my master be like Nabal. And let this gift, which your servant has brought to my master, be given to the men who follow you." (25:26-27)

She offers the food for David's men as a gift – a bribe, if you will. She has one chance to turn David away from destroying Nabal and his household, and she gives it everything she has. She asks forgiveness for Nabal. Then she points to the certainty of David's kingship – if he operates justly and doesn't have blood on his hands!

> "The LORD will certainly make a **lasting dynasty** for my master, because he fights the LORD's battles. **Let no wrongdoing be found in you** as long as you live.... The life of my master will be bound securely in the bundle of the living by the LORD your God.

> When the LORD has ... appointed him leader over Israel, **my master will not have on his conscience the staggering burden of needless bloodshed or of having avenged himself.**" (25:28-31)

David is overwhelmed, thanks Abigail, and grants her request to forgive Nabal.

Observe that David doesn't keep his foolish oath (25:22) – and we have no indication that God is displeased by this. Sometimes in our foolishness we can vow things that are wrong. God is more interested in keeping us from sin, than in making sure that we observe the terms of a foolish vow. An example of carrying vow-keeping too far is Jephthah, who killed his own daughter to keep a foolish vow (Judges 11:30-31).

Bloodguilt

David recognizes that unless Abigail had intervened he would have been guilty of Nabal's death.

> "[32] Praise be to the LORD, the God of Israel, who has sent you today to meet me. [33] May you be blessed for your **good judgment** and for **keeping me from bloodshed** this day and from **avenging myself with my own hands**. [34] Otherwise, as surely as the LORD, the God of Israel, lives, who has kept me from harming you, if you had not come quickly to meet me, not one male belonging to Nabal would have been left alive by daybreak." (25:32-34)

The moral issue here is bloodguilt, the sin of shedding innocent blood. As we trace this through Scripture, we see the principle enshrined in the Ten Commandments: "You shall not murder" (Exodus 20:13), that is, commit unlawful killing. The word "murder" (NIV, NRSV) or "kill" is *rāṣaḥ*, "murder, slay, kill."[7] Of the 35 times it is used in the Old Testament, it is used 14 times in Numbers 35, where the person who has accidentally killed someone can find sanctuary in a "city of refuge," where he can't be killed by a relative, an "avenger of blood," before his case is heard in a court of law, before he "stands trial before the assembly" (Numbers 35:12). Numbers gives guidelines for determining whether a person was killed purposely or accidentally, whether the killer acted with hostility or "malice aforethought" (Numbers 35:21). This chapter concludes:

> "Do not pollute the land where you are. Bloodshed pollutes the land, and atonement cannot be made for the land on which blood has been shed, except by the blood of the one who shed it. Do not defile the land where you live and where I dwell, for I, the LORD, dwell among the Israelites." (Numbers 35:33-34)

This command not to murder, of course, precedes the Ten Commandments. In the beginning, God condemns Cain for killing Abel out of anger (Genesis 4). The Lord also instructs Noah:

[7] William White, *rāṣaḥ*, TWOT #2208. Its use in Numbers 35 "makes clear that *rāṣaḥ* applies equally to both cases of premeditated murder and killings as a result of any other circumstances, what English Common Law has called, "man slaughter."

"And for your lifeblood I will surely demand an accounting.... From each man, too, I will demand an accounting for the life of his fellow man. Whoever sheds the blood of man, by man shall his blood be shed; for in the image of God has God made man." (Genesis 9:5-6)

The command not to murder is rooted in respect for God, in whose image man is made.

The Old Testament does not include in this category of murder three types of sanctioned killing: capital punishment (Genesis 9:6), killing in time of war (in many places), and self-defense (Exodus 22:2-3).

This issue of taking innocent blood is quite important later in David's history. The slayers of Saul's son Ish-Bosheth are guilty of taking innocent blood (2 Samuel 4:11). Joab bears bloodguilt for killing both Abner and Amasa who were rivals, "shedding their blood in peacetime as if in battle, and with that blood stained the belt around his waist and the sandals on his feet" (1 Kings 2:5).

Now, in our narrative of Nabal and Abigail, David is about to kill for a petty insult, which would have made him guilty of murder before the Lord. He is thankful that Abigail's appeal saved him from bloodguilt. His heart is tender before the Lord his God!

Later, when his heart grows callous, he becomes guilty of the murder of Uriah (2 Samuel 12:9). In the great penitential Psalm 51, David calls out to God for forgiveness.

"Save me from bloodguilt,[8]
O God, the God who saves me,
and my tongue will sing of your righteousness." (Psalm 51:14)

Nabal's Death and David's Marriage to Abigail (25:36-44)

Abigail returns home to find Nabal drunk. When she tells him in the morning how his life has been saved by her intervention, "his heart failed him and he became like a stone. About ten days later, the LORD struck Nabal and he died" (25:37-28). It sounds like Nabal had a stroke. David interprets it as God's judgment on him.

David has the wisdom to see in Abigail a worthy wife. He asks for her hand in marriage, and she accepts, attended by her five maids. She is David's second wife. You can see David's other wives and descendants in Appendix 3, "Genealogy of the House of David."

Q3. (1 Samuel 25) What do we learn about David's character in this incident with Nabal and Abigail? What do we learn about Abigail's character? Nabal's character?

---

[8] *Dām*, literally, "blood."

Why do you think this story was included in 1 Samuel? What important knowledge does it add to our understanding?

http://www.joyfulheart.com/forums/index.php?showtopic=1174

Polygamy in the Bible

It's difficult for many of us in the twenty-first century to see how the Bible seems to pass over polygamy so easily. Does God approve of multiple wives?

Monogamy is expressed as God's intention in the earliest chapters of Genesis:

"The man said, 'This is now bone of my bones and flesh of my flesh; she shall be called 'woman,' for she was taken out of man.' For this reason a man will leave his father and mother and be united to his wife, and they will become one flesh." (Genesis 2:23-24)

Jesus quoted this passage when he discussed divorce to reinforce God's intention for marriage to continue between a man and a woman as "one flesh."

"So they are no longer two, but one. Therefore what God has joined together, let man not separate." (Matthew 19:6)

While there are provisions in the Torah to regulate polygamy (Deuteronomy 21:15-17), the ideal marriage in Israel consists of one man and one woman (Malachi 2:13-16). The only exception to this is the Levirate marriage with a brother's widow.

Reasons why polygamy was more common in some Biblical periods probably include the preponderance of females vs. males because of war, providing for destitute widows, and to maintain the culture's working force. Of course, lust was a primary driver. Polygamy was tolerated among the rich, who could afford multiple wives, but it wasn't considered Israel's ideal.

The New Testament presupposes monogamy. The bond between husband and wife is seen to typify the relationship of Christ and his church (Ephesians 5:22-33). Church leaders are required to be monogamous (1 Timothy 3:2, 12; Titus 1:6), as are widows whom the church supports (1 Timothy 5:9).

Polygamy in our day can be seen in break-off Mormon sects and in the African church. The unnatural character of polygamy in some Mormon sects is seen in the requirement that most of the young men are driven out of the polygamous community when they are teenagers so that the young women can be possessed by the older men. In

Africa today, it is not uncommon for church leaders to have more than one wife, in accord with tribal customs. In spite of the examples of polygamy seen in our day and in the Bible, God's plan has always been for the union of one man and one woman.

Polygamy in David probably should be understood in the way that Jesus explained a provision for divorce in the Mosaic Law:

> "Moses permitted you ... because your hearts were hard. But it was not this way from the beginning." (Matthew 19:8)

David Has a Second Chance to Kill Saul (26:5-10)

Through his marriage to Abigail, David is probably entitled to Nabal's lands and servants.[9] But he can't settle down because of Saul. He and his wives are still on the run. They travel north east from Abigail's home in Maon into the Desert of Ziph, to one of David's old haunts on the hill of Hakilah[10] (23:19-24a). And again, spies from Ziph betray David's location. Despite his declarations and promises, Saul pursues David there with his army. It's Saul's army of 3,000 again against David's 600, an established king against his presumed rival, the establishment seeking to crush the loyal subject who has been declared an outlaw.

But David is a wily foe. He doesn't remain in one place, but decamps to the wilderness until his scouts tell him that Saul himself has arrived. David does some scouting himself, and sees Saul and his army sleeping and vulnerable. Back with his men, he finds his nephew Abishai willing to volunteer for the dangerous mission of infiltrating Saul's camp. Together the two sneak into Saul's camp. The narrator tells us:

> "There was Saul, lying asleep inside the camp with his spear stuck in the ground near his head. Abner and the soldiers were lying around him." (26:7)

They were all asleep, the narrator tells us: "They were all sleeping, because the LORD had put them into a deep sleep." (26:12b)

Abishai and David engage in a hushed argument. Abishai boasts that he will kill Saul "with one thrust of my spear. I won't strike him twice!" (26:8). But David won't let him. Look carefully at David's reasoning, since it clearly explains the nature of his faith in Yahweh:

> "[9] Don't destroy him! Who can lay a hand on the LORD's anointed and be guiltless? [10] As surely as the LORD lives, **the LORD himself will strike him**; either his time will come

[9] Baldwin, *1 and 2 Samuel*, pp. 152-153.
[10] Jeshimon is a general word describing the barren desert east of the mountains.

and he will die, or he will go into battle and perish. [11] But the LORD forbid that I should lay a hand on the LORD's anointed." (26:9-11a)

David knows that he himself has been anointed by the Lord. But he realizes that this doesn't give him the right to kill another person God has anointed. He trusts God to take care of Saul on his own, rather than take matters into his own hands.

When you think about it, this is what separates David from any other local warlord of his time. David is not a mere opportunist. He is a man of devout faith.

Many times you and I are tempted to do the expedient thing rather than the right thing. We are tempted by power, by money, by sex, and when an opportunity comes to advance our own cause we take it. That's what Satan's followers do, not Christ's disciples. David, who is a type of Christ, provides an amazing Old Testament example of Jesus' obedience to the Father. The Apostle Paul wrote:

> "[3] Do nothing out of selfish ambition or vain conceit, but in humility consider others better than yourselves. [4] Each of you should look not only to your own interests, but also to the interests of others. [5] Your attitude should be the same as that of Christ Jesus:
>
> [6] Who, being in very nature God,
>   did not consider equality with God something to be grasped,
> [7] but made himself nothing,
>   taking the very nature of a servant,
>   being made in human likeness.
> [8] And being found in appearance as a man,
>   he humbled himself and became obedient to death –
>   even death on a cross!
> [9] Therefore God exalted him to the highest place
>   and gave him the name that is above every name...." (Philippians 2:3-9)

Dear friend, what do you do when you are tempted to get great gain, even if it means taking a shortcut that you know is out of God's will?

David Takes Saul's Spear and Water Jug (26:11-20)

But David has a noble purpose: to redeem his good name. Saul has, no doubt, been smearing David as a dangerous rebel and outlaw, in order to justify his paranoid – and expensive – pursuit. So David says to Abishai,

> "Now get the spear and water jug that are near his head, and let's go." (26:11b)

The spear seems to be Saul's symbol of kingly authority, something like a scepter[11] that he often holds or keeps nearby (18:10) – perhaps as a protection against assassins. We read earlier:

> "Saul, spear in hand, was seated under the tamarisk tree on the hill at Gibeah, with all his officials standing around him." (22:6)

Saul always seems to have his spear at his side, both indoors and out. He had thrown his spear at both David (18:10-11; 19:10) and Jonathan (20:33) when he was upset. In fact, Saul's spear is unique in Israel, since in this early Iron Age culture, the Philistines have a monopoly on ironsmiths, so only Saul and Jonathan possess iron-tipped spears (13:19, 22).

Thus, when David takes Saul's spear (representing his kingly power) and his personal water jug (representing life-sustaining resources), David is symbolically stripping Saul of both social standing and life.[12]

Once David has retreated from Saul's army a safe distance, he begins to taunt Saul's general, Abner, for the serious security breach of the king's bodyguard that would allow an enemy so close to the king's person. Abner is silent. But Saul recognizes David's voice and calls out to David as "my son."

David presents his case publicly before Saul and before his entire shamed army:

1. **David is innocent of any plot against the king** (25:18), proved by not killing him when he has the chance.

2. **David has been unjustly deprived of Yahweh worship**, "my share in the Lord's inheritance" (25:19b). Saul has driven him away from worship at the tabernacle at Nob.[13] (Soon he will have to leave Israel entirely, to take refuge with the Philistines.) Exclusion from the sanctuary is intensely painful to David. In the Desert of Judah he writes longingly, "I have seen you in the sanctuary and beheld your power and your glory" (Psalm 63:2). David pleads with Saul: "Now do not let my blood fall to the ground far from the presence of the LORD" (26:20a).

3. **Saul's expensive expedition is irrational**. I am no threat, David contends. He humbly refers to himself as an insignificant flea, while Saul is mercilessly pursing

---

[11] In ancient times, the scepter derived from a full-length staff held by the king.

[12] Bergen, *1 and 2 Samuel*, p. 245.

[13] Baldwin (*1 and 2 Samuel*, p. 155) observes: "David is not really in doubt that Saul's motivation come from within himself, but he tactfully suggests otherwise," that the motivation might have come from the Lord or from his counselors.

him like hunters on a partridge hunt – with 3,000 men. What a waste of time, men, and money! And while employing the army in this irrational quest, Saul is leaving Israel's towns and villages unprotected from the Philistines.

Saul Repents – Again (26:21-25)

Saul, to his credit, publicly humbles himself:

> "I have sinned. Come back, David my son. Because you considered my life precious today, I will not try to harm you again. Surely I have acted like a fool and have erred greatly." (26:21)

David isn't fooled. Saul has made promises before, and though he may mean them at the time he makes them, he doesn't keep them for long. David returns Saul's spear, and then David calls on Yahweh to reward him for his righteousness and faithfulness – Saul certainly won't reward him!

> "As surely as I valued your life today, so may the LORD value my life and deliver me from all trouble." (26:25)

Saul blesses David – still calling him "my son" – and returns home. "You will do great things and surely triumph," he says. But his words ring hollow. David "accepted the king's words for what they were – sincere, deadly lies."[14]

David Seeks Asylum with the Philistines (27:1-7)

David knows he'll never be safe as long as Saul is alive.

> "David thought to himself, 'One of these days I will be destroyed by the hand of Saul. The best thing I can do is to escape to the land of the Philistines. Then Saul will give up searching for me anywhere in Israel, and I will slip out of his hand.'" (27:1)

So David once more seeks asylum with Achish, king of the Philistine city of Gath, in the area just west of the Judean hill country. The first time David had sought refuge in Gath, he came alone and fled when he realized how vulnerable he was (21:10-15). This time he comes to Achish as a vassal, a warlord with 600 warriors. As a vassal of King Achish, he will be protected by Achish, but he will owe tribute to Achish and be required to defend Gath and fight with the Philistines when they go to war.

Achish welcomes him on the simple basis that "my enemy's enemy is my friend." And it has the desired effect: "When Saul was told that David had fled to Gath, he no longer searched for him" (27:4).

---

[14] Berger, *1 and 2 Samuel*, p. 258.

Achish must be struggling to feed David's 600 men and their families in Gath. And David doesn't like being so closely under Achish's eye. After all, he doesn't exactly share the Philistines' religion and values. So David brings a request to Achish:

> "If I have found favor in your eyes, let a place be assigned to me in one of the country towns, that I may live there. Why should your servant live in the royal city with you?" (27:5)

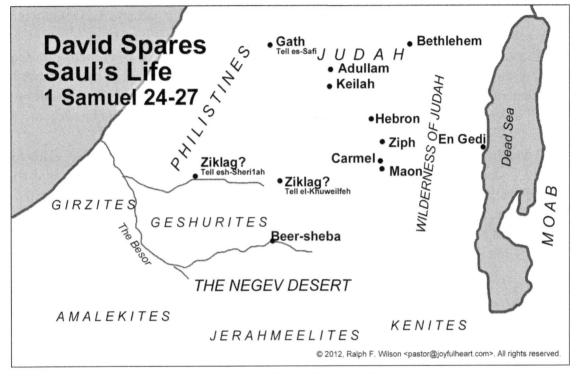

I expect that Achish is quite happy to send David a safe distance away.

> "So on that day Achish gave him Ziklag, and it has belonged to the kings of Judah ever since. David lived in Philistine territory a year and four months." (27:6-7)

The exact location of Ziklag is unknown, though it's surely a settlement in the Negev desert. It has been identified with Tell esh-Sheri'ah, about 20 miles ESE of Gaza. Others identify it as Tell el-Khuweilfeh, about 14 miles north of Beersheba,[15] but that may be too far east for the descriptions we have.[16] The Philistines control this area, so Achish gives the town over to David and his men and families as a base of operations.

---

[15] Oxford Bible Atlas, p. 142

[16] Tsumura, 1 Samuel, pp. 611-612. A.F. Rainey, "Ziklag," 4:1196. Student Map Manual shows it as Tell Sera (7-5, 7-6). It is listed as a city of Judah in Joshua 15:31, belonging to the Negev province. Ziklag, had been

David, as a Philistine Vassal, Raids Israel's Enemies (27:8-12; 28:1-5)

Now the narrator tells us what David and his men are doing while residing at Ziklag. They were engaged in raiding parties on Israel's enemies:

> "Now David and his men went up and raided the Geshurites,[17] the Girzites,[18] and the Amalekites. (27:8)

David would annihilate the enemy population and plunder their livestock, clothing, etc. The Amalekites, especially, were enemies of the Israelites. They had attacked them when they were being led by Moses in the Wilderness and the Israelites never forgot it.

When David brings Achish tribute and is asked about his raids, David tells him that he had raided the desert areas populated by people of the tribe of Judah (his own tribe), the clan of Jerahmeel,[19] or the clan of the Kenites.[20] (See Appendix 6. Considering David's Deceit.) As a result, Achish trusts David. He says to himself: "He has become so odious to his people, the Israelites, that he will be my servant forever" (27:12).

David has served as a vassal or servant of the Philistine king Achish of Gath for nearly a year and a half when active war breaks out between Saul's army and the Philistines. As you may recall, the Philistines were led by a confederation of five cities – Gath, Gaza, Ashkelon, Ashdod, and Ekron. As one of Achish's vassals, David is called up with his men to fight with the Philistine confederation against Israel. We'll consider David's dilemma and the outcome in the next lesson.

---

assigned to the tribe of Simeon at the Conquest under Joshua, but never been conquered (Joshua 19:5; 15:31).

[17] P.C. Hughes, "Geshur," ISBE 2:449. A tribe bordering the Philistines on the south (Joshua 13:2), raided by David.

[18] R. K. Harrison, "Girzites," ISBE 2:472. An otherwise unknown people living between the Philistines and the Egyptian border, not to be confused with Gezer.

[19] The Jerahmeelites (mentioned here and in 30:29) were a clan descended from Jerahmeel, who was a descendant of Judah by Tamar his daughter-in-law (1 Chronicles 2:9, 25-27, 33, 42; Genesis 38), considered as part of the tribe of Judah (R. K. Harrison, "Jerahmeel," ISBE 2:984).

[20] The Kenites were a tribe of nomads, perhaps smiths or metalworkers, who apparently lived in the mountains south of the Dead Sea and in the Sinai Peninsula. Moses' father-in-law is called a Kenite in some places (Judges 1:16; 4:11), so the Midianites and Kenites may have had a close relationship. Jethro's descendants went up with the people of Judah into the wilderness of Judah in the Negev near Arad (Judges 1:16) (John Arthur Thompson, "Kenites," ISBE 3:6-7).

Saul Seeks a Medium (28:7-14)

We conclude this lesson, however, with Saul. When he sees the Philistine armies begin to assemble in the Jezreel Valley at Shunem,[21] he is deathly afraid. "Terror filled his heart" (28:5).

Though Saul seeking a medium isn't technically part of David's life, we'll include it here, since it raises important questions about séances, spiritism, and channeling that Christians wonder about today.

God has forsaken Saul. He has given the Israelites several ways to receive guidance from God, but these are no longer available to Saul.

> "He inquired of the LORD, but the LORD did not answer him by dreams or Urim or prophets." (28:6)

The Spirit has left Saul so he doesn't receive dreams from the Lord (16:13-14). He has killed the priests who could inquire of the Lord for him. And Samuel, the prophet Saul has relied on for counsel, has died.

So Saul, desperate to determine the future of this coming battle with the Philistines by any means, turns from the Lord to illicit means, thus damning him further (1 Chronicles 10:13).

> "Saul then said to his attendants, 'Find me a woman who is a medium, so I may go and inquire of her.' 'There is one in Endor,'[22] they said. So Saul disguised himself, putting on other clothes, and at night he and two men went to the woman." (24:7-8a)

Occult Practices in the Ancient Near East

Seeking to learn the future from a deity was common in David's time. The Old Testament describes at least seven occult practices:

1. **Hepatoscopy**, divination by inspecting the liver of a sacrificed animal (Ezekiel 21:21), a widespread practice. Archaeologists have found clay models of livers at Megiddo and elsewhere.

2. **Hydromancy**, divining by water, perhaps seen in Genesis 44:5.

3. **Rhabdomancy**, divination using a divining rod (Hosea 4:12).

4. **Belomancy**, divination by casting of arrows (Ezekiel 21:21).

---

[21] B.R. and P.C. Patten, "Shunem," ISBE 4:497. Scholars identify it with Sôlem, a village 9 miles N of Jenin, overlooking the Valley of Jezreel.

[22] Endor ("fountain of dwelling") is a town assigned to western Manasseh, identified with the modern village of Endor, on the northern slope of the hill of Moreh (J. F. Prewitt, "Endor," ISBE 2:80).

5. **Teraphim**, household gods or images, widespread in the ancient Near East, used as a symbol of authority, land ownership, and for divination (Ezekiel 21:21; Zechariah 10:2).

6. **Astrology**, common in Babylon, seeking the future in the stars and planets (Isaiah 47:13; Jeremiah 10:2).

7. **Necromancy**, consultation with the dead to determine the future, as is practiced by the "witch of Endor."[23]

The word "medium" (NIV, NRSV), "familiar spirit" (KJV) that occurs in 28:7, 9 is 'ôb, "spirit of the dead,"[24] which occurs in the feminine gender in Hebrew. The word is often paired with yidde'ônî (as in 28:9), which occurs in the masculine gender in Hebrew.[25] Together they probably refer to females and males who conduct occult practices.[26] The prophet Isaiah describes how perverted people have become in his day, who prefer mediums and wizards to true prophets.

> "When men tell you to consult mediums and spiritists,
> who whisper and mutter,
> should not a people inquire of their God?
> Why consult the dead on behalf of the living?" (Isaiah 8:19)

The Mosaic law is clear that the Israelites were to stay away from these occultists, and to stone them (Leviticus 19:31; 20:27; Deuteronomy 18:10-11). We Christians, too, must stay away from any kind of sorcery or necromancy that seeks the future by occult means or by consulting the dead, a practice common in the New Testament world (Acts 8:9-24; 13:6-12, 16-18; 19:18-19; 1 Corinthians 10:20-21; Revelation 9:21; 21:8; 22:15).

Saul had rightly banished mediums from his realm, but they had only gone underground. With a bit of inquiry, Saul's attendants are able to find one rather quickly.

Saul asks the woman to "bring up Samuel" for him. She does so, but what happens is nothing like what she suspected – that's why she shrieks at the top of her lungs and realizes that her client is none other than King Saul.

The question arises whether this passage of scripture validates the practice of necromancy, that is, trying to communicate with the dead, which is forbidden in Deuteronomy 18:11. There seem to be four possibilities:

---

[23] This section draws on Davis, *Kingdom*, p. 95; and David E. Aune, "Divination," ISBE 1:-971-974; Ann Jeffers, "Magic and Divination," DOTHB, pp. 670-674.
[24] 'Ôb, Holladay 6.
[25] Yidde'ônî is derived from the root "to know" (yāda').
[26] Robert L. Alden, 'ôb, TWOT #37a.

1. **Psychological.** This was real, but the product of psychological impressions, so real that the medium herself is convinced by them.

2. **Hoax.** This is a hoax perpetrated by the medium upon Saul. But the medium herself is terrified by it, since it is out of the ordinary.

3. **Demonic.** A demon or Satan impersonates Samuel (2 Corinthians 11:14).

4. **Genuine.** This is a genuine appearance of Samuel brought about by God himself to declare again his judgment upon Saul.[27]

Though the last interpretation troubles us because necromancy was forbidden by God, it seems to fit the text the best. Bergen observes:

1. The text says the medium did in fact see Samuel.

2. The medium reacts to Samuel's appearance as though it were a genuine experience.

3. The speeches attributed to Samuel contain allusions to a prior exchange between Samuel and Saul.

4. Samuel's role and message as a prophet is unchanged in his encounter with Saul here.[28]

Nevertheless, this passage should not be considered an endorsement of the practice of necromancy, because (1) necromancy is specifically prohibited in Scripture – here and elsewhere, and (2) it is clear that this event wasn't normal at all! Baldwin says,

> "The incident does not tell us anything about the veracity of claims to consult the dead on the part of mediums, because the indications are that this was an extraordinary event for her, and a frightening one because she was not in control."[29]

Dear friend, if you've been involved in communicating with the dead through séances channeling, etc. – even Ouija boards – I urge you to repent before God and ask forgiveness. These are dangerous practices that can harm you spiritually![30]

Q4. (1 Samuel 28:7-14) Why do you think God condemns occult practices of communicating with the dead and channeling spirits of the dead? How might such practices

---

[27] Discussed by Davis, *Kingdom,* pp. 96-99.

[28] Bergen, *1 and 2 Samuel,* p. 267.

[29] Baldwin, *1-2 Samuel,* p. 159.

[30] It's pretty common for people to speak to their departed loved ones and even feel their presence. That's not what I'm talking about. But when we seek to communicate through occult practices, we open ourselves to demonic influences. Beware!

open Christians to victimization and oppression by evil spirits? What should you do if you've been involved in such practices in the past?
http://www.joyfulheart.com/forums/index.php?showtopic=1175

Samuel's Apparition Condemns Saul (28:15-25)

Saul doesn't see or speak to Samuel, but the medium purports to see him and hear his words. Saul explains through the medium about the Philistine threat and his aloneness, forsakenness by God, and wants to know what to do. Samuel's answer is several fold:

1. **A rebuke**. Why do you consult me through a medium?

2. **A fulfillment**. As God had said, because of your disobedience, Yahweh in his wrath has transferred the kingdom to David.

3. **A prediction**. The Philistines will defeat the Israelites in battle; Saul and his sons will be killed.

Saul is terror-stricken. The lady feeds him; then he and his men go out into the night. Saul realizes that the next day he will be killed and face God alone – a pretty sobering situation for anyone.

Praise God, that when we stand before God, we have an advocate, Jesus Christ the Righteous One, who has died for our sins (1 John 2:1-2). If you have put your trust in Jesus Christ and become his disciple, your name is written in the Lamb's Book of Life (Revelation 20:11-14). You have a Friend who will stand with you on that Day. Hallelujah.

Lessons for Disciples

In these chapters we find several lessons that we can apply to our lives.

1. **Respect.** We are to respect the leaders that God has appointed over us, even if they aren't perfect – which they never are (Hebrews 13:17a). David had respect for Saul as the Lord's anointed. God will judge those who rebel against His leaders, slander them, or speak evil of them (Acts 23:5b; Exodus 22:28).

2. **Appeal.** We can, however, respectfully disagree with our leaders, as David did before Saul, and appeal to their reason. And we can also appeal to God when a

leader is out of line. God, who put the leader in place can (and perhaps will) re-move that leader. Leaders must answer to God! (Hebrews 13:17b).

3. **Humility.** When we humble ourselves before a leader about to make a mistake, like Abigail did before David, and speak clearly and boldly, we can sometimes influence the outcome positively. Humility is appropriate for two reasons. First, leaders often struggle with pride. Second, we don't see everything the leader sees and may be wrong in our assessment.

4. **Steadfastness.** When God shows us one of his principles, we must stand up for it, even if others don't understand us or criticize us, as David's men did when he spared Saul. We aren't to cave in under pressure.

5. **Faithfulness.** When we make a promise, we must do our very best to be true to our word, not like Saul, whose promise not to harm David was made and broken again and again. Neither God nor man have respect for a person who makes a promise and then changes his mind and does the opposite.

6. **The Occult.** We are to stay away from occult practices of any kind, and thor-oughly repent of any involvement in the past that may have contaminated us spiritually or made us vulnerable to Satan's deception or oppression.

In this lesson, we've traced David during his Wilderness wanderings. He has been challenged, he has seen God's mercy, and he has grown stronger in the process. In the next lesson, we'll watch as David faces one of the greatest challenges of his life.

Prayer

Father, David's incredible faith allowed him to spare Saul – twice. Give us that kind of conviction and faith that we might stand against our great temptations. We seek your will. We renounce and repent of any occult practices. Forgive us for our sins and cleanse us, we pray. Teach us to walk close to you. In Jesus' name, we pray. Amen.

Key Verses

"[David] said to his men, 'The LORD forbid that I should do such a thing to my master, the LORD's anointed, or lift my hand against him; for he is the anointed of the LORD.' With these words David rebuked his men and did not allow them to attack Saul. And Saul left the cave and went his way." (1 Samuel 24:6-7)

"May the LORD judge between you and me. And may the LORD avenge the wrongs you have done to me, but my hand will not touch you." (1 Samuel 24:12)

"David said to Abigail, 'Praise be to the LORD, the God of Israel, who has sent you today to meet me. May you be blessed for your good judgment and for keeping me from bloodshed this day and from avenging myself with my own hands.'" (1 Samuel 25:32-33)

6. David Strengthens Himself in the Lord (1 Samuel 29-2 Samuel 1)

David, a fugitive from King Saul in exile among the Philistines, is perhaps 30 years old[1] when his protector, Achish, king of the Philistine city of Gath, calls up the military forces of all his vassals to fight against the Israelites. Up to this point, David has tried to be loyal to Saul, while at the same time pledging fealty to Achish (chapter 27). Now David faces a terrible dilemma.

James J. Tissot, "The Women of Ziklag Taken into Captivity" (1896-1902), gouache on board, The Jewish Museum, New York.

"Achish said to David, 'You know, of course, that you and your men are to go out with me in the army.' David said to Achish, 'Very well, then you shall know what your servant can do.' Achish said to David, 'Very well, I will make you my bodyguard for life.'" (28:1b-2)

Notice David's answer: "Then you shall know what your servant can do." David himself doesn't know what he will do, but he trusts the Lord to guide him. He gives Achish an ambiguous answer. Achish takes it as assent and full commitment to battle Israel. But David means it as a willingness to subvert the Philistine forces while within them, if need be. The die is cast. David's 600 men will join the massing armies of Philistia – or will he?

Framing the Battle of Gilboa

In the previous lesson we read,

[1] 1 Samuel 5:4. For more on David's ages at different points, see Appendix 4: A Chronology of David's Life.

"The Philistines assembled, and came and encamped at Shunem. Saul gathered all Israel, and they encamped at Gilboa. When Saul saw the army of the Philistines, he was afraid, and his heart trembled greatly." (28:4-5)

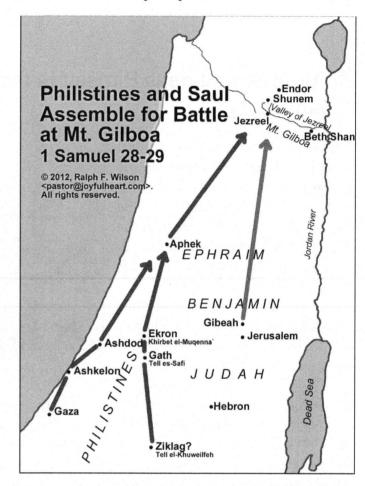

Philistines and Saul Assemble for Battle at Mt. Gilboa
1 Samuel 28-29

© 2012, Ralph F. Wilson
<pastor@joyfulheart.com>.
All rights reserved.

The place where this show-down battle takes place is north of the Philistine's core territory – and north of Saul's capital. The Philistines begin to mass their troops in the Jezreel Valley for several reasons:

1. Chariot advantage. The flat river valley was a much better place for the 3,000 Philistine chariots (13:5); the Israelites had no chariots. Chariots couldn't operate effectively in the hill country where Saul lived, so the Philistines chose the valley.

2. Split Israel. If the Philis-tines win the battle they can seriously weaken Saul by splitting off the Israelite tribes south of the Valley of Jezreel (Ephraim, Benjamin, Judah, etc.) from those north of it, around the Sea of Galilee (East Manasseh, Asher, Naphtali). Saul is forced to fight on this ground or lose control over much of his kingdom.

3. Opportunity for a decisive battle. If the Philistines can defeat Saul in this all-out battle, they can subdue Israel in the future and take over Judean towns in the Shepelah or low hills to the east of the coastal plain where the Philistines live. What is shaping up is not just a skirmish, but a major battle pitting the massed troops of the Philistine confederation and their vassals against the less organized, smaller, and poorly equipped force that Saul is able to put in the field. Add to this the fact that the Philistines have more advanced weaponry – iron vs. bronze – the battle can bring about Philistine dominance in the region for decades.[2]

Saul had no choice but to fight, but his odds of winning are poor. No wonder Saul is terrified!

David and His Men Are Sent Home (chapter 29)

> "[1] The Philistines gathered all their forces at Aphek, and Israel camped by the spring in Jezreel. [2] As the Philistine rulers marched with their units of hundreds and thousands, David and his men were marching at the rear with Achish." (29:1-2)

The Yarkon River is considered the northern extent of Philistine occupation.[3] Aphek, where the Philistine troops gather, is identified with Tell Ras el-'Ain about 10 miles east of present-day Tel Aviv, an area of springs providing the main source of the Yarkon River.

On the other hand, Saul's forces assemble near "the spring in Jezreel" (29:1b), probably the present 'Ain Jalud, just under the northern cliffs of Mount Gilboa, at the south edge of the Jezreel Valley. Dugan says, "A plentiful and beautiful spring of clear cold water rises in a rocky cave and flows out into a large pool, whence it drains off, in Nahr Jalud, down the valley past Beisan to the Jordan."[4] Where Saul's troops now camped, Gideon had camped with his troops centuries before as they prepared to fight the Midianites (Judges 7:1).

The Philistine march begins, but then reports of Israelites among the troops reach other generals in the Philistine confederation. Achish defends David and his record of loyalty, but the other Philistine leaders will have none of it. After all, with 600 men, David could do great damage behind Philistine lines once the battle begins. The generals aren't fooled:

> "Send the man back, that he may return to the place you assigned him. He must not go with us into battle, or he will turn against us during the fighting. How better could he regain his master's favor than by taking the heads of our own men? Isn't this the David

---

[2] Bright says, "The Philistine tactics are intelligible. The route into Esdraelon [that is, the Jezreel Valley] was in their control, and along it they might count on the support of Sea Peoples and Canaanite city-states allied with them. Furthermore, it offered terrain upon which their chariots could maneuver (2 Samuel 1:6), together with the possibility of cutting Saul off from the Galilean tribes to the north. Why Saul let himself be drawn into battle at such a place is less obvious" (John Bright, *History of Israel*, p. 194).

[3] J.F. Prewitt, "Aphek," ISBE 1:150; Tsumura, *1 Samuel*, pp. 188-189.

[4] Quote from R.P. Dugan, "Harod," ISBE 2:618. See also Arthur E. Cundall and Leon Morris, *Judges-Ruth: An Introduction and Commentary* (Tyndale Old Testament Series; Inter-Varsity Press, 1968), p. 109.

they sang about in their dances: 'Saul has slain his thousands, and David his tens of thousands'?" (29:4b-5)

Now Achish faces the delicate task of explaining the situation to David without offending him. David appears hurt, but inwardly he is relieved. So in the morning, the Philistine armies advance toward the Jezreel Valley, while David and his men begin the long trek back to Ziklag, far south in the Negev desert. Somehow, the Lord has helped David out of a ticklish situation!

David and His Men Mourn the Raid on Ziklag (30:1-5)

It is a three-day, 50-mile journey from north of Aphek to Ziklag, and by the time they return home, David and his men are worn out.

But when they arrive, they find Ziklag destroyed with smoke arising from the ashes, perhaps in retaliation for the raids David had made on the Amalekites (27:8). The narrator explains:

> "Now the Amalekites had raided the Negev and Ziklag. They had attacked Ziklag and burned it, and had taken captive the women and all who were in it, both young and old. They killed none of them, but carried them off as they went on their way." (30:1-2)

The exhausted warriors are beside themselves with exhaustion and grief.

> "So David and his men wept aloud until they had no strength left to weep." (30:4)

In our culture it is considered a sign of weakness for men to weep in public. But in the Middle East, men mourn just as openly as women. And David's men have lost everything that is dear to them.

The Men Blame David (30:6a)

Predictably, the men begin to blame David.

> "David was greatly distressed[5] because the men were talking of stoning him; each one was bitter[6] in spirit because of his sons and daughters." (30:6a)

"If David hadn't made us go north with our Philistine enemies, this wouldn't have happened," you can hear them say. "David should have insisted that we leave some of our men here to defend our families. It's his fault!" Some talked of stoning him.

---

[5] "Distressed" (NIV, KJV), "in great danger" (NRSV) is *yāṣar*, "bind, be narrow, be in distress" (TWOT #1973). I think the author is talking about David's internal distress, rather than an outward danger from his men here.

[6] The phrase "bitter in spirit" (NIV, NRSV), "soul ... was grieved" (KJV) uses the verb *mārar*, "to be bitter, embitter." It is interesting to note that the Hebrews expressed tragic, unpleasant experiences in terms of the sense of taste, the bitter (Victor P. Hamilton, *mārar*, TWOT #1248).

It's pretty human to assign blame, even when it isn't warranted. We blame ourselves if a child is killed by a drunk driver for not keeping him closer to home – even when the driver was clearly at fault. We blame others for events that impact us negatively, even if they couldn't have reasonably foreseen them. Politicians take credit for the jobs "they" have created, but they are also blamed for a downturn in the economy that they couldn't have reasonably prevented. Blame is natural, even if it's unfair. Nevertheless, it hurts when people blame you unjustly.

Strengthening Yourself in the Lord (30:6b)

One of my favorite verses in David's life is this one:

"But David found strength in the LORD his God." (30:6b, NIV)

Other translations are that he "strengthened himself" (NRSV) or "encouraged himself" (KJV) in the LORD his God. The verb is *ḥāzaq*, "be(come) strong, strengthen, prevail, harden, be courageous." The Hithpael stem of this word here is usually the reflexive idea, of "strengthening oneself."[7]

I can imagine David's 600 men weeping, cursing, blaming, and talking rebellion. But over at the side by himself is David. He sits in the dust with tears running down his face, but he is praying. He is singing quietly to himself and to the Lord. He cannot allow himself to become depressed and filled with hopelessness. He cannot allow himself to become defensive and react to his men's rebellious voices. He must connect with the Lord himself so that he can find strength to go on.

The Quaker tradition calls this "centering down," seeking to enter into a calm, quiet, reflective, receptive state.

Q1. (1 Samuel 30:1-6) Why do the men blame David? Why is the situation so explosive at this point. What does David do in the situation? What is David feeling? Why doesn't he act immediately?

http://www.joyfulheart.com/forums/index.php?showtopic=1176

---

[7] Carl Philip Weber, *ḥāzaq*, TWOT #636.

David Strengthening Himself in the Psalms

Just how do you go about strengthening or encouraging yourself in the Lord when everything is crashing in upon you? Here are some examples from the Davidic Psalms of David doing this very thing. Take the time to read these passages, for in them you'll find the secrets of strengthening yourself:

> "**In my distress I called to the LORD;**
> **I cried to my God for help.**" (Psalm 18:6a)

> "**The LORD is my light and my salvation** – whom shall I fear?
> The LORD is **the stronghold of my life** – of whom shall I be afraid?
> When evil men advance against me to devour my flesh,
> when my enemies and my foes attack me,
> they will stumble and fall." (Psalm 27:1-2)

> "I will **extol the LORD at all times**;
> his **praise will always be on my lips.**
> **My soul will boast in the LORD**;
> let the afflicted hear and rejoice.
> Glorify the LORD with me;
> let us exalt his name together.
> I **sought the LORD**, and he answered me;
> he delivered me from all my fears.
> Those who look to him are radiant;
> their faces are never covered with shame.
> This poor man **called**, and the LORD heard him;
> he saved him out of all his troubles." (Psalm 34:1-6)

> "I **waited patiently** for the LORD;
> he turned to me and heard my cry.
> He lifted me out of the slimy pit,
> out of the mud and mire;
> he set my feet on a rock and gave me a firm place to stand.
> He put a new song in my mouth,
> a hymn of praise to our God.
> Many will see and fear
> and put their trust in the LORD." (Psalm 40:1-3)

> "As the deer pants for streams of water,
> so **my soul pants** for you, O God.
> **My soul thirsts** for God, for the living God.
> When can I go and meet with God?
> My tears have been my food day and night,

while men say to me all day long, 'Where is your God?'
These things I remember as I pour out my soul:
how I used to go with the multitude,
leading the procession to the house of God,
with shouts of joy and thanksgiving among the festive throng.
Why are you downcast, O my soul?
Why so disturbed within me?
Put your hope in God, for I will yet praise him,
my Savior and my God." (Psalm 42:1-6a)

"Be merciful to me, O God, for men hotly pursue me;
all day long they press their attack.
My slanderers pursue me all day long;
many are attacking me in their pride.
When I am afraid, I will trust in you.
In God, whose word I praise, **in God I trust**;
I will not be afraid. What can mortal man do to me?" (Psalm 56:1-4)

"**My soul finds rest in God alone**;
my salvation comes from him.
He alone is my rock and my salvation;
he is my fortress, I will never be shaken." (Psalm 62:1-2)

Q2. (1 Samuel 30:6) From the Psalms of David, how does David seem to strengthen himself in the Lord when things are going bad? What devotional exercises does he adopt? What is the focus of his faith?
http://www.joyfulheart.com/forums/index.php?showtopic=1177

David Pursues the Amalekites (30:7-17)

First, David spends some time before the Lord getting his strength restored and his faith renewed. His first task isn't to find out what to do next. It's to receive refreshing from the Lord after a big emotional and spiritual blow.

But, second, David considers what action he should take. Often, we'll run off half-cocked. But David inquires of the Lord via the Urim and Thummim in the high priest's

ephod as he had done in the past when faced with a decision about what action to take
(23:9).

> "[7] Then David said to Abiathar the priest, the son of Ahimelech, 'Bring me the ephod.'
> Abiathar brought it to him, [8] and David inquired of the LORD, 'Shall I pursue this raid-
> ing party? Will I overtake them?'
> 'Pursue them,' he answered. 'You will certainly overtake them and succeed in the res-
> cue.'" (30:7-8)

Encouraged by the Lord, David and his army travel swiftly south to the Besor Ravine,
about a dozen miles south of Ziklag. The Wadi Besor (sometimes called Wadi Ghazzeh
near its mouth) is the largest stream in the northern Negev desert, considered the
southern boundary of Philistine territory.[8]

> "David and the six hundred men with him came to the Besor Ravine, where some
> stayed behind, for two hundred men were too exhausted to cross the ravine. But David
> and four hundred men continued the pursuit." (30:9-10)

Here, the desert floor has been deeply eroded during the occasional flash floods in the
Negev, so that crossing the wadi requires major effort. For about one third of David's
men, it is too much. They are exhausted physically and emotionally, and just can't go on.

But David and the rest of his men travel without stop through the wilderness, trying
to track the Amalekites, looking for signs of their passage. Finally, they find a half-dead
Egyptian, and give him water and food to revive him. It turns out he had been with the
Amalekites until he was left for dead. Now he leads David's men to the Amalekite
camp.

Apparently, the Amalekites are a much larger group than the 400 with David, since
the text tells us that *only* 400 young men escape on camels. Due to the element of initial
surprise and the ferocity of David's men, most of the Amalekites are slaughtered, as the
David's army "fought them from dusk until the evening of the next day" (30:17). The
victory is so complete that the Amalekites are not mentioned as an opponent of Israel for
300 years.

David Divides the Plunder (30:18-25)

Best of all, David's men recover every one of their wives and children unharmed.
Amazing! They also are entitled to plunder taken from Ziklag.

---

[8] This is the first major wadi southwest of Tell esh-Sheri1ah (which may be ancient Ziklag). Tsumura, *1
Samuel*, pp. 639-640. Modern Israeli maps identify it as Habesor, or "the Besor." J.F. Prewitt, "Besor
Brook," ISBE 1:463.

As leader, David gets the largest portion of plunder – the flocks and herds obtained from the Amalekites' other raids in the Negev; of course, the flocks and herds from Ziklag are returned to their owners. David's men divide up the rest of the plunder, which probably consists of jewelry, clothing, and slaves from other raided settlements in the Negev.

Some don't want to share the plunder with the 200 they had left exhausted at the Besor Ravine. But David insists. He attributed the victory to the Lord. By this action, David unifies his troops – even though he doesn't make them all happy.

> "The share of the man who stayed with the supplies is to be the same as that of him who went down to the battle. All will share alike." (30:24)

This policy became an established law in Israel.

David Sends Some of the Plunder to the Elders of Judah (30:26-31)

Notice what David does with his plunder. Instead of keeping it to enrich himself, he divides it up and sends it to the elders of the various cities and towns in Judah where he had roamed among during his fugitive sojourn.

> "Here is a present for you from the plunder of the LORD's enemies." (30:26)

There were two purposes. First, to cement his friendship with them; David has his eye on the kingship. Second, to demonstrate that David hasn't participated with the Philistines in fighting against Saul, but has only fought against their common enemies. David is a shrewd man when it comes to politics.

The Philistines Kill Saul and His Sons (31:1-6)

In the meantime, up north in the Valley of Jezreel, the armies of Israel experience a crushing defeat at the hands of the Philistines. Once the Philistines attacked and the Israelites realized they couldn't win, they broke ranks and ran for their lives, but "many fell slain on Mount Gilboa" (31:1) – including Saul and three of his sons: Jonathan, Abinadab and Malki-Shua.

Saul is wounded by Philistine archers. Realizing that he will be tortured and humiliated if captured, Saul asks his armor-bearer to kill him. But when the armor-bearer refuses, Saul falls on his sword and his armor-bearer follows suit. The narrator concludes:

> "So Saul and his three sons and his armor-bearer and all his men died together that same day." (30:6)

But the battle doesn't affect only the Israelite army. All the residents of the area flee as well, and the Philistines come and occupy these once-Israelite towns. The battle is a rout and changes the map of the areas now controlled by the Philistines. Israel is divided north from south, and greatly weakened.

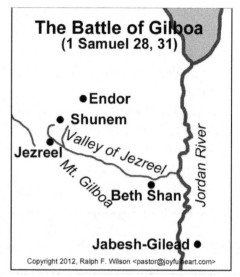

The Bodies of Saul and His Sons Are Buried (31:8-13)

The next day, the Philistines find Saul's body, gleefully cut off his head, and spread the word to all the Philistine towns. His armor is displayed in a heathen temple and his sons' bodies are dishonored by fastening them to the wall of the city of Beth Shan,[9] "the easternmost of the line of old Canaanite fortress cities across the country from the Mediterranean to the Jordan, which the Israelites had not conquered" (Joshua 17:11-13).[10]

"Valiant men" from the Israelite city of Jabesh Gilead,[11] about 10 miles south, remove the bodies from the wall, and take them home. Then they burn the bodies, bury the bones in honor under a tamarisk tree, and fast for seven days of mourning for their fallen king. It is a sad day in Israel!

David Hears of Saul's Death (2 Samuel 1:1-16)

On the third day after David and his men return to Ziklag after their victory over the Amalekites, a messenger arrives with the news of Saul's and Jonathan's deaths. David asks the circumstances. The messenger explains how the wounded Saul had asked him to finish him off.

> "So I stood over him and killed him, because I knew that after he had fallen he could not survive. And I took the crown that was on his head and the band on his arm and have brought them here to my lord." (2 Samuel 1:10)

---

[9] Beth Shan is a city located where the Jezreel Valley joins the Jordan Valley. The area contains numerous springs and wells, with rich soil, and intense summer heat. The ancient city is identified with the site of Tell el-Husn, about 650 feet north of modern Beit Shan (A. F. Rainey, "Beth-Shean," ISBE 1:475-476).

[10] Baldwin, *1 and 2 Samuel*, p. 171.

[11] Jabesh-Gilead was in the territory of the half-tribe of Manasseh and lies along the Wadi Yabis (Jabesh) (F.E. Young, "Jabesh-Gilead," ISBE 3:946).

The messenger probably expects a reward for his mercy killing and for bringing David the crown. But he badly misjudges David's reaction. Instead of rejoicing, David instinctively mourns:

> "Then David and all the men with him took hold of their clothes and tore them. They mourned and wept and fasted till evening for Saul and his son Jonathan, and for the army of the LORD and the house of Israel, because they had fallen by the sword." (1:11-12)

David asks the Amalekite,

> "'Why were you not afraid to lift your hand to destroy the LORD's anointed.' Then David called one of his men and said, 'Go, strike him down!' So he struck him down, and he died. For David had said to him, 'Your blood be on your own head. Your own mouth testified against you when you said, "I killed the LORD's anointed."'" (1:14-16)

Even when Saul had acted unrighteously, David would not slay him, even though twice he could have. That this opportunist would take killing Saul upon himself was an abomination to David! Being an Amalekite probably doesn't help, since David has just finished slaying hundreds of Amalekites whom he considers to be the "enemies of God's people." Probably the Amalekite is lying. He probably merely stripped the body and then brought the crown to David seeking a reward. Oops.

David's Lament for Saul and Jonathan (2 Samuel 1:17-27)

Take a few moments to read the amazing psalm that David wrote in honor of Saul and Jonathan. Note how gracious he is even to Saul, who had sought to kill him. He looks beyond Saul's dark and troubled side to Saul's greatness as a king and warrior in Israel.

> "[17] David took up this lament concerning Saul and his son Jonathan, [18] and ordered that the men of Judah be taught this lament of the bow (it is written in the Book of Jashar):
>
> '[19] Your glory, O Israel, lies slain on your heights.
> How the mighty have fallen!
> [20] Tell it not in Gath,
> proclaim it not in the streets of Ashkelon,
> lest the daughters of the Philistines be glad,
> lest the daughters of the uncircumcised rejoice.
> [21] O mountains of Gilboa, may you have neither dew nor rain,
> nor fields that yield offerings [of grain].
> For there the shield of the mighty was defiled,
> the shield of Saul – no longer rubbed with oil.

²² From the blood of the slain,
from the flesh of the mighty,
the bow of Jonathan did not turn back,
the sword of Saul did not return unsatisfied.

²³ Saul and Jonathan – in life they were loved and gracious,
and in death they were not parted.
They were swifter than eagles,
they were stronger than lions.

²⁴ O daughters of Israel, weep for Saul,
who clothed you in scarlet and finery,
who adorned your garments with ornaments of gold.
²⁵ How the mighty have fallen in battle!

Jonathan lies slain on your heights.
²⁶ I grieve for you, Jonathan my brother;
you were very dear to me.
Your love for me was wonderful,
more wonderful than that of women.

²⁷ How the mighty have fallen!
The weapons of war have perished!" (2 Samuel 1:19-27)

This psalm is an excellent example of the "lament genre" of Hebrew poetry.[12] There's a book in the Bible named "Lamentations." There are examples of lamentations in Anglo Saxon poetry. But in our present day, the closest lament literature we find is in country songs!

Lamenting in faith is an important art that we Christians need to reclaim, for we have hope after death, unlike the people around us.

Saul's Epitaph (1 Chronicles 10:13-14)

David's epitaph is gracious, but the Chronicler's epitaph on Saul's life and legacy speaks of the judgment of the Lord against him:

"Saul died because he was unfaithful to the LORD; he did not keep the word of the LORD and even consulted a medium for guidance, and did not inquire of the LORD. So the LORD put him to death and turned the kingdom over to David son of Jesse." (1 Chronicles 10:13-14)

---

[12] Laments begin with a complaint, but often conclude with praise. Examples of laments include: Psalm 3, 7, 13, 25, 22, 42-43, 44, 51, 74, 79, 80 and many others. Within a lament you may find several of the following elements: (a) invocation, (2) plea to God for help, (3) complaints, (4) confession of sin or assertion of innocence, (5) curse of enemies (imprecation), (6) confidence in God's response, and (7) hymn or blessing.

I wonder what will be your epitaph and mine. Have we been faithful to the Lord? Have we repented where we have sinned? It really doesn't matter how you start your Christian life. Because God is merciful and gracious, and Jesus died for your sins, you are forgiven. And it's how you finish your life that counts regarding your rewards. Finish well, my dear friend!

Q3. (2 Samuel 1:19-27; 1 Chronicles 10:13-14) David is gracious in his memorial psalm. How does he remember Saul's life? How does the Chronicler remember Saul's life? How do you think God evaluates Saul's life? What do we learn from this?
http://www.joyfulheart.com/forums/index.php?showtopic=1178

Lessons for Disciples

In this lesson, we've seen God's hand at work in David's life. Some lessons for disciples include:

1. We must learn to strengthen ourselves in the Lord when our lives seem like they're falling apart. There are many examples of how to do this in David's Psalms.

2. When we can, we should share the Lord's bounty with others, even with those who may not deserve it.

3. We need to learn to die well so that our epitaph brings glory to the Lord, rather than disgrace.

This lesson has taken us to both the highs and lows of emotions. We observe David honoring the Lord both in defeat and in victory. In the wilderness, David has been faithful, but his wilderness experience is nearly over. In the next lesson we'll see his rise to the throne of all Israel.

Prayer

Father, thank you that in the times that we are utterly shattered, you are with us. We ask you to help us to learn to strengthen ourselves in you, so that instead of just reacting, we make wise decisions about the future. Teach us to live well with you in the wilderness so that we might see your grace in the days to come. In Jesus' name, we pray. Amen.

Key Verses

"David was greatly distressed because the men were talking of stoning him; each one was bitter in spirit because of his sons and daughters. But David found strength in the LORD his God." (1 Samuel 30:6)

"The share of the man who stayed with the supplies is to be the same as that of him who went down to the battle. All will share alike." (1 Samuel 30:24)

"How the mighty have fallen in battle!
Jonathan lies slain on your heights.
I grieve for you, Jonathan my brother;
you were very dear to me.
Your love for me was wonderful,
more wonderful than that of women. How the mighty have fallen!
The weapons of war have perished!" (2 Samuel 1:25-27)

7. David Becomes King and Conquers Jerusalem (2 Samuel 2-5)

If you think national politics are nasty in our day, then take a look at the political intrigue going on behind the scenes that finally resulted in David becoming king of all Israel. Politics was bloody!

James J. Tissot, "The Valiant of Gibeon" (1896-1902), gouache on board, The Jewish Museum, New York.

David Is Anointed King over Judah at Hebron (2:1-7)

It has been at least 15 years since David has been anointed by Samuel. Finally, it is time for God's plan for David to be king to come to pass.

Life has changed for David. He has been a fugitive for probably more than five years. Now no one is hunting him down to take his life! It is time to move from the desert town of Ziklag on the perimeter of Judah. But before he does anything, he seeks the Lord.

> "¹ In the course of time, David inquired of the LORD. 'Shall I go up to one of the towns of Judah?' he asked. The LORD said, 'Go up.' David asked, 'Where shall I go?' 'To Hebron,' the LORD answered." (2:1-2)

Apparently, David is consulting the Lord through the Urim and Thummim. We think that these cast lots work with answers that could be yes, no, or maybe. The choice of Hebron could have been through asking the Lord about various possible cities one by one, or by a prophetic word, either through the prophet Gad or through David himself. We're not told.

So David and his wives and men and their families settle in the ancient city of Hebron and its surrounding villages, probably with the Philistines' consent, since David is still

Achish's vassal.[1] His final break with the Philistines doesn't seem to come until later (5:17).

Hebron was a walled city dating back to Early Bronze Age. It was a Canaanite royal city. In Abraham's time it was populated by Hittites. During the Conquest, Caleb led the Israelites who conquered the city (Joshua 11:21; 14:6-15). Later, David's son Absalom will be crowned king in this city. But for now, it serves as David's capital city for seven and a half years (2:11).

> "Then the men of Judah came to Hebron and there they anointed David king over the house of Judah." (2:4a)

This is David's second anointing of three. First, by the prophet Samuel (1 Samuel 16:13), and finally by the elders of the Israelite tribes (5:3), prior to moving his capital to Jerusalem.

As a new king of Judah, David graciously honors the men of Jabesh Gilead for burying Saul's body, even though he is not king over their tribe. In reaching out, David is seeking friends that will eventually make him king over all Israel. (2:5-7)

Now that he can settle down, David begins to raise a family in Hebron by his various wives. (See Appendix 3. Genealogy of the House of David.)

> "2b His firstborn was Amnon the son of Ahinoam of Jezreel; 3 his second, Kileab the son of Abigail the widow of Nabal of Carmel; the third, Absalom the son of Maacah daughter of Talmai king of Geshur; 4 the fourth, Adonijah the son of Haggith; the fifth, Shephatiah the son of Abital; 5 and the sixth, Ithream the son of David's wife Eglah. These were born to David in Hebron." (3:2-5)

(See the discussion of Polygamy in the Bible in Lesson 5 above.)

Ish-Bosheth Reigns over the Northern Tribes (2 Samuel 2:8-11)

However, at this point, Saul's only remaining son, Ish-Bosheth, reigns over the northern tribes.

> "8 Meanwhile, Abner son of Ner, the commander of Saul's army, had taken Ish-Bosheth son of Saul and brought him over to Mahanaim. 9 He made him king over Gilead, Ashuri [or Asher] and Jezreel, and also over Ephraim, Benjamin and all Israel.... The house of Judah, however, followed David." (2:8-9, 10b)

---

[1] "That [David] did this with the Philistines' consent is certain, for he was their vassal and could hardly have taken such a step without their approval. The Philistines, however, whose policy was 'divide and rule,' desired it" (Bright, *History of Israel*, p. 196).

Abner has been Saul's military commander, and the real power in the kingdom now that Saul is dead. Abner is Saul's uncle and Ish-Bosheth's great-uncle (1 Samuel 14:50).[2] Thus Ish-Bosheth is blood, he is family. And so, in loyalty to his family's house, Abner sets Ish-Bosheth on the throne, he "made him king." (see Appendix 2. Genealogy of the House of Saul).

Ish-Bosheth (elsewhere called Esh-Baal; 1 Chronicles 8:33; 9:39),[3] seems like a weak king, kept in power only by Abner's influence and military clout. For fear of the Philistines who now control much of the hill country, perhaps even Gibeah itself, Abner has moved Ish-Bosheth from Saul's capital of Gibeah to Mahanaim[4] on the east side of the Jordan, the place where Jacob had wrestled with the angel 800 years before (Genesis 32:1). Here the monarchy of Saul's house might be reestablished in relative safety.[5] Ish-Bosheth's territory, however, is substantially diminished. Though Gilead, east of the Jordan, is fairly secure, Asher and Jezreel, plus part of Ephraim and Benjamin are now under the control of the Philistines.

The chronology isn't clear to us at this point, since Ish-Bosheth reigns in Mahanaim for only two years, while David reigns in Hebron for 7-1/2 years before becoming king over all Israel (2:10-11). What is going on among the northern tribes during this interval, we just don't know.

However, David is working to heal his relationship with Saul's followers. Bright notes that:

> "[David] made overtures to the men of Jabesh-Gilead, whose loyalty to Saul he knew (2:4b-7). He also took in marriage (3:3) the daughter of the king of Geshur, an Aramean

---

[2] Ner could be interpreted as Kish's brother in 1 Chronicles 9:36, thus Saul's cousin. However, in 1 Chronicles 8:33 and 9:39, Ner is clearly the father of Kish. Thus Abner is Saul's uncle (1 Samuel 14:50-51). The word is *dôd*, "beloved uncle." The word is used in the Old Testament 58 times – 38 are "beloved" (all in Song of Solomon), 8 are "love," and 17 are "uncle" (Earl S. Kalland, *dwd*, TWOT #410a). It is possible, however, that there may have been two men named Kish, one being Ner's brother and the other his son – we just don't know ("Ner," ISBE 3:519-520; M.L. Margolis, "Abner," ISBE 1:12-13).

[3] Ish-Bosheth means literally "man of shame," though elsewhere he is called Esh-Baal, "fire of Baal" or perhaps "man of Baal" (1 Chronicles 8:33; 9:39). Probably it was offensive for the editor of 2 Samuel to use the name of Baal, a Canaanite god, in the name of the king, so the word *bōshet*, "shame," was substituted for Baal. We see the same kind of substitution in 1 and 2 Samuel of Mephibosheth ("exterminator of shame," 2 Samuel 9:6) for Meribbaal ("contender with Baal," 1 Chronicles 8:34) (John N. Oswalt, *bosh*, TWOT #222c).

[4] Mahanaim is a city in Gilead, which lies somewhat east of the Jordan, perhaps on the north bank of the Jabbok River, in the territory of Gad, a city assigned to the Merarite clan of the Levites (Joshua 21:38). Two possible suggestions for its location are Tell edh-Dhahab el Gharbi or Tell Hajjaj, but we just don't know (W.D. Mounce, "Mahanaim," ISBE 3:222-223; Anderson, *2 Samuel*, p. 33).

[5] Anderson, *2 Samuel*, p. 32.

state east of the Sea of Galilee, presumably to gain an ally in Eshbaal's (Ishbosheth's) rear. He also – and probably at this time – entered into friendly relations with Ammon (10:2), doubtless for the same purpose."[6]

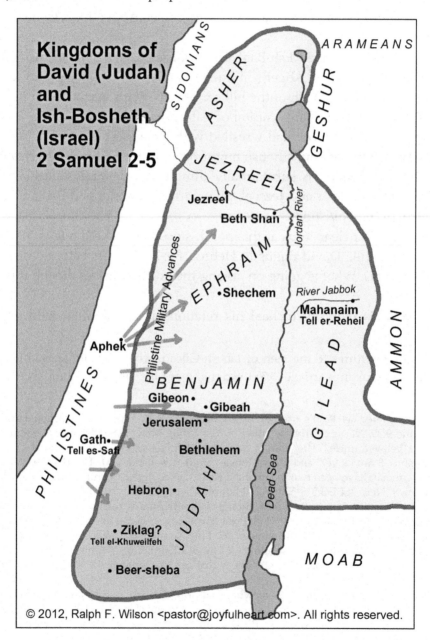

Kingdoms of David (Judah) and Ish-Bosheth (Israel) 2 Samuel 2-5

[6] Bright, *History of Israel*, p. 197.

War at the Pool of Gibeon (2 Samuel 2:12-17)

Now the level of conflict increases between David's kingdom of Judah and Ish-Bosheth's kingdom of Israel. Abner, Ish-Bosheth's general, moves his troops from Mahanaim closer to Judah at Gibeon, though still within Israel's territory. Joab, David's general, brings David's army to confront them, though all-out war has not broken out. The two generals sit down at the pool of Gibeon to talk.

Abner suggests a kind of hand-to-hand combat contest between a dozen men on each side. Perhaps this is more than just a game or mock battle. It may have been "a serious representative battle involving twelve pairs of chosen warriors."[7] The conclusion, however, is indecisive, as each of the contestants kills his opponent, leaving 24 dead bodies. As soon as this happens, the armies engage each other in a major skirmish.

> "The battle that day was very fierce, and Abner and the men of Israel were defeated by David's men." (2:17)

Abner's army retreats back to Mahanaim, but not before losing 360 men, compared to only 19 losses for David's army (2:30-31).

Abner Slays Asahel (2:18-3:1)

Joab's army pursues the retreating soldiers. Joab's brother Asahel is intent on killing Abner, Ish-Bosheth's general. If he can do so, Ish-Bosheth's kingdom will crumble, since it is utterly dependent upon Abner's support. Asahel draws on his greatest gift, his speed, "as fleet-footed as a wild gazelle" (2:18).

Asahel chases Abner to the point that he is so close that he is in danger of Abner killing him. Abner warns him. He doesn't want to kill him, he says. Asahel is young and fast, but Abner is a skilled warrior; he knows Asahel is no match for him, so he suggests Asahel fight one of the younger warriors. Abner knows the family; these brothers, Joab, Abishai, and Asahel have been his friends. But Asahel won't stop.

Finally, his life at risk, Abner apparently stops suddenly and Asahel impales himself on Abner's spear.[8] Defending himself in war, Abner's killing of Asahel wouldn't constitute bloodguilt by any objective judge.[9] But all Joab is able to see is that Abner has killed his brother, and seeks revenge when he gets a chance (3:27).

---

[7] Anderson, 2 Samuel, p. 43, citing similar trials at arms in the ancient Near East.

[8] "Butt end" (NIV, NRSV), "hinder part" (KJV) is 'ahar, "after, behind" (TWOT #68b). Whether this is the butt end of the spear, or Abner points his spear backwards isn't clear.

[9] See my discussion of bloodguilt in Lesson 5.

For now, however, Abner calls on Joab to restrain his army from this internecine conflict.

> "Must the sword devour forever? Don't you realize that this will end in bitterness? How long before you order your men to stop pursuing their brothers?" (2:26)

Abner had started it by moving his troops close to Judah, but now he calls for a halt. Joab agrees and sounds the trumpet or shofar to signal his army to halt. Now both armies march throughout the night to their respective capitals.

But the conflict continues. The narrator tells us:

> "The war between the house of Saul and the house of David lasted a long time. David grew stronger and stronger, while the house of Saul grew weaker and weaker." (3:1)

Ish-Bosheth Angers Abner (2 Samuel 3:6-11)

Finally, Ish-Bosheth does something stupid. He rebukes Abner who is the only reason he remains as king. Ish-Bosheth is justified, of course. Abner had been sleeping with Saul's concubine[10] Rizpah, which was probably construed (perhaps correctly) as Abner asserting a claim to the kingship himself. Elsewhere in the David saga, taking a king's wife or concubine was a political act of asserting the rights of a king (2 Samuel 12:8; 16:21; 1 Kings 2:13-22).[11] This act immediately follows the narrator's observation: "Abner had been strengthening his own position in the house of Saul" (3:6).

Although Abner is clearly guilty of overreaching, he deeply resents Ish-Bosheth's rebuke. "You owe your very life to me," Abner is thinking, "and you accuse me of something so petty?" Abner has probably been looking for some kind of provocation and Ish-Bosheth provides it. Abner says:

> "Am I a dog's head[12] – on Judah's side? This very day I am loyal to the house of your father Saul and to his family and friends. I haven't handed you over to David. Yet now you accuse me of an offense involving this woman! May God deal with Abner, be it ever so severely, if I do not do for David what the LORD promised him on oath and transfer

---

[10] Though we're not sure of the status of a concubine during this period, it probably refers here to "a legitimate wife of second rank" (Anderson, *2 Samuel*, p. 56).

[11] Anderson (*2 Samuel*, p. 56) questions this interpretation. "This is possible, but far from certain. There is no clear indication of it in the text itself; if anything, Abner's protestation of loyalty seems to exclude this interpretation." I disagree.

[12] The probable meaning is "worthless dog" (2 Kings 6:25), not some reference to a dog's proverbial promiscuity.

the kingdom from the house of Saul and establish David's throne over Israel and Judah from Dan to Beersheba."[13] (3:8-10)

Ish-Bosheth is afraid to say another word.

David Demands the Return of His Wife Michal (2 Samuel 3:12-16)

Abner, who had just sworn in his anger to establish David on the throne, sends a delegation to David to work out terms to transfer the kingdom to him. Abner has had enough of Ish-Bosheth! The message is:

> "Whose land is it? Make an agreement with me, and I will help you bring all Israel over to you." (3:12)

The question, "Whose land is it?" is difficult. Abner could mean either:

1. **The land is David's.** Yahweh has already promised the kingdom and its land to David when Samuel anointed him, as Abner had just said: "what the LORD promised [David] on oath" (3:9b).

2. **The land is Abner's.** Though Ish-Bosheth is king in name, Abner is "the de facto lord of the land,"[14] and he is the one with whom David will have to deal.

I think it's more likely that Abner sees himself fulfilling Yahweh's destiny for David, not placing himself in the role of acting ruler. Clearly, however, the land is not Ish-Bosheth's, in Abner's view.

David is happy to discuss a peaceful transfer of the kingdom to him. But he makes a precondition to talks.

> "Do not come into my presence unless you bring Michal daughter of Saul when you come to see me." (3:13)

If you remember, when David had fled, Michal's father Saul had arbitrarily (and unjustly) annulled the marriage and given Michal instead to Paltiel, son of Laish (1 Samuel 25:44).[15]

---

[13] Dan in the north and Beersheba in the south represent the extremes of Israel's territory – from north to south!

[14] Anderson (2 Samuel, p. 57) cites Kirkpatrick, Kennedy, and Hertzberg as holding this view, though Anderson himself sees the first interpretation as the most probable.

[15] Saul's annulment was unjust since David had not initiated the divorce nor had the bride's price of 100 Philistine foreskins been returned to him, as would have been required. There is precedent from ancient Near East law of a remarriage after a husband's return from captivity or exile, even though the wife had in the meantime married another man and had children by him. Anderson (2 Samuel, p. 58) cites Z. Ben-Barak, "The Legal Background of the Restoration of Michal to David," Vetis Testamentum Supplements 30 [1979] 21-25.

David's demand could be construed as David's desire to assert and strengthen his own claim to the kingship as Saul's rightful son-in-law. But John Bright says:

> "His reason for demanding the return of Michal was certainly the hope that a male issue would unite the claims of his house and Saul's – a vain hope as it turned out."[16]

This isn't love; this is politics.

Abner apparently agrees to David's precondition, so David sends a demand for his legal wife directly to Ish-Bosheth, who has no choice. Ish-Bosheth gives orders for her to be returned to David. When her grieving husband Paltiel follows her, Abner orders him to go home. Affairs of state take precedence over affairs of the heart.

No doubt, Ish-Bosheth sees the transfer of the kingdom to David as inevitable now, since Abner has decided to move in that direction. Both Ish-Bosheth and Abner expect mercy from David. After all, David had publicly pledged to Saul not to kill Saul's sons (1 Samuel 24:21-22). This is likely to be better future than what could result by holding out and being defeated by David in war.

Abner Meets with David in Hebron (2 Samuel 3:17-22)

Abner actively works to negotiate the peace. Now that both David and Ish-Bosheth are in agreement, Abner needs to convince the elders of Israel and the leaders of the tribe of Benjamin – Saul's tribe. He recognizes that they yearn for David to lead them to victory over their Philistine oppressors rather than to continue in a losing war against David for the kingdom. Abner says:

> "For some time you have wanted to make David your king. Now do it! For the LORD promised David, 'By my servant David I will rescue my people Israel from the hand of the Philistines and from the hand of all their enemies.'" (3:17b-18)

Abner seems to be referring to some prophetic word, known to the elders, that isn't recorded elsewhere in the Bible.

Now that all the stakeholders are in agreement to make David king, Abner himself travels to Hebron to seal the agreement with David face-to-face. David puts on a feast in Abner's honor, then David sends Abner home "in peace" to finalize arrangements by means of "a compact." "Compact" (NIV), "covenant" (NRSV), "league" (KJV) is *berît*, the word for covenant used throughout the Pentateuch. Here it connotes a "treaty." We don't know the exact terms, but it might involve making Ish-Bosheth a vassal of David's or, at least, an honored place at David's table.

---

[16] Bright, *History of Israel*, p. 198.

Joab Slays Abner in Hebron (2 Samuel 3:22-27)

But Joab, who has been away during these final negotiations, returns to Hebron, and realizes that his blood enemy Abner isn't far away. It doesn't seem to matter to Joab that Abner has diplomatic status and the promise of peaceful transit from David, and that Abner is just about to consummate a peace that will end a war simmering for years. All that matters to Joab is revenge for his brother Asahel's death.

Joab is livid. He goes to the king and rebukes David for the agreement, accusing Abner of deception and spying, rather than seeking true peace. David is unconvinced.

So Joab takes matters into his own hands. He sends messengers deceitfully in the name of the king to intercept Abner on his journey home, and ask him to return to Hebron for some last-minute clarifications. When Abner returns, Joab acts with treachery:

> "Joab took him aside into the gateway, as though to speak with him privately. And there, to avenge the blood of his brother Asahel, Joab stabbed him in the stomach, and he died." (3:27)

This is the equivalent of stabbing a person in the back without warning. It is clearly murder, not a righteous avenging. Later, he does something similar to Absalom's general Amasa (2 Samuel 20:9-12). Years later on his deathbed, David instructs his son Solomon to punish Joab for this, and indicts him as follows:

> "[Joab] killed them, shedding their blood in peacetime as if in battle, and with that blood stained the belt around his waist and the sandals on his feet." (1 Kings 2:5)

David Laments Abner (2 Samuel 3:28-39)

When David hears what Joab has done, he publicly disassociates himself from it, and pronounces a terrible curse upon Joab and his descendants:

> "I and my kingdom are forever innocent before the LORD concerning the blood of Abner son of Ner. May his blood fall upon the head of Joab and upon all his father's house! May Joab's house never be without someone who has a running sore or leprosy or who leans on a crutch or who falls by the sword or who lacks food." (3:28b-30)

Then David instructs his courtiers to publicly mourn Abner with fasting and wearing sackcloth, instead of their fine garments. David himself weeps as he follows Abner's body in procession to his tomb. Then he composes a special song for the occasion – in this case a special kind of psalm, a lament:

> "Should Abner have died as the lawless die?
> Your hands were not bound,

> your feet were not fettered.
> You fell as one falls before wicked men." (3:34)

> "Do you not realize that a prince and a great man has fallen in Israel this day?" (3:38)

The narrator observes:

> "So on that day all the people and all Israel knew that the king had no part in the murder of Abner son of Ner." (3:37)

Q1. (2 Samuel 3:22-39) Why does Joab slay Abner? Is he justified in doing so? How does this affect his king's unification plans? Why do you think Joab is so blind? How can our spiritual blindness get in the way of God working out His plan in our lives?
http://www.joyfulheart.com/forums/index.php?showtopic=1179

Why Doesn't David Punish Joab?

What I find hard to understand is why David doesn't punish Joab for his treacherous murder. On the surface, David's public explanation seems lame:

> "And today, though I am the anointed king, I am weak (*rak*), and these sons of Zeruiah are too strong (*qāsheh*) for me. May the LORD repay the evildoer according to his evil deeds!" (3:39)

Key to understanding this is to look at the pair of Hebrew opposites translated "weak" and "strong." David characterizes himself as *rak*, meaning "tender, soft, delicate, sensitive." It can also be used of "soft" words.[17] This doesn't seem to refer to political or moral weakness, but perhaps refers to his tendency towards restraint,[18] rather than going off "half-cocked." On the other hand, Joab and his brother Abishai are *qāsheh*, that is, "hard, cruel, obstinate, stiff, severe,"[19] rash and rough, ruthless! David is tender, while they are harsh and cruel. Rather than try to punish them himself, David calls on Yahweh to repay them for their evil deeds.

That is David's explanation of his actions. But I still wonder why David doesn't punish Joab's treachery and treason? There are several possibilities:

---

[17] William White, *rak*, TWOT #2164a; Holladay, p. 339, 2.
[18] So Bergen, *1 and 2 Samuel*, p. 318.
[19] Leonard J. Coppes, *qāsheh*, TWOT #2085a; Holladay, p. 327, 2.

1. **Politics**. Though Ish-Bosheth is utterly dependent upon his general Abner, David doesn't seem beholden to Joab in the same way – at least at this point in his life. David is his own man and has a lot of support from the elders of Judah who have anointed him king. I think David had the political clout to have Joab punished.

2. **Legality**. It seems more likely to me that David doesn't believe his legal grounds are clear-cut enough to take action. Even though Joab murdered Abner with treachery, Joab's action is understandable enough – and perhaps marginally legal as "justifiable homicide." The Torah created cities of refuge where a person guilty of manslaughter could be protected. But if he ventured outside the city, the "avenger of blood" could kill him without being guilty of murder (Numbers 35: 9-8; Deuteronomy 19:6; Joshua 20:1-6). This may be so, but Joab is guilty of going directly against his king's desire to bring peace between these two kingdoms. Why can't David enforce his will upon his closest lieutenant?

3. **Family**. David is constrained by his kinship ties with Joab. Perhaps he throws up his hands and says, "He's family, and you can't be responsible for what your relatives do. Joab and his brothers are headstrong! But since Joab is a relative, I can't punish him." When David became a fugitive, his father's family was hunted too (1 Samuel 22:1). Indeed, Joab and his brothers had been loyal to David through his very hardest times.

David has a technical right to punish Joab for murder and treason, but he feels somehow constrained, perhaps for some of the reasons above. So he says, I'll let the Lord repay him. He not only fails to punish Joab, he doesn't remove him from his position as head general of the army, even though he can't be trusted to carry out David's wishes. He continues to allow him to serve as a top advisor and officer.

I think this represents a serious character flaw and a severe leadership weakness. David can't seem to punish the crimes of those close to him, even though they deserve it. We'll see several examples in the future. David fails to punish Amnon for his rape, Absalom for murdering Amnon, and Joab for murdering both Abner and (later) Amasa. Finally, he can't seem to take decisive action against his son Absalom who usurps his throne and seeks to kill him.

We'll continue to ponder this as we consider David's life as king. We need to ask ourselves: What is the appropriate balance between justice and mercy and faithfulness?

Ish-Bosheth Is Assassinated (2 Samuel 4:1-12)

Joab's murder of Abner destroys the hoped-for peace between the two kingdoms. The narrator tells us:

"When Ish-Bosheth son of Saul heard that Abner had died in Hebron, he lost courage, and all Israel became alarmed." (4:1)

Abner is the essential support of Ish-Bosheth's throne. Now that he is gone, the future looks dim.

At this point, the narrator introduces two brothers, Baanah and Recab, military leaders under Ish-Bosheth from Saul's tribe of Benjamin. They decide to take advantage of the power vacuum to gain favor with the new power – David. They are opportunists, and completely unscrupulous. The brothers gain access to Ish-Bosheth's house, stab him in his bed during a noonday rest, cut off his head, and bring it to David as proof that they have killed David's enemy for him. They are hoping for a big reward. The problem is, they don't know David very well.

David is outraged! He had slain the Amalekite opportunist who had claimed to kill Saul. He said:

"How much more – when wicked men have killed an innocent man in his own house and on his own bed – should I not now demand his blood from your hand and rid the earth of you!" (4:11)

The brothers are guilty of treason against their king. This is not blood shed in war, but blood shed in treachery and is by no means innocent. The men are slain, and their bodies are mutilated and exposed publicly in the capital city. But Ish-Bosheth's head is buried with honor in Abner's tomb.

David has a keen sense of righteousness when it involves the kingship. He would not raise his hand against Saul out of respect for the Lord who appointed him as king, and he punishes anyone else who takes it upon himself to kill the Lord's anointed. It doesn't matter that Ish-Bosheth hadn't been anointed king by a prophet. He is an innocent son of the true king and one David had vowed to protect (1 Samuel 24:21-22).

Other Tribes Support David's Claim to the Kingdom (2 Samuel 5:1-5)

We are not told much about the process of David being made king over all Israel. But the Chronicler gives us some clues.

"These are the numbers of the men armed for battle who came to David at Hebron to turn Saul's kingdom over to him, as the LORD had said." (1 Chronicles 12:23)

Then he lists the numbers of armed warriors that come to Hebron to swear loyalty to David from all the tribes: Judah, Simeon, Levi, Benjamin, Ephraim, Manasseh, men of Issachar "who understood the times and knew what Israel should do," Zebulun, Naphtali, Dan, Asher, Reuben, and Gad. All the tribes are represented.

> "They came to Hebron fully determined to make David king over all Israel. All the rest
> of the Israelites were also of one mind to make David king." (1 Chronicles 12:38)

It may have taken some time for this to occur, as the various tribal elders decide what to do in the absence of a king from Saul's house. But finally they gather at Hebron. The narrator describes the formality as follows:

> "All the tribes of Israel came to David at Hebron and said, 'We are your own flesh and
> blood. In the past, while Saul was king over us, you were the one who led Israel on their
> military campaigns. And the LORD said to you, "You will shepherd my people Israel,
> and you will become their ruler."' When all the elders of Israel had come to King David
> at Hebron, the king made a compact with them at Hebron before the LORD, and they
> anointed David king over Israel." (5:1-3)

They spoke what they had concluded in their tribal councils, that David should be king because:

1. **Identity**. David is one of them, a true Israelite.

2. **Military prowess**. David has led Saul's troops against the Philistines.

3. **God's approval**. God has spoken prophetically that David should be their king.

We don't have a record of this prophecy, but Samuel may have spoken publicly before he died of what God had shown him. So a compact or covenant (*berît*) is made between the people and their king, and he is formally anointed king for the third time, now over all Israel.

Notice the words of the prophecy quoted: "You will shepherd my people Israel, and you will become their ruler" (5:2b). The image evoked by the verb "to shepherd" (NIV, NRSV), "to feed" (KJV) is common in the ancient Near East, where this figure for the king is found in Sumerian king lists, in Babylonian court documents, and in Egyptian pyramid texts.[20] The concept of shepherd is used to illustrate God's care for his people in the early poetry of Genesis (48:15; 49:24), as well as in the poetry of the Psalms (23, 74:1; 77:20; 78:52; 80:1; 95:7). The image of shepherd carries a high model of faithfulness, justice, and loving kindness.

Then the assembled tribes enjoy a three-day party:

> "The men spent three days there with David, eating and drinking, for their families had
> supplied provisions for them. Also, their neighbors from as far away as Issachar,
> Zebulun and Naphtali came bringing food on donkeys, camels, mules and oxen. There
> were plentiful supplies of flour, fig cakes, raisin cakes, wine, oil, cattle and sheep, for
> there was joy in Israel." (1 Chronicles 12:39-40)

---

[20] E. Beyreuther, "Shepherd," *New International Dictionary of New Testament Theology* 3:564.

The narrator now informs us of the duration of David's reign:

> "David was thirty years old when he became king, and he reigned forty years. In Hebron he reigned over Judah seven years and six months, and in Jerusalem he reigned over all Israel and Judah thirty-three years." (5:4-5)

Q2. (2 Samuel 5:1-5) Approximately how long has it been since David had been anointed king by Samuel? (See Appendix 4. Chronology of the Life of David). Why did the fulfillment of God's word take so long? How would you evaluate David's patience concerning this prophecy that he would be king? How would you measure your own patience concerning what you believe God has promised you?
http://www.joyfulheart.com/forums/index.php?showtopic=1180

Jerusalem (5:6-8)

David's kingdom is now secure. One of the first things he does is to move his capital from the city of Hebron in the center of Judah's territory to a new site that isn't really identified with any tribe – Jerusalem. Bright observes: "The new capital undoubtedly served to elevate the government to a degree above tribal jealousy."[21]

The city is known by various names in the Bible:

- **Jerusalem** is the most-frequently mentioned name. It appears in Egyptian Execration texts of nineteenth-eighteenth centuries BC, in diplomatic correspondence from Tell el-Amana in Egypt, and in the Assyrian account of Sennacherib's 701 BC siege of the city.[22]

- **Salem** is probably a shortened form of this (Genesis 14:18; Psalm 76:2).

- **Jebus** recalls the Jebusites that lived there (Joshua 18:28; Judges 19:10-11; 1 Chronicles 11:4-5).

---

[21] Bright, *History of Israel*, p. 200.

[22] The name "Jerusalem" apparently derives from West Semitic words meaning "foundation of [the god] Shalem," a Canaanite deity mentioned in the Ugaritic texts, though in Hebrew times this part of the name was identified with the Hebrew word *shālôm*, "peace" (Anderson, 2 Samuel, p. 82).

- **Zion** refers to the stronghold[23] taken by David (2 Samuel 5:7; 1 Kings 8:1). The term "Zion" has some etymological connection with Arabic terms for "ridge," or perhaps "fortified ridge."[24] Later Zion comes to refer to the whole city, not just the east ridge.

- **City of David** is used to name the city after its conqueror (2 Samuel 5:7), though the term sometimes refers specifically to the original city David captured (2 Chronicles 32:5).[25]

Jerusalem had its origins in the late fourth or early third millennium BC, with small settlements in the Chalcolithic and early Bronze I and II periods. By the early second millennium BC (Middle Bronze II), archaeologists have found evidence of a sizeable 12 acre walled town with a three foot thick wall with towers to protect the Gihon spring, as well as an underground water channel bringing water from the spring into the settlement at times when the city was under siege. The city also begins to show up in Egyptian texts as a small and minor part of Egyptian colonial rule, governed by a mayor rather than a king.

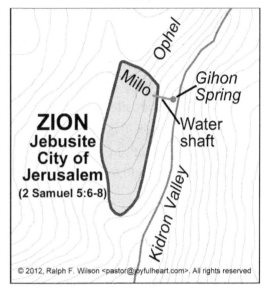

ZION
Jebusite
City of
Jerusalem
(2 Samuel 5:6-8)

Ophel

Millo

Gihon
Spring

Water
shaft

Kidron Valley

A "stepped stone structure" as part of the citadel apparently dates from the time of Jebusite rule in the late thirteenth to early twelfth centuries BC, at the end of the Late Bronze Age.[26]

During the time of the Conquest under Joshua, Jerusalem had remained in Jebusite hands. Neither the tribe of Judah nor the tribe of Benjamin could dislodge[27] them (Joshua 15:63; Judges 1:21), though at one point Judah had a successful raid against it (Judges 1:8). In David's time, the Jebusites and Israelites probably coexisted with some

---

[23] *Meṣûdâ*, "fastness, stronghold." Masada, the fortress-palace plateau of Herod near the Dead Sea, is related to this word (John E. Hartley, *meṣûdâ*, TWOT #1885i).

[24] Carol Meyers, "Jerusalem," DOTHB 547-556, especially p. 549.

[25] Meyers, DOTHB, p. 549.

[26] Mcycrs, DOTHB, p. 550.

[27] *Yārash*, Hiphil stem, "inherit, drive out, cast out, dispossess, destroy, make poor" (John E. Hartley, TWOT #920).

kind of state of truce between them, the Jebusites controlling the city and Judah controlling the land around the city.

We don't know much about the Jebusites, members of the Canaanite clan of Jebus. While they were considered Canaanites because they lived in Canaan (Genesis 10:16), they may have been a non-Semitic people related to the Hurrians or the Hittites.[28] We may see a trace of this in Ezekiel's prophecy:

> "Thus says the Lord God to Jerusalem: 'Your origin and your birth were in the land of the Canaanites; your father was an Amorite, and your mother a Hittite.'" (Ezekiel 16:3)

Conquering Jerusalem through the Water Shaft (5:6-8)

Because of the Jerusalem citadel's natural strength as a fortress, defended by walls as well as a steep slope on either side, the city felt impervious to attack. The narrator records that the Jebusites had taunted David's men:

> "You will not get in here; even the blind and the lame can ward you off." (5:6b)

We might say something like, "Resisting you will be like child's play."

You can also read David's words to his men as a response to this taunt, as he laid out his strategy:

> "Anyone who conquers the Jebusites will have to use the water shaft[29] to reach those 'lame and blind' who are David's enemies." (5:8a)

Trying to piece together David's strategy is hindered because the noun ṣinnôr, has been translated variously as "water shaft" (NIV, NRSV), "gutter" (KJV), and "grappling iron" (New English Bible).[30] But I think that "water shaft" or "water supply"[31] is probably correct, since the use of grappling hooks would mean scaling the impregnable fortress in full view of its defenders.

Ancient walled cities needed access to a water supply in order to survive in time of siege. Jerusalem relied on a single source, the Gihon spring, which was outside the Canaanite city walls, near the bottom of the Kidron Valley to the east of the city.

In 1998, excavations by Israeli archaeologists Ronny Reich and Eli Shukron demonstrated that the Gihon spring outside the city had been heavily fortified by the Canaanites with a massive tower (termed the "Spring Tower"). A complex system of

---

[28] Meyers, DOTHB, p. 550; R.K. Harrison, "Jebus, Jebusite," ISBE 2:973-974.

[29] Baldwin, *1 and 2 Samuel*, p. 196; In 1922, W.F. Albright argued that the word probably referred to a grappling hook (W.F. Albright, "The ṣinnôr in the Story of David's Capture of Jerusalem," *Journal of Palestine Oriental Society* (JPOS), 2 (1922), pp. 286-290.)

[30] ṣinnôr, "pipe, spout, conduit" (BDB 857), based on Psalm 42:7 and a related word in Zechariah 4:12.

[31] Anderson, *2 Samuel*, p. 84.

underground passages, entered from within the city walls, took people to the edge of a pool fed by the spring, where they could draw water by letting down a bucket.[32]

Of course, we don't know exactly how Joab and his men got into the city, but I expect that it reads like an episode from "Mission Impossible." Here's my attempt at a possible scenario, based on what we've learned from Reich's and Shukron's excavations:

> Joab and his men somehow breach the massive Spring Tower and overcome its guards. They creep along a narrow water-filled channel (Channel II), then move up a narrow water-filled tunnel (Tunnel III) to get into the large underground water-storage pool. Here, they scale its walls to get to the cave-tunnel above, creep along a curved tunnel, its pitch blackness lit only by flickering lamps. Now they climb the tunnel's steep steps into a guard tower inside the city and overcome the guards. From there they creep out secretly, overcome more guards, and open the city gates so that David's troops can flood into the city and overwhelm it.

David laid out the strategy, and Joab volunteered for the assignment, with the promise that, if he succeeded, he would become David's commander (1 Chronicles 11:6).[33]

Of course, we can only speculate on how the city fortress was entered. Perhaps they simply forced the city to surrender because they were able to cut off its water supply.[34] But we know that David indeed captured it. Apparently, the existing Jebusite population was neither slaughtered nor displaced, for later David purchased a threshing floor from a Jebusite named Araunah (24:18-25), land that eventually became the site of Solomon's temple.

David's Palace in Jerusalem (5:9-16)

In addition to "Zion," its Canaanite name, Jerusalem is now called "The City of David," probably because David captured it with his own personal troops, rather than with an army gathered from levies on the various tribes. It becomes David's capital.

> "David then took up residence in the fortress and called it the City of David. He built up the area around it, from the supporting terraces inward. And he became more and more powerful, because the LORD God Almighty was with him." (5:9-10)

---

[32] Ronny Reich and Eli Shukron, "Light at the End of the Tunnel: Warren's Shaft Theory of David's Conquests Shattered," *Biblical Archaeology Review*, vol. 25, January/February 1999, pp. 22-33, 72. They determined that Warren's Shaft, discovered in 1867 by Sir Charles Warren, long thought to be the water shaft, was never used for drawing water, but was a widening of a natural fissure in the rock.

[33] This is the author's reconstruction of events – purely speculation – but it would make a great scene in an adventure movie!

[34] Anderson, *2 Samuel*, p. 84.

The narrator explains that David "built up the area around it, from the supporting terraces inward." The word translated "supporting terraces" (NIV) or "the Millo" (NRSV, KJV, from Hebrew *millō*), apparently means "what is full" or "what fills the gap," or both. British archaeologist Kathleen Kenyon contends that this complex of terracing on the eastern slope of Ophel[35] is a Jebusite structure built to support houses on the incline of the hill,[36] retaining walls with leveled filling. David, Solomon, and later kings repair and extend these terraces.

David's palace is built by Hiram, king of Tyre, who sends timber from the cedars of Lebanon, as well as skilled carpenters and stonemasons. This aid no doubt represents a treaty that David has made with the descendants of the Phoenicians, Israel's neighbors to the northwest along the coast.

The children born to David in Jerusalem are mentioned here also.

The First Battle with the Philistines (5:17-21)

Now that David is king over all Israel and established in the fortress city of Jerusalem, the Philistines become alarmed.

> "When the Philistines heard that David had been anointed king over Israel, they went up in full force to search for him, but David heard about it and went down to the stronghold." (5:17)

David has been a Philistine vassal for nearly nine years – nearly 1-1/2 years in Ziklag and another 7-1/2 years as king of Judah in Hebron. But now that David has become king over all Israel, the Philistines realize that David has become too powerful. He not only refuses to send tribute to Gath. He now poses a substantial threat to his Philistines overlords themselves.

By taking Jerusalem, David is able to "eliminate the foreign wedge between the northern and southern tribes."[37] Bright observes:

> "The Philistines understood perfectly that David's acclamation constituted a declaration of independence on the part of a reunited Israel. And this they could not tolerate. They knew that they would have to destroy David, and destroy him at once."[38]

---

[35] Ophel is another name for the original City of David, a narrow promontory beyond the southern edge of Jerusalem's Temple Mount and Old City, with the Tyropoeon Valley on its west, the Hinnom valley to the south, and the Kidron Valley on the east.

[36] Anderson (*2 Samuel*, p. 85) cites Kathleen Kenyon, *Digging Up Jerusalem* (1974), p. 100.

[37] Aharoni and Avi-Yonah, *Macmillan Bible Atlas*, p. 66, map 100.

[38] Bright, *History of Israel*, p. 198.

"All the Philistines," that is, the combined armies of the five Philistine city-states, go out to find David and crush him. Probably, David's army is greatly outnumbered by the determined Philistines. The Philistine armies have assembled in the Valley of Rephaim, an agricultural plain just southwest of Jerusalem.[39]

But David doesn't stay within Jerusalem to await a Philistine siege. He "went down

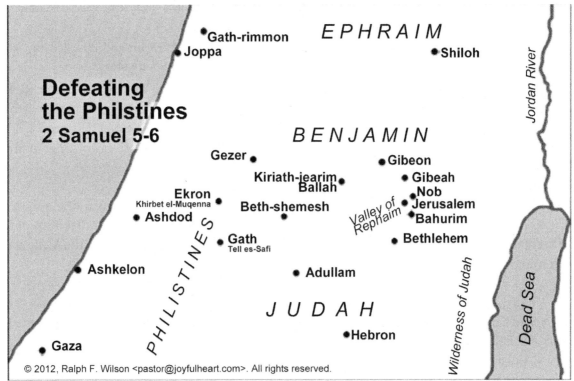

to the stronghold," probably referring to the stronghold at Adullam (cf. 1 Samuel 22:1, 4).[40] This time he went to the stronghold as a tactical move, rather than to hide or escape. Here he inquires of the Lord using the Urim and Thummim from the ephod. He asks,

> "'Shall I go and attack the Philistines? Will you hand them over to me?' The LORD answered him, "Go, for I will surely hand the Philistines over to you." (5:19)

---

[39] The Valley of Rephaim appears to be the plain immediately southwest of Jerusalem, the modern el Baq'a, now a quarter of Jerusalem. It was once the main agricultural area for Jerusalem (Isaiah 17:5), and at one time belonged to the Jebusites (Joshua 15:8; 18:16. A. van Selms, "Rephaim, Valley of," ISBE 4:137-138).

[40] One can scarcely go "down" to the stronghold at Jerusalem! In Bible language always go "up" to Jerusalem, due to its elevation.

Now David moves his troops to nearby Baal Perazim,[41] attacks the Philistine forces, and defeats them. The narrator quotes David's exclamation lauding what Yahweh has done:

> "'As waters break out, the LORD has broken out against my enemies before me.' So that place was called Baal Perazim." (5:20)

Baal Perazim means "lord of the breakings through." Though we're not told the details of the battle, Anderson speculates,

> "It is possible that David and his men rushed down Mount Perazim and attacked the surprised enemy in the valley, sweeping them away like raging floodwaters."[42]

However it happened, the Philistines fled so quickly that they "abandoned their idols there and David and his men carried them off" (5:21), a counterpart to how the Israelites' ark had been captured in battle by the Philistines years before (1 Samuel 4:11). The Chronicler tells us that they were burned (1 Chronicles 14:12), according to the command of the Torah (Deuteronomy 7:5, 25; 12:3).

The Second Battle with the Philistines (5:22-25)

The Philistines attack a second time, perhaps several years later. They must eliminate David as a threat to their control over the hill country. They gather again in the Valley of Rephaim. David inquires of the Lord again. This time the answer is different.

> "Do not go straight up, but circle around behind them and attack them in front of the balsam trees. As soon as you hear the sound of marching in the tops of the balsam trees, move quickly, because that will mean the LORD has gone out in front of you to strike the Philistine army." (5:23-24)

Yahweh's answer is so specific here that it surely doesn't come via the Urim and Thummim, but through a prophetic word, either from the prophet Gad, David's seer (2 Samuel 24:11), or through David himself (Acts 2:29-30).

> "So David did as the LORD commanded him, and he struck down the Philistines all the way from Gibeon to Gezer." (5:25)

I find it fascinating that David inquires of the Lord the second time. So often, we seek the Lord the first time we have a problem. But then we think we have it figured out and

---

[41] The location of Baal Perazim is uncertain, but may refer to the mountains to the east of the Valley of Rephaim, or perhaps refer to Mt. Perazim near the valley of Gibeon (Isaiah 28:21), possibly Sheikh Bedr, about 3 miles northwest of Jerusalem (R.E.W. Bason, "Baal-Perazim," ISBE 1:380; Anderson, 2 *Samuel*, p. 93).

[42] Anderson, 2 *Samuel*, p. 93.

don't need to seek God's wisdom again. Part of David's genius is that he seeks the Lord for every major crisis that he faces. What's more, he is obedient. He doesn't think he knows better than the Lord.

Conditions change. The Philistines perhaps expected David to do what he had done before. But this time David is to come around *behind* the Philistine army and only come when the wind comes up to rustle the leaves of the balsam trees in this valley. David's attack results in a rout, in which his troops slaughter the retreating Philistines all the way to their walled city of Gezer. In this second battle – because he did it God's way – David breaks the back of Philistine dominance of the entire region.

Q3. (2 Samuel 5:17-25) Why does David inquire of the Lord before he attacks the Philistines the first time? What would have happened if he thought he knew how to attack the Philistines, and didn't inquire of the Lord the second time? Why do we often want to figure out the process so we can act independently, rather than wait on God as a way of life? What does that say about God? What does that say about us?
http://www.joyfulheart.com/forums/index.php?showtopic=1181

David Comes to Dominate the Philistines

Later, we read:

"In the course of time, David defeated the Philistines and subdued them, and he took Metheg Ammah [a title for Gath] from the control of the Philistines" (8:1).

According to Bright, David eventually:

1. Occupies the coastal plain to a point south of Joppa (1 Kings 4:9-11).

2. Clears Philistines from Israelite soil in the south (including, at one time, Bethlehem, 2 Samuel 23:14), and thrusts his frontiers deep into their territory.

3. Captures Gath,[43] the city to which David was once a vassal (8:1; 2 Chronicles 18:1). David incorporates mercenaries from Gath into his army – the Gittites –

---

[43] In 8:1 Gath is termed Metheg Ammah, "bridle of the mother" = "mother city" of the Philistines. The NASB renders the term "chief city."

who are personally loyal to him (15:18), as well as other Philistine military contingents, the Cherethites and the Pelethites.[44]

4. Reduces the territory of Ekron if not occupying it altogether.

David, however, does not seize the Canaanite cities of Gezer, Ashdod, Ashkelon, and Gaza, perhaps knowing that Egypt still claims suzerainty over them.[45] Under David, the Philistines are obliged to recognize Israelite supremacy in the region and some become his vassals and bring him tribute (8:12).

Discipleship Lessons

What are we as disciples supposed to learn from these chapters? I see at least four important applications:

1. **Patience.** Samuel had anointed David as king when he was perhaps 15, but he doesn't become king over Judah until he is 30, and doesn't become king over all Israel until he is 37. We have to be patient as God works out His will in His time.

2. **Diplomacy.** Sometimes we have a very simplistic view of doing God's will. Sometimes our efforts on God's behalf look like "a bull in a china shop." Just as David developed relationships and worked through careful diplomacy to bring about a united kingdom, so our ministries must be characterized by grace, wisdom, and love in the way that we work with people and groups as agents of God's Kingdom. Knowing God's will isn't enough; how we facilitate it is important, too.

3. **Seeking God.** David inquires of the Lord on three occasions in these chapters: (1) Where to settle after his exile, (2) How to attack the Philistine troops, and (3) How to attack the Philistines when they come again. If we think we know it all and stop seeking God, we get in a lot of trouble.

4. **Self-interest.** One of David's biggest obstacles to uniting all Israel is Joab's single-minded intention to avenge Abner's killing of his brother Asahel. Joab not only lacked the right to extract blood vengeance, but by his actions he delayed David's peace initiative by months or years. We have to surrender our own priorities if we are to serve the King.

---

44 2 Samuel 8:18; 15:18; 20:7, 23.
45 Bright, *History of Israel*, p. 199.

David has established Jerusalem as the political and civic capital of a united Israel. In the next lesson we'll see how he seeks to make Jerusalem the center of worship for Yahweh, his beloved King.

Prayer

Father, sometimes we discount politics as unspiritual and dirty. And it often is! But we know that wise and just governing is what you desire. You are the just Judge and the righteous King. We pray for our country and for our leaders, that you would bring out of your church, righteous leaders who can cause our nation to be blessed. In Jesus' name, we pray. Amen.

Key Verses

"Then the men of Judah came to Hebron and there they anointed David king over the house of Judah." (2 Samuel 2:4a)

"All the tribes of Israel came to David at Hebron and said, 'We are your own flesh and blood. In the past, while Saul was king over us, you were the one who led Israel on their military campaigns. And the LORD said to you, "You will shepherd my people Israel, and you will become their ruler."' When all the elders of Israel had come to King David at Hebron, the king made a compact with them at Hebron before the LORD, and they anointed David king over Israel." (2 Samuel 5:1-3)

8. David Brings the Ark to Jerusalem (2 Samuel 6)

Saul had become king primarily because the Israelites felt a need for a military commander to lead them in battles (1 Samuel 8:20). At that point, Israel was a loose confederation of tribes who looked to Samuel as Judge and worshipped Yahweh together. Saul united them to some degree and led them in an united army, primarily in defensive battles against their enemies.

James J. Tissot, "David Dances before the Ark" (1896-1902), gouache on board, The Jewish Museum, New York.

However, David has a larger vision for his kingdom. He establishes a new capital city in Jerusalem in neutral territory, designed to unite all the tribes. Under him, the Philistines are not just resisted, but vanquished. But more than just being a successful military leader and diplomat, David loves the Lord.

Under Saul, worship of the Lord had languished. Saul had disobeyed the Lord's direction through Samuel (1 Samuel 13:13; 15:11). The ark had been lost a generation before and never returned to its place in the Tabernacle (1 Samuel 4-6). In his paranoia, Saul had slaughtered the priests who tended the tabernacle at Nob (1 Samuel 22:18-19), and no longer was able to seek the Lord because Abiathar, the remaining priest, had taken the ephod with him when he had fled to David (1 Samuel 22:20; 23:6). The worship of Yahweh was so diminished that Saul is reduced to seeking guidance from the witch of Endor, a spiritualist medium (1 Samuel 28).

David longs to renew the nation in the worship of Yahweh. To do that he wants to bring the long-neglected ark into his new capital city as a sign that the Lord, the true

King over Israel, is once again in the midst of his people.[1] He also wants to unite the people, with Jerusalem as both their political *and* religious center.[2]

Bringing the Ark from the House of Abinadab (6:1-2)

This is not just an idle whim. David brings together "the whole assembly of Israel," as well as representatives from his army, and seeks to get their "buy-in" to a decision to bring the ark back. The Chronicler records his speech to the assembled multitude:

> "If it seems good to you and if it is the will of the LORD our God, let us send word far and wide to the rest of our brothers throughout the territories of Israel, and also to the priests and Levites who are with them in their towns and pasturelands, to come and join us. Let us bring the ark of our God back to us, for we did not inquire of it during the reign of Saul." (1 Chronicles 13:2-3)

The assembly agrees. As a wise leader, David elevates the restoration of Yahweh worship to be a national goal, not just the fulfillment of a king's pet project.

As you may recall, the Philistines had captured the ark when Samuel was a child. The glory had departed from Israel" (1 Samuel 4:21-22). The Philistines had paraded the ark as a trophy of war in Ashdod, Gath, and Ekron, but as long as they kept it, sickness followed (1 Samuel 5). No Philistine city wanted it. Finally, after seven months, they returned it to Israelite territory on a new cart pulled by two cows. Initially it was in the priestly city of Beth-Shemesh, but because they were judged for treating the ark carelessly (1 Samuel 6), the ark was finally moved to the city of Kiriath Jearim (also known as Baalah), a town about nine miles west of Jerusalem.[3] (See Appendix 7. Locations of the Ark and the Tabernacle.)

> "They took it to Abinadab's house on the hill and consecrated Eleazar his son to guard the ark of the LORD." (1 Samuel 7:1)

There the ark remained throughout the judgeship of Samuel and the reign of Saul.

---

[1] Another reason may have been that since the Israelites had destroyed the Philistines' idols (5:21), David wanted to protect the ark, lodged only a few miles from their territory, from a reprisal (Bergen, *1 and 2 Samuel*, pp. 328-329). At this point David's subjection of the Philistines may not have been complete.

[2] "Where Saul had neglected the ark and driven its priesthood from him, David established both Ark and priesthood in the official national shrine. It was a masterstroke. It must have done more to bind the feelings of the tribes to Jerusalem than we can possibly imagine." (Bright, *History of Israel*, p. 201).

[3] Kiriath Jearim ("city of forests") was one of four cities in the Hivite confederation (along with Gibeon, Kepirah, and Beeroth) that deceived Joshua into thinking they weren't nearby neighbors (Joshua 9:17). It had been assigned to both Judah (Joshua 15:60) and later to Benjamin (Joshua 18:28). The city had been known for being a religious center, since it was also known as Baalah (Joshua 15:9) and Kiriath-baal (Joshua 15:60), that is "City of Baal." It is identified with the modern Deir al 'Azar (C.E. DeVries, "Kiriath-Jearim," ISBE 3:42).

Now, bringing back the ark becomes a national event:

> "So David assembled all the Israelites, from the Shihor River in Egypt to Lebo Hamath, to bring the ark of God from Kiriath Jearim. David and all the Israelites with him went to Baalah of Judah (Kiriath Jearim) to bring up from there the ark of God the LORD, who is enthroned between the cherubim – the ark that is called by the Name." (1 Chronicles 13:5-6)

Transporting the Ark Man's Way (6:3-10)

Apparently, David didn't seek the Lord – or read the Torah – about *how* the ark should be transported. Rather, his method of transport seems to be similar to the Philistine approach of putting the ark on a new cart pulled by two cows (1 Samuel 6:7). The celebration of bringing the ark to Jerusalem begins with great joy.

> "³ They set the ark of God on a new cart and brought it from the house of Abinadab, which was on the hill. Uzzah and Ahio, sons of Abinadab, were guiding the new cart ⁴ with the ark of God on it, and Ahio was walking in front of it. ⁵ David and the whole house of Israel were celebrating[4] with all their might before the LORD, with songs and with harps, lyres, tambourines, sistrums[5] and cymbals." (6:3-5)

Then things go terribly wrong.

> "⁶ When they came to the threshing floor of Nacon, Uzzah reached out and took hold of the ark of God, because the oxen stumbled. ⁷ The LORD's anger burned against Uzzah because of his irreverent act;[6] therefore God struck him down and he died there beside the ark of God." (6:6-7)

This recalls the severe punishment upon the men of Beth Shemesh for looking in the ark (1 Samuel 6:19). At that time, they had said: "Who can stand in the presence of the LORD, this holy God?" (1 Samuel 6:20). The Holy God insists that holy things be treated with reverence in the manner he has prescribed!

Notice David's reaction.

---

[4] "Celebrating" (NIV), "were dancing" (NRSV), "played" (KJV) in verses 5 and 21 is *śāḥaq*. "The simple stem of *śāḥaq* conveys the idea of laughter, whether in joy or incredulity. The stronger Piel stem connotes positively, "play and sport," or negatively, "mockery and derision." Here, of course, the sense is positive. The same word used to describe the Israelites' celebrating before the golden calf in at Sinai (Exodus 32:6), of children playing (Zechariah 8:5), and to play tambourines and dance (1 Samuel 18:6-7) (J. Barton Payne, *śāḥaq*, TWOT #1905).

[5] "Sistrums" (NIV), "castanets" (NRSV), "coronets" (KJV) is *mena'an'îm*, "a kind of rattle," from *nûa'*, "to shake" (Andrew Bowling, *nûa'*, TWOT #1328a). The word is found only here in the entire Old Testament.

[6] The NIV's explanatory phrase, "because of his irreverent act," doesn't appear in the Hebrew text.

"Then David was angry because the LORD's wrath had broken out against Uzzah, and to this day that place is called Perez Uzzah. David was afraid of the LORD that day and said, 'How can the ark of the LORD ever come to me?'" (6:8-9)

Why is David angry? The text doesn't tell us, but we can surmise two reasons:

1. **Misunderstood.** David has done this with the best of intentions. He loves the Lord and wants Yahweh to be honored in Israel's capital of Jerusalem. His motives are right, he feels, so why would God bring judgment? He has been misunderstood.

2. **Humiliated.** David has been publicly humiliated. The national celebration he has planned in front of 30,000 onlookers has ended with disaster, as if God doesn't approve of moving the ark. In people's eyes, David's relationship with God is being questioned.

David is angry, but he isn't stupid. He sends everyone home – if they haven't fled already – and makes arrangements to move the ark to the nearby home of Obed-Edom the Gittite. In this case, the Gath referred to is probably not the nearby Philistine city of Gath, but rather the Levitical city of Gath-Rimmon, a few miles east of Joppa (Joshua 21:24; 1 Chronicles 6:59).[7] This is likely, because we hear later of an Obed-Edom who is a prominent Levite who had seven sons, "**for God had blessed Obed-Edom.**" (1 Chronicles 26:5),[8] seemingly referring to the next verse in our text:

"The ark of the LORD remained in the house of Obed-Edom the Gittite for three months, and **the LORD blessed him and his entire household**." (6:11)

Q1. (2 Samuel 6:1-10) Why does God strike Uzzah? Why is David so angry?
http://www.joyfulheart.com/forums/index.php?showtopic=1182

---

[7] Gath-Rimmon is identified with Tell ej-Jerisheh on the south bank of the river Yarkon, about five miles northeast of Joppa (D.H. Madwig, "Gath-Rimmon," ISBE 2:414-415).

[8] Obed-Edom later became a doorkeeper for the ark in Jerusalem, in charge of 68 associates in ministry there (1 Chronicles 15:18, 24; 16:37-38).

Transporting the Ark God's Way (6:11-13)

> "Now King David was told, 'The LORD has blessed the household of Obed-Edom and everything he has, because of the ark of God.'" (6:12a)

When David learns that Obed-Edom is being blessed with the "dangerous" ark at his house, David realizes that the ark itself is not the problem. He wants that blessing in the City of David! He begins to research in the Torah about how the ark is supposed to be transported, and discovers:

> "No one but the Levites may carry the ark of God, because the LORD chose them to carry the ark of the LORD and to minister before him forever." (1 Chronicles 15:2)

This is the way the ark was carried across the Jordan River as Joshua led the people into the Promised Land (Joshua 3:3; 6:6). However, since this had been hundreds of years before, people had forgotten. Nevertheless, instructions for carrying the ark are found several times in the Pentateuch (Numbers 4:4-15, 19-20; 7:9; Deuteronomy 10:8; 31:9). Specifically, the Kohathite clan of the Levites is charged with carrying the sacred objects from the tabernacle, and it just happens that Obed-Edom is a Levite from the Kohathite town of Gath-Rimmon (Joshua 21:20-24).[9]

David now instructs the Levites:

> "It was because you, the Levites, did not bring it up the first time that the LORD our God broke out in anger against us. We did not inquire of him about how to do it in the prescribed way." (1 Chronicles 15:13)

He makes sure that the priests and Levites consecrate themselves according the Torah before this ceremony (1 Chronicles 15:14). Then David tries a second time:

> "12 So David went down and brought up the ark of God from the house of Obed-Edom to the City of David with rejoicing. 13 When those who were carrying the ark of the LORD had taken six steps, he sacrificed a bull and a fattened calf." (6:12-13)

This time, David makes sure to do God's will in God's way. It's interesting that they're rejoicing,[10] after their previous aborted celebration. But David knows what he had done wrong and he has made it right. He and the people come with faith before the Lord and God honors them in it.

---

[9] It's possible that Obed-Edom the Gittite (2 Samuel 6:10-12) is a different person from Obed-Edom son of Jeduthun (1 Chronicles 16:38). We're not sure. However, it looks that way when you put together 1 Chronicles 26:5 with 2 Samuel 6:11.

[10] "Rejoicing" (NIV, NRSV), "gladness" (KJV) is *śimḥâ*, "joy (both the emotion and its manifestation)" (Holladay, p. 353). "The root *ś-m-ḥ* denotes being glad or joyful with the whole disposition as indicated by its association with the heart" (Bruce K. Waltke, TWOT #2268b).

Q2. (2 Samuel 6:11-13) How should the ark have been transported? How are Uzzah and David responsible if they don't know the provisions of the Mosaic Law? What does David's mistake in this incident teach us about seeking to do God's will?
http://www.joyfulheart.com/forums/index.php?showtopic=1183

David Dances before the Lord (6:14)

David leads his people in worship in the procession.

"David, wearing a linen ephod, danced[11] before the LORD with all his might, [15] while he and the entire house of Israel brought up the ark of the LORD with shouts and the sound of trumpets." (6:14)

David is personally absorbed in joyful worship of his God. This is not some formal exercise, but worship from the heart – and with the arms, legs, and feet. David is dancing, and doesn't seem to care that it might seem undignified. When David's wife Michal questions him about behavior below the dignity of a king, he responds:

"I will become even more undignified than this, and I will be humiliated in my own eyes...." (6:22)

A few years ago, Matt Redman wrote "Undignified." I have never really liked the song, but I must admit that the lyrics reflect the scripture rather accurately:

"I will dance, I will sing
To be mad for my King.
Nothing, Lord, is hindering
The passion in my soul

And I'll become even more
Undignified than this.
Some would say it's foolishness but
I'll become even more
Undignified than this."[12]

[11] "Danced" is *kārar*, a word that occurs only here in the Old Testament, both verses 14 and 16 in the Pilpel stem, "dance," literally, whirling (Gerard Von Gronigen, *kārar*, TWOT #1046).
[12] Matt Redman, "Undignified," © 1995, Thankyou Music.

Often we are inhibited in our worship by what others might think of us. What will people think if I say "Amen" or if I lift my hands in worship? What will people think if I am so entranced with worship that I forget everyone around me and just focus on Him? It is before the Lord that we worship!

Free church Protestants don't understand Anglicans, Lutherans, Catholics, and the Orthodox who worship liturgically – and vice versa! Pentecostals accuse quieter evangelicals of being "God's frozen people," while the quieter judge the Pentecostals as "holy rollers." Foolishness! Our worship reflects both our culture and our traditions. God had to remind Samuel on one occasion:

> "The LORD does not look at the things man looks at.
> Man looks at the outward appearance,
> but the LORD looks at the heart." (1 Samuel 16:7)

When we worship, we focus on an "audience of One."[13] It doesn't really matter what others think. But it matters greatly what God thinks of our worship!

One of the great lessons of the Psalms is the importance of praise. The Psalms were not designed to be read silently, but to be sung out, at the very least, to be read aloud. The Psalms are designed to help us experience praise, to enter into it ourselves.

One of the revolutions we have seen in the church since the Jesus Movement of the 60s and 70s is how we worship God. Praises to God are more prominent now that the testimony songs characteristic of gospel music of a previous era. It is common in churches of all varieties to see people lift their hands in worship as they sing and pray.

Q3. (2 Samuel 6:14, 22) How would you describe David's approach to worship? What does his dancing here teach us? What do we learn about praise from the psalms he wrote? Does what others might think affect your ability to worship? How has God been working in your life to teach you to worship him in spirit and in truth?
http://www.joyfulheart.com/forums/index.php?showtopic=1184

---

[13] The phrase, "Audience of One" probably derives from a worship song by the same name composed by Michael Weaver (© 2002 Word Music, LLC)

David Brings the Ark into a Tent (6:17-19)

David can't very well return the ark to the tabernacle at Shiloh. Shiloh had been destroyed! (Jeremiah 7:12). The tabernacle had been moved to the priestly city of Nob, but the ark had never been there and Saul had slaughtered the town's priests and their families. The ancient tabernacle is now to be found at "the high place at Gibeon" (1 Chronicles 16:39-40; 21:29; 2 Chronicles 1:3, 13; 1 Kings 3:4), in a Levitical city where personnel continued sacrifices.[14]

David wants the center of Yahweh worship to be in the capital at Jerusalem, not in some priestly town. So he sets up a tent for the ark in Jerusalem, in hopes of eventually building a proper temple to house it.

> "17 They brought the ark of the LORD and set it in its place inside the tent ('ōhel) that David had pitched for it, and David sacrificed burnt offerings and fellowship offerings before the LORD. 18 After he had finished sacrificing the burnt offerings and fellowship offerings, he blessed the people in the name of the LORD Almighty. 19 Then he gave a loaf of bread, a cake of dates and a cake of raisins to each person in the whole crowd of Israelites, both men and women. And all the people went to their homes." (6:17-19)

Worship in the Tent in Jerusalem (1 Chronicles 16:4-6)

David is the great architect of worship before the Lord in Jerusalem. Compared to the emphasis on sacrifice at the Tabernacle in the Wilderness, worship before the ark in Jerusalem is characterized by praise music, much of it written by David and his musical successors – Asaph and others.

This passage will give you the flavor of this worship that David instituted:

> "He appointed some of the Levites to minister before the ark of the LORD, to **make petition, to give thanks, and to praise** the LORD, the God of Israel.... They were to **play the lyres and harps**, Asaph was to **sound the cymbals**, 6 and Benaiah and Jahaziel the priests were **to blow the trumpets** regularly before the ark of the covenant of God." (1 Chronicles 16:4-6)

However, David didn't restrict praise-worship only before the ark. Sacrifices continued at the high place in Gibeon – along with musical praise.

> "Heman and Jeduthun were responsible for the sounding of the trumpets and cymbals and for the playing of the other instruments for sacred song. The sons of Jeduthun were stationed at the gate." (1 Chronicles 16:42)

---

[14] Gibeon is the modern el-Jib. After the Conquest, Gibeon had become a Levitical city in the tribal territory of Benjamin. The name gib 'ōn ("hill") suggests a height, and the site is atop a limestone outcropping in the Judean hills (Keith N. Schoville, "Gibeon," ISBE 2:462-463).

Some see "David's Tabernacle" being renewed in our day. I have spelled out my understanding of this in Appendix 5. The Tabernacle of David Today (2 Samuel 6:17; Acts 15:16).

Michal Despises David (6:20-23)

David is the great Praise Leader of Israel. But sadly, that very praise is misunderstood by one of the people closest to him, Michel, David's wife.

> "And when she saw King David leaping and dancing before the LORD, she despised him in her heart." (6:16b)

"Despised" is *bāzâ*, "to despise, disdain, hold in contempt ... to accord little worth to something."[15] When David comes home, happy in the Lord, ready to share his joy with his family, he is met by a rebuke from his wife.

> "When David returned home to bless his household, Michal daughter of Saul came out to meet him and said, 'How the king of Israel has distinguished himself today, uncovering[16] in the sight of the slave girls of his servants as any vulgar[17] fellow would!'" (6:20)

Here is David's response:

> "[21] David said to Michal, 'It was before the LORD, who chose me rather than your father or anyone from his house when he appointed me ruler over the LORD's people Israel – I will celebrate before the LORD. [22] I will become even more undignified than this, and I will be humiliated in my own eyes. But by these slave girls you spoke of, I will be held in honor.' [23] And Michal daughter of Saul had no children to the day of her death." (2 Samuel 6:21-23)

David's answer indicates that there is no longer any great love between the two. His response involves three elements:

1. God's choice of David over Saul's dynasty. It sounds like Michal resents David. She had loved him once, when he was the young warrior honored by her father the king (1 Samuel 18:20). However, for years she had been the wife of Paltiel, one of Saul's supporters and a fellow Benjamite. Paltiel obviously loved her deeply, for when she was to be returned to her legitimate husband, David, Paltiel "went with her, weeping behind her all the way to Bahurim" (3:16). Though she had been David's first wife, by the time Michal was returned, she seems to have been David's seventh wife in terms of status –

---

[15] Bruce K. Waltke, *bāzâ*, TWOT #224.

[16] "Disrobe" (NIV), "uncover" (NRSV, KJV) is *gālâ*, "uncover." In the reflexive sense it can mean "to expose oneself" (Bruce K. Waltke, *gālâ*, TWOT #350).

[17] "Vulgar" (NIV, NRSV), "vain" (KJV) is *rêq*, "empty, vain, worthless." William White, *rîq*, TWOT #2161a.

and all the rest bore him children! (3:2-5). Her once high status as a king's daughter is but a memory – and she resents it! David understands this, and that is why he reminds her that God had made him king in the place of her father Saul:

> "... The LORD ... chose me rather than your father or anyone from his house when he appointed me ruler over the LORD's people Israel." (6:21)

2. Humility vs. pride. David isn't afraid to humble himself before the Lord. He knows Yahweh's character:

> "You save the humble
> but bring low those whose eyes are haughty." (Psalm 18:27)

Some commentators believe that David's short ephod exposed his genitals to the eyes of the low-class slave girls when he leaped in dance. That's possible, of course, but I think it's more likely that Michal is objecting to the fact that David takes off his royal robe to wear the simple ephod of a priest, and thus "uncovers" himself as if he were a commoner, rather than wearing the royal robes of a king.[18] The NIV's translation "vulgar" misleads us, I think. The word *rêq* doesn't suggest sexual vulgarity, only the idea of being common ("empty, vain, worthless"), rather than dignified as a king might be expected to be. Assuming that David is wearing the priestly ephod specified in the Torah, he will also be wearing a linen undergarment prescribed for this very reason – to prevent a priest from exposing himself (Exodus 20:26).

David had spent years in desert camps fleeing Michal's father Saul. He knows homelessness and hunger. He knows fear and faith. However, all her life, Michal has been pampered as a king's daughter, and later as the wife of an important person the king chose to favor. She knows only luxury and has developed a sense of class superiority that sometimes accompanies wealth and position.

It is significant that David doesn't defend himself against a charge of exposing his sexual organs, as some believe happened. Rather, his answer justifies humbling himself before the Lord. The word translated "undignified" (NIV), "contemptible" (NRSV), "vile" (KJV) has the idea of being of little account, that is abased, or seen as humble.[19]

3. The priority of worship. David defends his act of worship as not for anyone's benefit but God's. Michal sees only the exterior – because she isn't a co-worshipper, only an observer. God sees David's heart.

---

[18] Baldwin, *1 and 2 Samuel*, p. 209.

[19] "Undignified" (NIV), "contemptible" (NRSV), "vile" (KJV) is *qālal*, "be slight, swift, trifling, of little account," here, ""to be light or slight" (Leonard J. Coppes, *qālal*, TWOT #2028). It is used in parallel to "humiliated" (NIV), "abased" (NRSV), "be base" (KJV) is *shāpāl*, "be low, sink, be humbled" (Hermann J. Austel, *shāpāl*, TWOT #2445).

'It was before the LORD.... I will celebrate before the LORD." (6:21)

Q4. (2 Samuel 6:16, 20-23) What has happened to Michal that she is so bitter at David? How does her bitterness cause her to misjudge what she sees? Are you bitter towards God about something in your past? What effect might it have on your spiritual life? How can you find healing from the bitterness? What would have happened if David had conformed his worship expression to his wife's preferences?
http://www.joyfulheart.com/forums/index.php?showtopic=1185

Discipleship Lessons

What are we as disciples supposed to learn from these chapters?

1. **Seeking God's Way**. David brings the ark to Jerusalem, but he doesn't take time to study the Word to see how it should be done. When he consults the Word, God blesses his efforts. We are to do God's will God's way!

2. **Desire to Worship**. David sets an example before us of joyful, self-less worship. He doesn't seem to care what others think; he will worship his God! So often we are passive about worship. One of the messages of this lesson and the Book of Psalms is involvement in and love of worship.

3. **Bitterness and Despising**. Michal despises her husband's enthusiastic worship of Yahweh because she allowed bitterness into her heart. We should search and cleanse our hearts so that our hurts don't keep us from understanding what God loves and desires of us.

We have traced David's journey from exile to Hebron and finally to king in the new capital of Jerusalem. He has capped this return to power by making central the joy of his life – worship. In the next lesson, we'll see what happens when David seeks to take his love for the Lord to the next level – to build Him a temple.

Prayer

Father, I want to learn to worship you in a way that pleases You, that allows a humble and loving heart to express itself unfettered before You. Help me. Heal me so that I might worship You truly! In Jesus' name, we pray. Amen.

Key Verses

"David and the whole house of Israel were celebrating with all their might before the LORD, with songs and with harps, lyres, tambourines, sistrums and cymbals." (2 Samuel 6:5)

"David, wearing a linen ephod, danced before the LORD with all his might, while he and the entire house of Israel brought up the ark of the LORD with shouts and the sound of trumpets." (2 Samuel 6:14-15)

9. The Davidic Covenant (2 Samuel 7)

If you were to select ten of the most important chapters in the Old Testament, 2 Samuel 7 would be among them. The theme of the Davidic dynasty upon whose throne the Messiah would finally reign – the true Son of David – runs throughout the remainder of the Bible.

David Desires to Build a Temple for the Lord (7:1-3)

The story of the Davidic covenant begins with David's desire to build a temple to house the ark he has brought to Jerusalem. His motives are, no doubt mixed – like most of ours.

Gerrit van Honthorst (1590-1656), King David Playing the Harp (1611), .82x65cm, Centraal Museum, Utrecht, Holland.

1. **Love**. David loves the Lord! He composes and sings love songs to the Lord that now comprise much of our Book of Psalms. He is overjoyed to have the ark in his capital city. He loves God's presence and wants to honor God.

2. **Guilt**. But David feels guilty. Once he has conquered Jerusalem, Hiram, King of Tyre, offers to build him a suitable palace fit for a king (5:11). But, in the meantime, the earthly symbol of the presence of the Almighty and Glorious God dwells in a tent. No doubt it is a beautiful, fitting tent from David's perspective, but it is still merely a temporary structure – not like the palace David inhabits. God's glory requires something more, David feels.

3. **Boredom**. For all of his adult life David had been consumed with war – fighting the Philistines, then protecting himself from Saul's army, then establishing his kingdom by defeating neighboring kingdoms that sought to encroach on Israel's

territory. But for now, the fighting has settled down some and David has time on his hands.

The narrator sets the scene:

> "¹ After the king was settled in his palace and the LORD had given him rest from all his enemies around him, ² he said to Nathan the prophet, 'Here I am, living in a palace of cedar, while the ark of God remains in a tent.' ³ Nathan replied to the king, 'Whatever you have in mind, go ahead and do it, for the LORD is with you.'" (7:1-3)

This is the first time we see Nathan the prophet. We know little about his past, except that he seems to have been from a priestly family (1 Kings 4:5). But from this point on, he serves, along with Gad, as a prophet of the Lord with access to the king. Later, he reproves David for his sin with Bathsheba (12:1-15), conveys God's name (Jedidiah) for their child (12:24-25), and later still, he helps Bathsheba put David's chosen successor, Solomon, on the throne (1 Kings 1:11-30). He is also a writer, recording the history of both David's and Solomon's reigns (1 Chronicles 29:29; 2 Chronicles 9:29). His sons later hold trusted positions in Solomon's court (1 Kings 4:5).

David expresses his desire to Nathan to build a temple for the Lord. David is seeking God's will, and thus discusses it with God's spokesman, the prophet. And Nathan, well aware of the spiritual anointing upon David, says, "Whatever you have in mind, go ahead and do it, for the LORD is with you" (7:3). In other words, I know that you hear from God. Follow what God is telling you.

David Will Not Build the Temple (7:4-11)

But Nathan has spoken in the flesh, not in the Spirit. He was too quick to give a "word" from the Lord. Later that evening God corrects him.

> "⁴ That night the word of the LORD came to Nathan, saying: ⁵ 'Go and tell my servant David, 'This is what the LORD says:
>
> "Are you the one to build me a house to dwell in? ⁶ I have not dwelt in a house from the day I brought the Israelites up out of Egypt to this day. I have been moving from place to place with a tent as my dwelling. ⁷ Wherever I have moved with all the Israelites, did I ever say to any of their rulers whom I commanded to shepherd my people Israel, Why have you not built me a house of cedar?'"" (7:5-7)

God's word to Nathan makes three points:

1. **Wrong person.** David isn't the one God will choose to build him a temple. Much later, David explains to his son Solomon that God had told him about this:

"You have shed much blood and have fought many wars. You are not to build a house for my Name, because you have shed much blood on the earth in my sight." (1 Chronicles 22:8)

2. **Wrong time.** God doesn't want a temple at this point. The tent is a symbol of God's ability to be with his people wherever they go – it is portable.

3. **Wrong initiator.** God hadn't commanded David or any previous shepherd or leader of God's people to build a cedar temple such as David is proposing. This is something for which God desires to provide the initiative – not man.

So often – especially when we are in places of power and authority – we think somehow that whatever we want to do is okay with God. After all, we think, I am the leader God has put in this place. Our people might even rubber-stamp our ideas because they think we are spiritual. Often, if we are walking with God, our ideas *will* have been inspired by the Holy Spirit. But often we have just a portion of the idea, as David did.

There is no substitute for seeking God for his will, rather than going forward our own with what we've got, without his clear leadership. David's heart is right. And indeed, a temple *is* on God's mind, but not quite yet. And David isn't to be the builder. But as we'll see, David is to be both the architect and the supplier of the material for the temple built by Solomon.

Q1. (2 Samuel 7:1-7) Why is Nathan so quick to give David approval to build the temple? What should have Nathan done instead? What is the danger of leaders and followers too quickly approving major spiritual directions without really waiting upon the Lord? David's heart is *partly* right about building the temple though. Which part does David have right?
http://www.joyfulheart.com/forums/index.php?showtopic=1186

David's Plan for David (7:8-11a)

What follows is known as the Davidic Covenant that God gave by prophetic word through Nathan. The first three promises (7:9-11a) are to find realization during David's lifetime:

1. **A great name** (7:8b-9; cf. 8:13).

"8b This is what the LORD Almighty says: I took you from the pasture and from following the flock to be ruler over my people Israel. 9 I have been with you wherever you have gone, and I have cut off all your enemies from before you. Now I will make your name great, like the names of the greatest men of the earth." (7:8-9)

Indeed, in Lesson 10 David achieves great renown as emperor and overlord over most of the Eastern Mediterranean, an amazing rise for one who began as the youngest boy in a family of shepherds.

2. **A secure homeland for his people** (7:10-11a).

"10 And I will provide a place for my people Israel and will plant them so that they can have a home of their own and no longer be disturbed. Wicked people will not oppress them anymore, as they did at the beginning 11 and have done ever since the time I appointed leaders over my people Israel." (7:10-11a)

The kingdom under Saul and Ish-Bosheth had been insecure, with frequent need to secure the borders from the Philistines on the west, the Moabites on the east, the Edomites and Amalekites to the south, and the Aramean kings to the north. Saul seems to have developed friendly relations with only a few of his neighbors – perhaps the Phoenicians and Geshur.

3. **Peace** (7:11b).

"I will also give you rest from all your enemies." (7:11b)

Saul's whole reign was spent in constant wars. David's first few years are also consumed with war. In Lesson 10 we'll see David rise to his zenith of international power – and a period of relative peace.

Yahweh's Promise of a Perpetual Throne for David's Descendants (7:11c-17)

These three promises constitute a wonderful blessing that will be experienced by David and his people. But the next three promises talk about what God will grant David's descendants in the future – and these promises bring wonderful blessings to you and me, as we will see.

4. **A Dynasty** (7:11c).

"The LORD declares to you that the LORD himself will establish a house for you." (7:11c)

The term "house" in Hebrew has a double meaning – as it does in Greek and English. David uses it in a material sense, a physical "house" for the Lord – a temple. But God through Nathan uses the word in a figurative sense as dynasty, household, descendants – the House of David.

5. **A Son Who Will Build the Temple** (7:12-13).

"¹² When your days are over and you rest with your fathers, I will raise up your off-spring to succeed you, who will come from your own body, and I will establish his kingdom. ¹³ He is the one who will build a house for my Name." (7:12-13a)

God now speaks concerning David's natural descendant, in particular one of his own sons, who will build the temple. This promise is fulfilled in Solomon, a son not yet born, the second son of David and Bathsheba.

6. **An Everlasting Kingdom** (7:13).

"... And I will establish the throne of his kingdom forever." (7:13a)

The final – and amazing – provision of this covenant is a kingdom that will last forever. Most dynasties don't last more than a few centuries at the most. But this kingdom that God reveals will be eternal.

Ten psalms presuppose this covenant with David, the so-called Royal Psalms (2, 18, 20, 21, 45, 72, 89, 101, 110, 144).

Q2. (2 Samuel 7:8-13) What are the main promises of the Davidic Covenant? Are these promises conditional or unconditional? Why does conditionality make a difference? Which of these promises is most important to you as a Christian?
http://www.joyfulheart.com/forums/index.php?showtopic=1188

A Father's Discipline (7:14-16)

The next verses spell out the terms of the everlasting kingdom. David and his descendants don't get a "blank check" to do whatever they want without reprimand. God will act towards them as a Father. Seldom in the Old Testament is God referred to as a personal Father, but here is an exception. God will treat David's descendants as his special sons.

"¹⁴ I will be his father, and he will be my son. When he does wrong, I will punish him with the rod of men, with floggings inflicted by men. ¹⁵ But my love will never be taken away from him, as I took it away from Saul, whom I removed from before you. ¹⁶ Your house and your kingdom will endure forever before me; your throne will be established forever." (7:14-16)

With sonship comes a Father's discipline. Perhaps you recall a passage in Proverbs (quoted in Hebrews 12:5-6):

> "My son, do not despise the LORD's discipline
> and do not resent his rebuke,
> because the LORD disciplines those he loves,
> as a father the son he delights in." (Proverbs 3:11-12)

God will not reject David's dynasty because of one of his descendant's sins. He will punish him severely, but he will not remove David's dynasty from the kingship as he did Saul's dynasty.

We see in David's life an example of God "punishing him with the rod of men, with floggings inflicted by men." In David's case, the chastisement came in the form of family problems and suffering from a coup by his son Absalom.

Nevertheless, the result of the David Covenant is rather remarkable. The kingdom split under Solomon's son Rehoboam. The split-off Northern Kingdom went through nine different royal dynasties before it ended in exile by the Assyrians in 722 BC. The Southern Kingdom of Judah, on the other hand, experienced just a single dynasty throughout the approximately 400 years between David ascending the throne until the final exile to Babylon in 587 BC. You can read about the sad end of the kings of Judah in 2 Kings 24-25.

Q3. (2 Samuel 7:14-16) There is a conditional aspect in the Davidic Covenant – that God will discipline David's descendants when they sin. How did God discipline David and his descendants?

http://www.joyfulheart.com/forums/index.php?showtopic=1189

Did God Forsake His Covenant with David? (Psalm 89)

But what happened during and after the exile when the princes of David's dynasty were no longer upon the throne? Zerubbabel, grandson of Jehoiachin (one of the last kings of Judah), was governor of Judah during the exile and the restoration of the temple. But after 587 BC there were no sons of David upon the throne.

Did God's promise fail? The writer of Psalm 89 poses this tragic question by reciting God's promise to David, then comparing it to his present reality:

"[35] 'Once for all, I have sworn by my holiness –
and I will not lie to David–
[36] that his line will continue forever
and his throne endure before me like the sun;
[37] it will be established forever like the moon,
the faithful witness in the sky.'

[38] But you have rejected[1], you have spurned[2],
you have been very angry with your anointed one.
[39] You have renounced[3] the covenant with your servant
and have defiled his crown in the dust....

[46] How long, O LORD?
Will you hide yourself forever?
How long will your wrath burn like fire?" (Psalm 89:35-39, 46)

It certainly seemed like God had forgotten the Davidic Covenant – at least from the perspective of the person who wrote this psalm, probably either during or after the exile.

Renewing God's Promise Regarding David's Heir (Jeremiah 33)

But God had not renounced the covenant, as he clearly spoke to the prophet Jeremiah, who lived during the period of the last Davidic kings and the exile. The fulfillment was sure, but it would be in the future. The promise was of the Messiah whom God would send in the last days.

"[14] 'The days are coming,' declares the LORD, 'when I will fulfill the gracious promise I made to the house of Israel and to the house of Judah.

[15] In those days and at that time
I will make a righteous Branch sprout from David's line;
he will do what is just and right in the land.
[16] In those days Judah will be saved
and Jerusalem will live in safety.

---

[1] "Rejected" (NIV), "spurned" (NRSV), "cast off" (KJV) is *zānah*, "'reject, spurn, cast off.' Related to an Arabic root meaning 'be remote, repelled,' *zanah* carries the basic meaning of strong dislike or disapproval" (Leon J. Wood, TWOT #564).

[2] "Spurned" (NIV), "rejected" (NRSV), "abhorred" (KJV) is *mā'as*, "reject, despise" (Walter C. Kaiser, TWOT #1139).

[3] "Renounced" (NIV, NRSV), "made void" (KJV) is *nā'ar*, "abhor, spurn" (TWOT #1276). Derek Kidner believes this rare verb means something like "disdained" or "held cheap" (*Psalms 73-150*, Inter-Varsity Press, 1975, p. 324).

> This is the name by which it will be called:
> The LORD Our Righteousness.'
>
> [17] For this is what the LORD says:
>
> 'David will never fail to have a man to sit on the throne of the house of Israel, [18] nor will the priests, who are Levites, ever fail to have a man to stand before me continually to offer burnt offerings, to burn grain offerings and to present sacrifices.'
>
> [19] The word of the LORD came to Jeremiah:
>
> [20] 'This is what the LORD says: If you can break my covenant with the day and my covenant with the night, so that day and night no longer come at their appointed time, [21] then my covenant with David my servant – and my covenant with the Levites who are priests ministering before me – can be broken and David will no longer have a descendant to reign on his throne.
>
> [22] I will make the descendants of David my servant and the Levites who minister before me as countless as the stars of the sky and as measureless as the sand on the seashore.'" (Jeremiah 33:14-22)

Other prophets also look to the future Son of David, the Messiah whom God will send. Consider Isaiah's prophecy of the Child who is to be born:

> "Of the increase of his government and peace there will be **no end**.
> He will reign on David's throne and over his kingdom,
> establishing and upholding it with justice and righteousness
>   **from that time on and forever.** " (Isaiah 9:7)

Daniel spoke of "a kingdom that will never be destroyed" (Daniel 2:44). Later, Daniel shares his vision of the Son of Man that Jesus referred to concerning himself (Matthew 26:64):

> "In my vision at night I looked, and there before me was one like a son of man, coming with the clouds of heaven. He approached the Ancient of Days and was led into his presence. He was given authority, glory and sovereign power; all peoples, nations and men of every language worshiped him. His dominion is an **everlasting dominion** that **will not pass away**, and **his kingdom is one that will never be destroyed**." (Daniel 7:13-14)

John the Baptist's father Zechariah prophesied about Jesus:

> "He will be great and will be called the Son of the Most High.
> The Lord God will give him **the throne of his father David**,
> and he will reign over the house of Jacob **forever**;
> **his kingdom will never end**." (Luke 1:32-33)

The Davidic Covenant

Jeremiah refers to the Lord's "covenant" with David. Indeed, the term covenant (*berît*) and related terms are used a number of times to describe the promises of God toward David and his descendants (1 Chronicles 7:18; 2 Chronicles 21:7; 2 Samuel 23:5; Psalm 89:3, 28, 34; Psalm 132:11-12; Isaiah 55:3; Jeremiah 13:14, 20-21; cf. Acts 2:30; 13:34).

But what kind of covenant was this? Scholars have demonstrated convincingly that the Mosaic Covenant had its roots in the suzerain-vassal treaties of the ancient Near East. But attempts to find precursors of the Davidic Covenant have met with less success. Clearly, the Mosaic Covenant is conditional; the blessings of the covenant only come through the obedience of the vassal.

But the Abrahamic and Davidic Covenants are different. They are unconditional promises rather than conditional. The Davidic Covenant is clearly unconditional.[4] If David's descendants sin, they will be punished, but that won't terminate God's promise of "an everlasting covenant (*berît*), arranged[5] and secured[6] in every part?" (2 Samuel 23:5a).

The sacred authors clearly saw this as an authentic covenant, sealed by God's solemn oath to David (Acts 2:30; Psalm 89:3; 132:11).

Q4. The Davidic kingdom did end in 587 BC – temporarily. How did God fulfill his promises in the Davidic Covenant? In what ways is it fulfilled in Christ?
http://www.joyfulheart.com/forums/index.php?showtopic=1190

---

[4] In the 1970s Moshe Weinfeld of the Hebrew University in Jerusalem attempted to show that the Davidic covenant was modeled on royal land grants known from the Hittite and Mesopotamian realms (Moshe Weinfeld, "The Covenant of Grant in the Old Testament and in the Ancient Near East," *Journal of the American Oriental Society*, 90/2 (1970), pp. 184-203). But Knoppers pointed out enough weaknesses in Weinfeld's work that some scholars conclude, "the model probably should be abandoned" (J.J.M. Roberts, "Davidic Covenant," DOTHB pp. 208-209).

[5] "Arranged" (NIV), "ordered" (NRSV, KJV) is '*ārak*, "a verb of preparation, arranging (so its Phoenician cognate), setting in order; often used in martial contexts of drawing up in battle order" (TWOT #1694).

[6] "Secure/d" (NIV, NRSV), "sure" (KJV) is *shāmar*, "keep, guard, observe, give heed.... The basic idea of the root is 'to exercise great care over'" (TWOT #2414).

David's Prayer of Humility and Thanks (7:18-29)

David's response to God's promise is moving in its humility. I encourage you to read it aloud to catch something of its pathos and love. It begins: "Then King David went in and sat before the LORD" (7:18a). Apparently, he went into the tabernacle that housed the ark and sat in God's presence there. First, he is awestruck by God's grace – undeserved and unmerited:

> "18b Who am I, O Sovereign LORD, and what is my family,
> that you have brought me this far?
> 19 And as if this were not enough in your sight, O Sovereign LORD,
> you have also spoken about the future of the house of your servant.
> Is this your usual way of dealing with man, O Sovereign LORD?
> 20 "What more can David say to you?
> For you know your servant, O Sovereign LORD.
> 21 For the sake of your word and according to your will,
> you have done this great thing and made it known to your servant." (7:18b-21)

Now, he gives praise to God for his greatness.

> "22 How great you are, O Sovereign LORD!
> There is no one like you,
> and there is no God but you,
> as we have heard with our own ears.
> 23 And who is like your people Israel –
> the one nation on earth that God went out
> to redeem as a people for himself,
> and to make a name for himself,
> and to perform great and awesome wonders
> by driving out nations and their gods from before your people,
> whom you redeemed from Egypt?
> 24 You have established your people Israel as your very own forever,
> and you, O LORD, have become their God." (7:22-24)

Now he calls on God to keep this wonderful and hard-to-believe promise – though he knows that God will keep his word!

> "25 And now, LORD God, keep forever the promise
> you have made concerning your servant and his house.
> Do as you promised, 26 so that your name will be great forever.
> Then men will say, 'The LORD Almighty is God over Israel!'
> And the house of your servant David will be established before you." (7:25-26)

Finally, he asks God for the blessing upon him and his descendants forever.

"²⁷ O LORD Almighty, God of Israel,
you have revealed this to your servant, saying,
'I will build a house for you.'
So your servant has found courage to offer you this prayer.
²⁸ O Sovereign LORD, you are God!
Your words are trustworthy,
and you have promised these good things to your servant.
²⁹ Now be pleased to bless the house of your servant,
that it may continue forever in your sight;
for you, O Sovereign LORD, have spoken,
and with your blessing the house of your servant
will be blessed forever." (7:27-29)

Disciple Lessons

There are several lessons in this chapter for us as disciples:

1. **Partial Revelation**. We may have a glimmer of what God's plan is, but we must be patient until he reveals it and confirms it to us.

2. **Quick to Speak**. Don't be too quick to confirm someone else's vision, like Nathan was. Rather say, "Let me pray about that." Then seek God and listen for his voice. Don't speak before God speaks.

3. **Patience**. Don't be discouraged if God's promises don't seem to come to pass. If he has indeed promised something, he will fulfill it in his time.

4. **Jesus Christ**. Jesus the Messiah is the fulfillment of the Davidic Covenant, which will be complete when he returns.

The Davidic Covenant Is Fulfilled in Christ

David's heart is to build a "house," a temple for the Lord, but to his surprise, Nathan tells him that the Lord wants to build a "house," a dynasty for him. Solomon built a temple that was indeed glorious. But this temple, in all its glory, was destroyed and its treasures dispersed more than 2,500 years ago. That "house" is gone. But the more important "house" is still reigning over the Kingdom of God in the person of Jesus the Messiah, Son of David, and King of kings and Lord of lords.

The fulfillment of the Davidic covenant shall be complete when the angel shall proclaim at the Messiah's coming:

"The kingdom of the world has become the kingdom of our Lord and of his Christ, and he will reign for ever and ever." (Revelation 11:15)

Hallelujah!

Prayer

Thank you, Lord, for this amazing promise you made to David. We enjoy the fulfillment of this promise in Jesus Christ, Son of David and Son of God. Thank you! In Jesus' name, we pray. Amen.

Key Verses

"This is what the LORD Almighty says: I took you from the pasture and from following the flock to be ruler over my people Israel. I have been with you wherever you have gone, and I have cut off all your enemies from before you. Now I will make your name great, like the names of the greatest men of the earth." (2 Samuel 7:8-9)

"The LORD declares to you that the LORD himself will establish a house for you: When your days are over and you rest with your fathers, I will raise up your offspring to succeed you, who will come from your own body, and I will establish his kingdom. He is the one who will build a house for my Name, and I will establish the throne of his kingdom forever.... Your house and your kingdom will endure forever before me; your throne will be established forever." (2 Samuel 7:11-13, 16)

"I will be his father, and he will be my son. When he does wrong, I will punish him with the rod of men, with floggings inflicted by men. But my love will never be taken away from him, as I took it away from Saul, whom I removed from before you." (2 Samuel 7:14-15)

10. David's Rise, Fall, and Punishment (2 Samuel 8-12)

As king of all Israel, David finds success beyond his wildest dreams – but that doesn't seem to be enough for him. While he was a fugitive in the Judean desert, he had to rely closely on God, since his life was tenuous. But here in the palace, David is surrounded by wealth and luxury and any pleasure he could desire – and that becomes his downfall. I recall the thorny soil in Jesus' Parable of the Sower:

> "The worries of this life, the deceitfulness of wealth and the desires for other things come in and choke the word, making it unfruitful." (Mark 4:19)

It is a sad and cautionary tale from which we must learn, especially those of us from the relatively affluent West that allows us to become soft and feel sufficient in ourselves.

This is a long lesson. While the first part doesn't include many deep spiritual insights, I've tried to fill in some of the geopolitical background context so you can understand better the empire that David

James J. Tissot, "Nathan Reproaches David" (1896-1902), gouache on board, The Jewish Museum, New York.

developed. The real spiritual insights come later as we examine David's sin with Bathsheba.

David Subjugates the Philistines and Moabites (8:1-2)

When David took the throne, his first concern was the survival of his kingdom. But gradually he developed a policy of subjugating the nations around Israel, so they could not rise up against Israel. It is an expensive policy, but also extremely lucrative in terms of the tribute that these vassal nations send to David in his capital at Jerusalem.

David finally subdues the Philistines that have troubled Israel for centuries. We examined his victories over the Philistines in Lesson 7. (However, late in David's reign the Philistines trouble Israel again and are put down; 21:15-17).

David also defeats the Moabites. Despite the fact that David's ancestor Ruth was a Moabite (Ruth 4:17) and that the Moabites had protected David's parents while he was being hunted by Saul (1 Samuel 22:3-4), David enforces on Moab's conquered army a brutal punishment to reduce their numbers and end whatever threat they posed to Israel. Moab becomes a vassal state bringing tribute to David (8:11-12).

David defeats Zobah and the Arameans (8:3-6)

The Philistines and Moabites are nearby enemies. But now David begins to secure his borders to the far north, to Aram, a confederacy of Aramean kingdoms headed by the king of Zobah.

According to the ancient genealogies in Genesis, Aram was a son of Shem, thus a Semite people (Genesis 10:22). Abraham, born in Ur, was a Semite, but not an Aramean. However, Abraham moved to Haran, an Aramean region. And when Abraham and Isaac sought wives for their sons, they looked to "old country" around Haran, an Aramean region, in Aram Naharaim (that is, Aram of the Two Rivers, the Euphrates and the Tigris) and Paddan Aram (that is, the Plateau of Aram). Jacob is called an Aramean (Deuteronomy 26:5). Hebrew is a Semitic language, closely related to Aramaic, the language of the Arameans.

Over time, some Aramean peoples moved south from Mesopotamia into the area known as present-day Syria. In David's time, these Aramean kingdoms or city-states consisted of an alliance headed by the kingdom of Zobah.[1] Zobah was centered in the what is known today as the Beqaa Valley, watered by two rivers, the Orontes and the Litani. The area was rich in vineyards, grain fields, and minerals, especially copper.[2] Zobah's king acted as overlord to a vast territory extending northeast, along the Fertile Crescent to the Euphrates River. Saul had fought against Zobah in his day (1 Samuel 14:47); now it is David's turn.

Hadadezer, king of Zobah, is a powerful and aggressive king. So in order for David to secure the northern borders of Israel, it is necessary to subdue these Aramean kingdoms. It seems that David took the opportunity to attack Zobah from the south when Hadadezer's main army was away seeking to restore territory along the Euphrates River. Even when Zobah's troops were reinforced by allies from Damascus, David won an outstanding victory:

[1] William S. LaSor, "Syria," ISBE 4:686-694; Jerome A. Lund, "Aram, Damascus, and Syria," DOTHB, pp. 41-50.
[2] Barry J. Beitzel, "Zobah," ISBE 4:1203-1204.

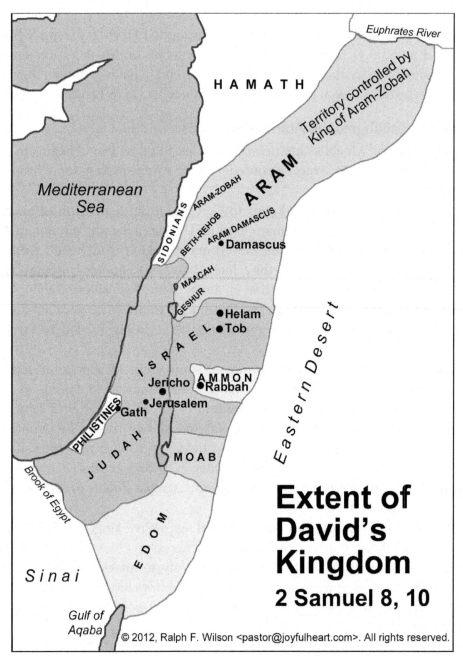

Extent of David's Kingdom
2 Samuel 8, 10

"4 David captured a thousand of his chariots, seven thousand charioteers and twenty thousand foot soldiers. He hamstrung all but a hundred of the chariot horses. 5 When the Arameans of Damascus came to help Hadadezer king of Zobah, David struck down twenty-two thousand of them. ⁶ He put garrisons in the Aramean kingdom of Damascus, and the Arameans became subject to him and brought tribute." (8:4-6)

We don't know much about the battle, except that David won a major victory, capturing a huge chariot division as well as 20,000 soldiers. In fact, the largest chariot battle in history in 1274 BC, took place between the Egyptians and the Hittites in the Beqaa Valley at Kadesh, involving 5,000 to 6,000 chariots. Chariots were a powerful military weapon in battles on flat river valleys – a mobile fighting platform that could destroy an army of foot soldiers.³ But David's kind of fighting, centered in the hill country, had no use for chariots, since they only were effective on flat ground. To weaken Zobah's ability to rebel, however, he hamstrung nearly all the chariot horses, a common military practice.

Since Hadadezer was the overlord of a number of vassal kingdoms extending all the way to the Euphrates River, when David conquered Hadadezer, David himself became the overlord of all these vassal kingdoms, and the influence of his reign extended over a huge territory, from the Brook of Egypt (probably Wâdī el-'Arîsh⁴) in the south to the Euphrates River in the northeast.

To ensure continued control of these Aramean kingdoms, David puts a garrison of soldiers in Damascus. However, keeping the Arameans subdued is a continual struggle. In 2 Samuel 10 (later in this lesson) we see further battles with Hadadezer and other Aramean city-states hired by Ammon.

As a result of David conquering the Aramean kingdoms, David receives an appreciative visit bearing gifts from the king of Hamath, a Hittite kingdom that often warred with the Arameans (8:9-10). This looks more like a strategic alliance between Hamath and Israel, rather than an actual suzerain-vassal relationship.

In 8:13-14 we read about a major victory over the Edomites inflicting 18,000 casualties. After that, the Edomites were put under submission by garrisons of troops.

When we read a single sentence in the Bible that reports a victory, it's easy to pass over it quickly. But to wage war hundreds of miles from his home base against such powerful enemies, requires David and his officers to manage supply lines, military units, strategy on unfamiliar ground, to motivate large numbers of soldiers, and to coordinate their movements against huge and well-equipped armies. True, in Joab,

---

³ Chariots could be used effectively along the coastal plain and in the valley of Jezreel. They were used at various times by the Egyptians, the Philistines (1 Samuel 13:5), and the Syrians (2 Samuel 8:4; 10:18). Solomon kept a stable of Egyptian horses and chariots, and exported them to the Hittites and Arameans (1 Kings 10:26, 39).

⁴ R.K. Harrison, "Brook of Egypt," ISBE 1:550.

David has a gifted general, but winning and then retaining such a vast kingdom says a lot about David's vision and abilities. Baldwin observes,

> "These military operations must have been time-consuming, occupying much of David's best years, and displaying his brilliance as a general."[5]

David is a military and administrative genius, rising from being a shepherd boy to becoming the head of a substantial empire. However, the narrator attributes it not to David, but to God.

> "The LORD gave David victory wherever he went." (2 Samuel 8:6b)

David Receives Tribute (8:7-12)

In the ancient Near East, a conquering king didn't usually rule conquered kingdoms directly. Rather, the existing kings would often continue to rule as vassal kings, who were now expected to support David's garrisons of soldiers and to send tribute regularly to David in Jerusalem. Here the narrator records tribute of gold and bronze that David then "dedicated" to the Lord. The word "dedicate" is *qādash*, that which is in the sphere of the sacred. So David transfers control from his own personal treasury to that of the Lord, apparently stockpiling materials that could be used later by Solomon to build the temple (1 Chronicles 22:14-16; 28:11-19).

David's Administrative Structure (8:15-18)

The narrator sums up David's role:

> "David reigned over all Israel, doing what was just and right for all his people." (8:15)

Verses 16-18 along with 20:23-26 delineate David's cabinet of chief ministers. Note the divisions:

1. **National army**. This is the army drawn from the tribes of Israel, under the generalship of Joab.
2. **Mercenaries** made up a large part of the troops David uses to conquer and to occupy his far-flung kingdoms. These forces are under the control of Benaiah, a legendary military leader (23:20). The mercenaries seemed to consist of three groups.
   a. **Gittites**. David's personal bodyguard is made up of Gittites (soldiers from Gath) under the leadership of Ittai (15:18-19). Using foreign troops to protect the king's person lessened intrigue that could have been based on tribal loyalties.

---

[5] Baldwin, *1 and 2 Samuel*, p. 223.

    b. **Kerethites or Cherethites**. This group probably consists of Philistines from the Negev desert (1 Samuel 30:14).[6]

    c. **Pelethites** are probably Philistine mercenaries also.[7]

This interesting administrative division between the regular army and the mercenary army has important historical implications. When David is old, Adonijah attempts to become king rather than Solomon. The regular army of Israelites under Joab supports Adonijah, while the mercenary troops (who didn't have tribal loyalties) under Benaiah support Solomon, David's hand-picked successor (1 Kings 1:7-8). Solomon win out.

3. **Priests**. Abiathar and Zadok shared this responsibility. Later, Abiathar is deposed for supporting Adonijah, and Zadok is given full responsibility as high priest (1 Kings 1:7-8; 2:35). David is a strong patron of Yahweh worship, and, as we have seen, prepares for the construction of a temple. He sets up a whole Levitical structure to ensure appropriate worship both in Jerusalem before the ark and at the tabernacle site at the high place at Gibeon (1 Chronicles 16:39).

4. **Recorder**, or perhaps "royal herald" (*mazkir*, literally, "one causing to remember"). We're not sure of the exact responsibilities of this officer,[8] though he may have been responsible for keeping the king informed, advising him, and communicating the kings commands.[9]

5. **Royal secretary or scribe** (*sōpēr*) or secretary of state.[10] He may have served as an assistant to the Recorder, but since this office doesn't follow right after the Recorder in this list, it probably has specific duties. Both offices seem to have been important in later administrations (1 Kings 4:3; 2 Kings 12:10; 18:18; 2 Chronicles 34:8; cf. Esther 6:1).

---

[6] Anderson, *2 Samuel*, p. 137. For etymological reasons, Klein (*1 Samuel*, 282-283) sees them as mercenaries from Crete in service of the Philistines. Later, the term "Kererthites" is used as a synonym for the Philistines (Ezekiel 25:16; Zephaniah 2:5).

[7] George Kroeze ("Pelethites," ISBE 3:736-737) sees this as a variant form of *pᵉlištî*, "Philistine," with the "š" assimilating to the "t", citing J. Montgomery, in his ICC commentary on Kings.

[8] *Zākar* can refer to inward mental acts ("think (about), meditate (upon), pay attention (to)" as well as outward speaking ("proclaim, invoke.") Thomas E. McComiskey, *zakar*, TWOT #551.

[9] Baldwin, *1 and 2 Samuel*, p. 224; Bergen, *1 and 2 Samuel*, p. 351.

[10] Bright, *History of Israel*, pp. 205-207.

6. **Royal advisors**, literally, "priests"[11] (NRSV). David's sons apparently serve in his cabinet also – which makes sense in developing them for a future role as king. The Chronicler mentions them as "chief officials."

A similar list in 20:23-26 reflecting a later period includes a couple more officers: a person in charge of forced labor and David's private priest, Ira the Jairite. Important roles that are *not* mentioned in these lists are instructive.

7. **Prime Minister** or vizier. Since this is omitted, it is likely that David heads his own government, rather than being a king who delegates all the day-to-day governance issues to others. David exercises strong personal administrative and leadership gifts.

8. **Judicial**. David, as was common in the ancient Near East, is the final judge. We see this role in Solomon, who famously proposed to settle a dispute about who was a child's true mother by cutting the child in half (1 Kings 3:16-28). Apparently, however, David delegates some judicial duties to a group of Levites (1 Chronicles 23:4; 26:29). In later years, however, David may not have taken his responsibility to judge disputes seriously enough – at least according to his son Absalom, who offers to intervene on the behalf of people seeking the king's justice (2 Samuel 15:2-4).

9. **Taxation**. David doesn't have a Department of Internal Revenue, since much of the income for his government comes from tribute from surrounding vassal nations. However, David's census (chapter 24) may have had implications for taxation as well as conscription of soldiers.

David did have a lot of expenses. By the end of his reign, he has a growing number of clients and pensioners eating at his table (19:32-38). Mephibosheth, whom we'll consider next, is one of these.

David Honors Jonathan's Son Mephibosheth (9:1-13)

Perhaps the following story about Mephibosheth is placed here because the narrator has just been talking about David's cabinet – and Mephibosheth becomes, if not a member of the ruling council, at least a member of the royal household.

---

[11] Though there is occasional precedent for non-Levites performing priestly functions (Samuel, for example), it's more likely that *kōhēn* is used here in its early secular usage with the idea of the root being "serving as a minister" (J. Barton Payne, *kōhēn*, TWOT #959a, citing S. R. Driver, *Notes on the Hebrew Text of the Books of Samuel*, pp. 284-285).

If you recall in Lesson 3, David and Jonathan had made a covenant with each other (1 Samuel 18:3), renewed again when David had to flee from Saul (1 Samuel 20:14-17; 20:42). Jonathan knew that David would become king, and had asked of David:

> "Do not ever cut off your kindness from my family – not even when the LORD has cut
> off every one of David's enemies from the face of the earth." (1 Samuel 20:15)

Jonathan had kept his promises to protect David from Saul's anger and David does not forget his promises to Jonathan. David even honors his promise to Saul not to kill his offspring when he gets the chance (1 Samuel 24:21-22; 2 Samuel 4).

Apparently, David is recalling his sweet friendship with Jonathan, which prompts him to ask his staff:

> "Is there anyone still left of the house of Saul to whom I can show kindness for Jona-
> than's sake?" (9:1)

Inquiries are made and a man named Ziba, who had formerly been "a servant of Saul's household," is summoned to the palace. Presumably, Ziba had been a capable part of Saul's paid household staff, not an owned slave, for now Ziba appears to be a wealthy man with 15 sons and 20 servants (9:10). David asks him if anyone is left from Saul's family. Ziba informs him, "There is still a son of Jonathan; he is crippled in both feet" (9:3b).

This son is named Mephibosheth.[12] When he was a boy of five, word came to the palace that Saul and Jonathan had been slain. In order to protect the prince from the Philistines, who were expected to overrun the capital at Gibeah, his nurse had dropped him in her haste to flee and he became crippled (4:4).

Mephibosheth had been staying in Lo Debar, a town east of the Jordan, in the home of Makir son of Ammiel, a wealthy, generous, and hospitable man who later assists David when he flees from Absalom (17:27-29).

When Mephibosheth is summoned to appear before David, he is probably terrified. As the rightful heir of the previous king, he could be considered in line for the throne. Such offspring from a former dynasty were usually killed to insure the security of the new king (19:28). But David isn't motivated by fear. Rather, he is motivated by his love for Jonathan and his honor in keeping the covenant he has made with Jonathan. David says to Mephibosheth:

---

[12] Mephibosheth ("dispeller of shame") is called Merib-Baal ("quarreler of Baal") in 1 Chronicles 8:34. The author of 1 Samuel apparently is offended by the name of Canaanite god Baal in his name, and substitutes for it the word *bōshet*, "shame." In a similar way as Ish-Bosheth in 2 Samuel 2:8, 10 is Eshbaal in 1 Chronicles 8:33.

"Don't be afraid, for I will surely show you kindness for the sake of your father Jonathan. I will restore to you all the land that belonged to your grandfather Saul, and you
will always eat at my table." (9:7)

The privilege of eating at the king's table is a high honor (19:28; 1 Kings 2:7) that Saul
had once bestowed upon David (1 Samuel 20:5, 18). Now David accords this honor to
the son of his friend Jonathan.

Moreover, David restores all of Saul's land to Mephibosheth (which, presumably, had
become David's as the new king), and commands Saul's former servant Ziba to manage
these farmlands for him. Ziba may not like this change in status, but he wisely obeys
David's edict. Later, however, he tries to get free from this obligation (16:1-4), and
apparently succeeds (19:17, 26-29).

David not only spares Mephibosheth from death; he honors and blesses him. That's
how David keeps the spirit of his covenant with Jonathan (Psalm 15:4).

**Q1. (2 Samuel 9:1-13) Why does David honor Mephibosheth? What does this teach us
about David's character?**

http://www.joyfulheart.com/forums/index.php?showtopic=1191

David Fights the Ammonites – and the Arameans Again (10:1-19)

Up to this point, David had an alliance with the king of Ammon, whose capital was
at Rabbah (Rabbath-Ammon). Today it is Amman, capital of the modern Hashemite
Kingdom of Jordan.

But the former friendly king had died, so David sends a delegation to Rabbah to
express his sympathy and to cement good relations with Hanun, his son, who reigns in
his place.

But the son wants to assert the independence of Ammon from the increasing power
of Israel. The new king's advisors interpret David's delegation as being spies trying to
find the city's weaknesses so David can later attack to overthrow this walled city. On
that provocation, Hanun thoroughly humiliates David's delegates by cutting off one half
the beard of each man and cutting off their robes in such a way that their nakedness is

exposed. Then he sends them home in disgrace. How stupid! Wise rulers don't insult the most powerful king in the entire region.

Finally, however, the Ammonite king realizes his stupidity. In order to defend his kingdom from David's inevitable retaliation, he pays some of his allies to send their armies:

- Beth Rehob and Zobah send 20,000 Aramean foot soldiers from a kingdom David had previously subdued (8:3-8). This constitutes an act of rebellion of vassals against David their suzerain.
- Maacah[13] sends 1,000 men.
- Tob[14] sends 12,000 men.

David responds to the Ammonites' insult with his entire army under Joab.

When the Israelite army arrives at the gates of Rabbah, they find that their enemies threaten them from two directions. The Ammonites are arrayed in front of Rabbah's city gates, while their Aramean allies are deployed *behind* the Israelite army. The Israelite army is in extreme jeopardy!

Joab is forced to divide his army to fight a two-front battle. Joab commands the division that will attack the Aramean forces deployed behind them, while his brother Abishai, a valiant man in his own right (1 Samuel 26:6-12; 2 Samuel 23:18-19), commands the division that will attack the Ammonites stationed in front of their city. In Joab's words to the troops, you can sense the seriousness of the situation. They are in a fight for their very lives:

> "If the Arameans are too strong for me, then you are to come to my rescue; but if the Ammonites are too strong for you, then I will come to rescue you. Be strong and let us fight bravely for our people and the cities of our God. The LORD will do what is good in his sight." (10:11-12)

And God is with them! When Joab advances on the Arameans, they flee, and the Ammonites then retreat into their city to avoid slaughter. Rather than put the walled city under siege at this point, Joab returns to Jerusalem. The Israelites have won the first round, though the Ammonites remain a dangerous enemy on Israel's eastern borders.

---

[13] Maacah was a small Aramean kingdom situated between Gilead in the south and Mount Hermon in the North (Anderson, *2 Samuel*, p. 147, citing B. Mazar, "Geshur and Maacah," *Journal of Biblical Literature*, 80 (1961), 16-28).

[14] Tob was a small Aramean city-state – perhaps subject to or allied with Maacah – apparently located at et-Tayîbeh (Anderson, *2 Samuel*, p. 147; William S. LaSor, "Tob," ISBE 4:865).

But David is aware that he not only has the Ammonites to cope with. Now his Aramean vassals are in full rebellion, trying to throw off his yoke as their suzerain.

The Arameans regroup. King Hadadezer of Zobah calls on troops from Aramean allies north of the Euphrates River (ancient Mesopotamia), and they assemble for battle at Helam, east of the Jordan,[15] with Zobah's chief general in command. It is a huge force, with tens of thousands of soldiers and hundreds of chariots.

Instead of leaving this battle to Joab, David himself gathers troops from all over Israel for the showdown and leads them personally. Israel's massed troops cross the Jordan at a ford and march towards the Arameans massed at Helam.

We don't know the details of the battle, but we know the result:

> "They fled before Israel, and David killed seven hundred of their charioteers and forty thousand of their foot soldiers. He also struck down Shobach the commander of their army, and he died there." (10:18)

It is a decisive victory. As a result, all the city-states and kingdoms that had been loyal to Hadadezer of Zobah now transfer their allegiance to David and become his vassals. Baldwin observes:

> "This means that the consolidated Israelite tribes had ... secured control over the main trade routes that connected Egypt and Arabia with Syria and further afield. As a result, Israel gained political dominance and economic advantage."[16]

And the Ammonites at Rabbah now have nowhere to turn for help. It is time to move against them.

Joab Lays Siege to the Ammonite Capital of Rabbah (11:1)

David returns to Jerusalem. But the next spring, when the rains are over, the weather is warm enough for an extended campaign, and the troops can sustain themselves from the ripening fields of wheat and barley surrounding Rabbah, David's troops move to besiege Rabbah.

David sends his own troops (perhaps his Philistine mercenaries – the Gittites, Kerethites, and Pelethites), as well as troops from the various tribes of Israel, all under the command of Joab. They go with one purpose: to put down the Ammonite threat.

I've often heard David criticized for staying in Jerusalem rather than going off to war with his troops. That's unfair. David had gone out with the troops when threatened by a

---

[15] The location of Helam is uncertain, but it may be a region (rather than a city) in northern Transjordan. (Anderson, *2 Samuel*, p. 148). It may be identical with Alema (1 Maccabees 5:26, 35), `Alma, northeast of Der`a (Edrei) in Ḥaurân (B.E. Hovey, "Helam, ISBE 2:676).

[16] Baldwin, *1 and 2 Samuel*, p. 231.

massive Aramean force that could have destroyed the Israelite army at Helam (10:17-18). But the siege of Rabbah doesn't require him to be present personally. After all, he has an empire to administer.

Joab is certainly competent to conduct the siege of Rabbah. No fancy strategies are required – just a considerable period of time, even years in some cases (2 Kings 17:5). Typically, a besieging army would build earthworks (a line of circumvallation) to completely encircle their target, preventing food, water, and other supplies from reaching the besieged city. The plan would be to starve them for several months – and, if possible, cut off their water supply and get them to surrender – or get someone inside to betray the fortification.

If that failed, siege ramps would be built (Isaiah 37:33; Ezekiel 4:2; 21:22), from which battering rams might be able to break down the city walls or gates (2 Samuel 20:15; Ezekiel 26:8-9). Siege towers filled with archers could be erected (Isaiah 29:3; 2 Kings 25:1; Jeremiah 52:4). Sappers could dig tunnels to undermine and weaken a wall's foundations. Ropes and grappling hooks could pull down a wall (2 Samuel 17:13). The dangerous task of breaching the walls with assault ladders would take place only if surrender couldn't be achieved by other means.[17]

When it came time to finally enter the city, Joab would call David to bring the rest of the army and enter the city with a massive force, so that the king could take personal credit for the victory. And that's what happened (12:26-30). David wasn't shirking his duties by staying in Jerusalem. He would come when it was time.

The narrator tells the story of the siege of Rabbah here to introduce the story of David and Bathsheba, to explain why Bathsheba's husband wasn't at home, and to explain how he was murdered.

David Commits Adultery with Bathsheba (11:2-5)

David does a very bad thing.

"[2] One evening David got up from his bed and walked around on the roof of the palace. From the roof he saw a woman bathing. The woman was very beautiful, [3] and David sent someone to find out about her. The man said, 'Isn't this Bathsheba, the daughter of Eliam and the wife of Uriah the Hittite?' [4] Then David sent messengers to get her. She came to him, and he slept with her. (She had purified herself from her uncleanness.) Then she went back home." (11:2-4)

---

[17] Details from Keith N. Schoville, "Siege, Siegeworks, Besiege," ISBE 4:503-505.

It's springtime. David can't sleep. He gets up and goes out on the roof, where he is refreshed by the cool breezes blowing up the ridges from the Mediterranean. From his palace, probably at the highest point of Zion, he has a wonderful view of the city and the hills beyond.

Tonight he looks down into the city below and sees a woman bathing. Hollywood would portray Bathsheba bathing openly and immodestly, but that would have been contrary to Hebrew views about nudity. She is probably in her own courtyard or home, and doesn't have any idea that the king is peering down at her. She is a very beautiful woman. David is entranced. And the intimacy of bathing must have captured David's lustful imagination.[18] Suddenly he wants her – and her alone.

It's not that David is starved for female companionship. By this time as a wealthy king, he has many women: Ahinoam of Jezreel, Abigail the widow of Nabal, Maacah daughter of a king from Geshur (east of Galilee), Haggith, Abital, Eglah – that's six while he was living in Hebron – and then "David took more concubines and wives in Jerusalem, and more sons and daughters were born to him" (5:13). In addition he has Saul's concubines in his harem (12:8). (See the discussion of "Polygamy in the Bible" in Lesson 5 above.)

But David is overtaken by lust. He sees a beautiful woman and wants her – now.

He doesn't recognize her, so David sends one of his courtiers to find out who she is. It turns out that she is apparently related to three people close to David:

1. Her father, Eliam, is one of David's thirty elite warriors (23:35).

2. Her grandfather, Ahithophel the Gilonite, is David's chief counselor (16:23; 23:34).[19]

3. Her husband, Uriah the Hittite, is also one of David's mighty men, one of the renowned group known as The Thirty (23:39). Though he was a Hittite by race, Uriah had a good Hebrew name meaning "Yahweh is my light."[20]

When David's courtier identifies Bathsheba, David sends for her – even though he knows how intricately her family is tied to David's life and kingdom! Stupid!

---

[18] There is an apocryphal addition to the Book of Daniel that tells the story of Susanna and the Elders. Susanna is spied upon by two elders while bathing in her private garden. Then they attempt to blackmail her into having sex with them – which she refuses to do.

[19] Later, Ahithophel supports Absalom against David when Absalom rebels (2 Samuel 15:12, 31), perhaps because he is angry at David over David taking advantage of his granddaughter Bathsheba.

[20] Uriah may have belonged to Jerusalem's nobility which may have had Hittite associations (Ezekiel 16:3) (Anderson, 2 Samuel, p. 153).

Some commentators have blamed Bathsheba. Keil and Delitzsch faulted her because "she came without any hesitation and offered no resistance to his desires."[21] That's an argument from silence. The text doesn't blame her, so we have no cause to judge her. When the king sends for you, you come, since the king's word is absolute. The king would have the power of life or death – though David had the reputation of being a righteous king up to this point.

In my opinion, Bathsheba is forced to submit to the king's sexual advances. She doesn't really have a choice. To blame her would be the same as blaming a woman for being raped, or blaming a woman under your supervision for instigating a sexual liaison with you. The person with the power here is David, not Bathsheba – and David is held solely responsible for the sin by the Lord himself (12:9).

Bathsheba's bathing is probably part of her purifying herself from her menstrual period or "uncleanness" (11:4b). This demonstrates to the reader that she had not been pregnant previously. But it also gives us a hint as to her fertility, since the time seven days after her menstrual flow had ceased (Leviticus 15:19) puts her at the most fertile day of her monthly cycle when ovulation is most likely to occur – about 14 days from the beginning of menstruation. A couple of months after this episode, Bathsheba realizes she indeed is pregnant and sends word to David.

David Attempts to Cover Up Bathsheba's Pregnancy (11:6-13)

David feels he must cover up his sin – for Bathsheba's sake as well as his own. Plan A is to have Uriah come home, sleep with his wife, and then – more or less – nine months later (who is counting?) Uriah will have a child. He'll be happy. Bathsheba will be happy. And David will have complete deniability. No one will be able to prove anything.

Not that David is really in any danger. Though the penalty for adultery was death (Leviticus 20:10; Deuteronomy 22:22), no court in Israel has authority to convict the king of adultery. And David would surely intervene to protect Bathsheba from being convicted. But it would be messy. It would hurt Bathsheba's marriage and sully the king's reputation as a righteous follower of Yahweh.

So he sends for Uriah, who returns the 40 or so miles from the siege of Rabbah to Jerusalem. When he arrives, David asks some general questions about how the siege is going, and then encourages Uriah, "Go down to your house and wash your feet." In

[21] Keil and Delitzsch, *2 Samuel* (reprinted, Eerdmans, 1976), vol. 2, p. 383.

other words, the king is encouraging him to go home, relax with his wife, and refresh himself – and have sex!

The problem is that Uriah doesn't go home, but rather sleeps in the guardhouse at the gate to David's palace.[22] When David is informed and summons Uriah, the man explains:

> "The ark and Israel and Judah are staying in tents, and my master Joab and my lord's men are camped in the open fields. How could I go to my house to eat and drink and lie with my wife? As surely as you live, I will not do such a thing!" (11:11)

Uriah is a man of honor. He doesn't feel right to relax at home when his fellow soldiers are undergoing the rigors of war "in the open fields."

There is also, likely, a ban against soldiers on duty having sex – even if David has seemed to give him permission. Since serving as a soldier in Israel's army was considered service to Yahweh, for which one must be consecrated (Exodus 19:15; Leviticus 15:18), apparently David did not allow his soldiers to have sex while on duty (1 Samuel 21:4-5; Deuteronomy 23:9-11). So Uriah is being faithful to his God.

David doesn't give up. So he detains him another night and gets him drunk. Still Uriah won't go home and sleep with Bathsheba.

David Conspires to Have Uriah Killed (11:14-27)

Now David resorts to Plan B. He writes a letter to Joab:

> "Put Uriah in the front line where the fighting is fiercest. Then withdraw from him so he will be struck down and die." (11:15)

David seals the letter so it cannot be opened, and sends Uriah back to Joab and the siege carrying his own death warrant! Joab complies with David's order, and Uriah is killed. Now there is no evidence of David's adultery.

However, palace gossip has surely told and embellished the true story so that the king's sordid acts are widely known (12:14). Certainly, David's palace servants will know that the child is David's. Even back then, people could count as high as nine (11:27). David marries Bathsheba after a period of mourning[23] and she becomes part of his harem. Everything seems to settle down and the baby is born.

> "But the thing David had done displeased the LORD." (11:27b)

David, who had somehow avoided bloodguilt by God's grace up until now, is covered with the blood of Uriah!

---

[22] 1 Kings 14:27.
[23] The period of mourning probably lasted for seven days (Genesis 50:10; Book of Judith 16:24).

Q2. (2 Samuel 11) How can a "man after God's own heart" do something so ugly, so despicable as this – first adultery and then murder by proxy to cover it up? What does this teach us about our human condition? What is our problem as humans? How can David ever recover his integrity after this?
http://www.joyfulheart.com/forums/index.php?showtopic=1192

Nathan's Story of the Poor Man with One Ewe Lamb (12:1-6)

The "man after God's own heart" has fallen and become hardened to God's voice. How will God restore him? "The LORD sent Nathan to David" (12:1a). Praise God that God's servants can hear the voice of the Lord and respond to Him!

Nathan has an extremely sensitive assignment: to help David repent of his sins without making him defensive and shutting off communication. It's hard enough to reason about such a sensitive subject with a normal man or woman. But a king has supreme authority, and doesn't *have* to listen to people who annoy him.

So Nathan tells David a story, a so-called "juridical parable."[24] On the surface it is a story that might have come from the local courts, though no names are mentioned. As king, David would often be asked to decide on more difficult civil cases such as this. So he listens with his "judge hat" on – not realizing that this story is a mirror, a parable of his own sin!

> "1b There were two men in a certain town, one rich and the other poor. 2 The rich man had a very large number of sheep and cattle, 3 but the poor man had nothing except one little ewe lamb he had bought. He raised it, and it grew up with him and his children. It

---

[24] There are several of these juridical parables in the Bible which disguise a real-life violation of the law as a parable told to the guilt person in order to lead him to pass judgment upon himself (Anderson, *2 Samuel*, p. 160). They are: (1) the woman of Tekoa to David, to get him to welcome Absalom back (2 Samuel 14:1-20); (2) a prophet to Ahab (1 Kings 20:35-43); and (3) the song of the vineyard, a parable of Israel (Isaiah 5:1-7). Each of these parables shares an introduction, the supposed legal case, the judgment elicited, and then the judgment reapplied to the real culprit himself.

shared his food, drank from his cup and even slept in his arms. It was like a daughter to him.

> [4] Now a traveler came to the rich man, but the rich man refrained from taking one of his own sheep or cattle to prepare a meal for the traveler who had come to him. Instead, he took the ewe lamb that belonged to the poor man and prepared it for the one who had come to him." (12:1b-4)

Nathan sets up the comparisons: The rich man (David), who has numerous cattle (wives), takes the only lamb (Bathsheba) of the poor man (Uriah).

Painted in those terms, the decision is what American slang might call a "no-brainer." David responds with the obvious judgment – not realizing that in so judging, he is judging himself. Angry, now, David says:

> "[5b] As surely as the LORD lives, the man who did this deserves to die! [6] He must pay for that lamb four times over,[25] because he did such a thing and had no pity." (12:5-6)

Sigmund Freud developed a theory of human behavior known as "projection." This is a psychological defense mechanism where a person subconsciously denies his or her own attributes, thoughts, and emotions, which are then ascribed to the outside world, usually to other people. Though I don't subscribe to most of Freud's theories, this is an astute observation that has been generally accepted by psychologists. We can see it in action! David condemns his own sin as seen in another person.

Nathan Confronts David with Adultery and Murder (12:7-9)

Once David has stated his judgment on the rich man in the parable, Nathan nails him!

> "[7] Then Nathan said to David, 'You are the man! This is what the LORD, the God of Israel, says: "I anointed you king over Israel, and I delivered you from the hand of Saul. [8] I gave your master's house to you, and your master's wives into your arms. I gave you the house of Israel and Judah. And if all this had been too little, I would have given you even more."'" (12:7-8)

Look at the verbs in verses 7 and 8: "anointed – delivered – gave – gave - gave." David is not deprived like the poor man. He is anointed. He has been protected by the Lord. He has been blessed and is rich. He has Saul's harem in addition to his own. He is king of Israel and Judah – and God is prepared to give him even more.

---

[25] This is the Torah's penalty for theft of a sheep (Exodus 22:1).

> "Why did you despise the word of the LORD by doing what is evil in his eyes? You struck down Uriah the Hittite with the sword and took his wife to be your own. You killed him with the sword of the Ammonites." (12:9)

David is guilty of adultery. But the cover-up is even worse. He is guilty of deliberate, premeditated murder.

What is the kernel of David's sin? What is the kernel of our sins? Despising the Lord's word. "Despise" (bāzâ) in verses 8 and 10 is a strong word. It means "to despise, distain, hold in contempt." The basic meaning of the root is "to accord little worth to something."[26] When we go against God's commands, we elevate ourselves to a place of greater worth, while demoting the Lawgiver's words and values to a place of lesser worth.

When we sin willfully – that is, something more than an inadvertent slip-up – we count ourselves as independent of God's rules. We despise our Ruler. We are in rebellion.

This has to do with love. Jesus said,

> "If you love me, you will obey what I command." (John 14:15)

Christian love (agapē) is not just an emotion. It is not even *primarily* an emotion. It is not about feelings, but it is about commitment to another person. When we break these commitments, even though we feel the emotion of love, we have sinned against people.

My dear brother and sister. You and I are guilty before God. Though we may not be adulterers and murderers, we are not righteous, church-going people who are "pretty good" and "deserve heaven." We have each rebelled in our own way. We are sinners who desperately need a Savior! And Jesus is that Savior! Praise God.

Q3. (2 Samuel 12:1-10) Why might it be dangerous for Nathan the prophet to confront the king? What device does Nathan employ get the king to listen to him? How does David's condemnation of the rich man's greed help him acknowledge and condemn his own actions?
http://www.joyfulheart.com/forums/index.php?showtopic=1193

---

[26] Bruce K. Waltke, bāzâ, TWOT #224.

Nathan Pronounces David's Punishment (12:10-14)

Nathan continues:

> "'10 Now, therefore, the sword will never depart from your house, because you despised me and took the wife of Uriah the Hittite to be your own.' 11 "This is what the LORD says: 'Out of your own household I am going to bring calamity upon you. Before your very eyes I will take your wives and give them to one who is close to you, and he will lie with your wives in broad daylight. 12 You did it in secret, but I will do this thing in broad daylight before all Israel.'" (12:10-12)

To his credit, David doesn't bluff and bluster. Though he has the power to kill the messenger, he doesn't. David's conscience has been seared by his sin and cover-up. But his heart is still hungry for the Lord he has spurned. So he confesses immediately:

> "I have sinned against the LORD." (12:13a)

Nathan responds:

> "The LORD has taken away your sin. You are not going to die. 14 But because by doing this you have made the enemies of the LORD show utter contempt, the son born to you will die." (12:13b-14)

Forgiveness and punishment are two different things. I remember disciplining my older son. He told me, "I said I was sorry. Why are you going to spank me?" Forgiveness has to do with relationship. God has restored the relationship between himself and David. But the spanking is necessary because that is the way children learn that their actions have consequences. If we parents are always protecting our children from the consequences of their actions, we don't let them learn and grow up.

There are consequences for David's sin. That David and Bathsheba's son dies is part of it. That David's sons follow in his footsteps of sexual sin and murder is another. It seems hard. But dear friends, that's life.

Before we leave Nathan's words to David, consider Nathan's indictment:

> "You have made the enemies of the LORD show utter contempt." (12:14a)

Our actions reflect on the Lord we claim to serve. One of the reasons that so many people are closed to the gospel in our day is because of hypocritical actions by church people. By our lives we have brought "utter contempt" on Jesus. God be merciful to us.

The phrase, "utter contempt" (NIV), "utterly scorned" (NRSV), "blaspheme" (KJV) consists of two words derived from the same stem. When a word is doubled like this in Hebrew, it indicates a more intense degree than just one word alone – not just "scorned," but *utterly* scorned." Here the verb is *nāʾas,* "despise, abhor." The root "signifies the action or attitude whereby the former recipient of favorable disposition and/or service is consciously viewed and/or treated with disdain."[27]

Notice how personally the Lord brings the punishment:

"... I will do this thing in broad daylight before all Israel." (12:12b)

The Lord doesn't bring the punishment directly by zapping David from on high. Rather he uses people, as he indicated in the Davidic Covenant that he would:

"When he does wrong, I will punish him with the rod of men, with floggings inflicted by men." (2 Samuel 7:14)

I've heard naive Christians say – and actually believe their words: "God never punishes people!" How foolish! Such people have a completely unbiblical and unbalanced understanding of God's love and justice. God's judgment here comes to pass when David's son Absalom tries to take the kingdom away from his father, and sleeps with all of his concubines publicly (16:21-22). Is God responsible for doing evil? No. Absalom sinned against his father. But God orchestrates these events, just as he did when Assyria attacks the Northern Kingdom centuries later and takes them into exile. On that occasion, through Isaiah, God says:

"Woe to the Assyrian, the rod of my anger,
in whose hand is the club of my wrath!" (Isaiah 10:5)

The Assyrian oppressors are not waived of responsibility for their evil attacks. Nevertheless, they fulfill God's purposes.

Q4. (2 Samuel 12:10-14) What punishment does David deserve? What does he get instead? How does this punishment relate to the provisions of the Davidic Covenant in 2 Samuel 7:14-15? How do David's sins hurt God's glory? How do our sins reflect on Jesus Christ?
http://www.joyfulheart.com/forums/index.php?showtopic=1194

David's Son by Bathsheba Dies (12:15-25)

Immediately after Nathan's departure, the newborn falls ill.

[27] Leonard J. Coppes, *nāʾas*, TWOT #1273.

> "David pleaded with God for the child. He fasted and went into his house and spent the
> nights lying on the ground." (12:16)

He does this for seven days until the child dies. But when he realizes that the child has
died, he gets up, takes a shower, changes clothes, and worships. Then he resumes
eating.

His courtiers can't understand it. They misinterpret David's fasting as mourning. It
isn't. David explains,

> "While the child was still alive, I fasted and wept. I thought, 'Who knows? The LORD
> may be gracious to me and let the child live.' But now that he is dead, why should I fast?
> Can I bring him back again? I will go to him, but he will not return to me." (12:22-23)

David isn't mourning. Rather he is humbling himself before God and petitioning God
for mercy. Why? Because he knows that even when God pronounces judgment, he
sometimes relents if we humble ourselves before him. He is seeking God in repentance
to change his mind, ask him to relent. In this case God doesn't. But many times in
Scripture, indeed he does.[28]

This story shows us several things.

1. David believes in God's grace – that we sometimes receive blessings much more
    than we deserve with God. He knows that God sometimes relents and shows
    mercy.

2. David knows that humbling himself before God for his former arrogance to-
    wards God – "a broken and contrite heart" (Psalm 51:17) – will be noticed by
    God.

3. David accepts the Lord's punishment without complaint. He doesn't nurse anger
    against God like we sometimes do.

4. David immediately worships. This is his response to trouble – even trouble he
    has brought upon himself and his family. David worships the Lord.

The Birth of Solomon (12:24-25)

Notice how the Lord doesn't hold a grudge against David.

> "24 Then David comforted his wife Bathsheba, and he went to her and lay with her. She
> gave birth to a son, and they named him Solomon. The LORD loved him; 25 and because

---

[28] Examples of God relenting upon repentance are: Nineveh in the time of Jonah (Jonah 3:10), Ahab (1 Kings
21:27-29), the people of Israel when Moses interceded for them (Exodus 32:14; Psalm 106:45), punishment
upon Israel when David interceded (2 Samuel 24:16). See Jeremiah 18:8; 26:3, 13, 19; Joel 2:13; Amos 7:3, 6.

the LORD loved him, he sent word through Nathan the prophet to name him Jedidiah." (12:24-25)

Verse 24 is interesting: David comforts[29] Bathsheba by having sex with her. Sex, here, is an act of love, not of a man using a woman. And God comforts her by allowing her to conceive Solomon and have a new child to love.

God expresses his love for Solomon and gives him a special name – Jedidiah, "loved by Yahweh" – to demonstrate this. That God would bring blessing through David and Bathsheba – what had begun as an adulterous relationship – shows God's great mercy. It's interesting to see some of the people mentioned in Jesus' family tree – women including Rahab the prostitute, Tamar who prostituted herself, Ruth the foreigner, and Bathsheba – as well as all the male sinners among the kings of Israel and Judah! We are what God makes us; we are not doomed to repeat our parents' sins or exhibit their same weaknesses, that is, if we yield ourselves to God.

David's Psalms help us understand spiritually how to humble ourselves and repent. If you like, you or your group can study two of these psalms in Appendix 8. David's Psalms of Repentance (Psalms 51 and 32).

David Defeats Rabbah of the Ammonites (12:26-31)

This lesson concludes with the defeat of Rabbah, the besieged Ammonite capital where Uriah had been killed. Joab captures the city water supply and the royal citadel. Then he calls on David to come quickly with the rest of the army, so David gets credit for taking the city, not he. The fall of Ammon's capital brings glory and riches to David:

> "He took the crown from the head of their king – its weight was a talent of gold, and it
> was set with precious stones – and it was placed on David's head." (12:30)

A talent of gold weighted approximately 75 pounds! In addition, he takes much plunder from the city and consigns the Ammonite people to forced labor.

The glory of Ammon's crown is great, but it seemed somehow tarnished for David, the once-righteous king of Israel.

Lessons for Disciples

These chapters are full of lessons for us to take hold of.

---

[29] "Comforted" (NIV, KJV), "consoled" (NRSV) is *nāḥam*, in the Piel stem, "to comfort." The word is used in "Comfort ye, my people" (Isaiah 40:1) and in the twenty-third Psalm, "your rod and your staff they comfort me" (Psalm 23:4). The origin of the root seems to reflect the idea of breathing deeply," hence the physical display of one's feelings, usually sorrow, compassion, or comfort (Marvin R. Wilson, *nāḥam*, TWOT #1344).

1. **Faithfulness**. God expects us to fulfill our promises, as David does when he honors Jonathan's son Mephibosheth – at his own risk.

2. **Arrogance**. God's blessings can make us feel self-sufficient, arrogant, and spiritually dull to God's voice unless we are very careful to remain humble and thankful. Don't let blessing make you spiritually soft.

3. **Temptation**. Even godly men and women can be tempted and fall. We must put a guard around ourselves so that we don't ruin what God by his grace has built in our lives. You are not immune.

4. **Confession**. Covering up our sin can be worse than the sin itself. Honesty and confession are better than covering up (Psalm 32:3-5).

5. **Confrontation**. Confronting people with their sins is a delicate task that God sometimes asks his servants to perform – with gentleness (Galatians 6:2-3). Don't take this upon yourself, but if God shows you how to do it, you can save a precious believer from ruin.

6. **Repentance**. God will honor repentance, if we come with humility and turn away from our sin. Psalm 51 can help you do this. (See Appendix 8. David's Psalms of Repentance.)

7. **Mercy**. Our God is merciful, slow to anger, and abounding in love and faithfulness (Exodus 34:607; Numbers 14:18; Psalm 86:15; 103:8). You can trust your future into the hands of such a God, even if you have sinned grievously. Jesus is your Savior!

In this lesson we've seen David fulfill his promises to Jonathan to protect his children. David has reached the pinnacle of his kingdom, attained power over a huge realm. The narrator keeps reminding us:

> "The LORD gave David victory wherever he went." (8:6b, 14b)

But from here on out, though David has been forgiven for his sin and his heart is right with God once more, he faces trouble of a different kind, from within his own family, as prophesied by Nathan. The once glorious story turns sad. Nevertheless, it still instructs how God relates to men and women for whom Christ died.

Note: If you like, you can follow this with an optional lesson, Appendix 8. David's Psalms of Repentance (Psalms 51 and 32).

Prayer

Lord, thank you that you forgive our sins. David didn't know how you could forgive his sin, that his own Descendant, Jesus, would bear his awful sins. But we know. Thank you for your great love that sent Jesus to the cross for our sins. In his holy name, we pray. Amen.

Key Verses

"The thing David had done displeased the LORD." (2 Samuel 11:27b)

"Nathan said to David, 'You are the man!'" (2 Samuel 12:7a)

"Then David said to Nathan, 'I have sinned against the LORD.' Nathan replied, 'The LORD has taken away your sin. You are not going to die. But because by doing this you have made the enemies of the LORD show utter contempt, the son born to you will die.'" (2 Samuel 12:13-14)

11. Rape, Murder, and Conspiracy in David's Family (2 Samuel 13:1-15:13)

In the following narrative we see several things going on. Most apparent is the affair between Amnon and his sister Tamar, and his death at the hands of his brother Absalom. But beneath this drama is a struggle for succession to the throne.

Amnon is the firstborn and heir apparent to the throne. The second-born, Kileab or Chileab, isn't mentioned. Perhaps he died young. But Absalom, the third-born, is eager to gain the throne, and that lies behind his action to murder his brother Amnon.

I wish I could point to some deep spiritual learnings that we will take hold of in this lesson, but, alas, the narrative is a sad one with little redeeming value. Probably, the main lessons are two-fold. First, that Nathan's prophecy to David comes to pass with withering severity:

> "Now, therefore, the sword will never depart from your house.... Out of your own household I am going to bring calamity upon you." (12:10-11)

John J. Tissot, "Absalom" (1896-1902), gouache on board, The Jewish Museum, New York.

Second, that the sins of the father often become the sins of the son. We do not sin in isolation! Each sin tends to foster more sin, and provide precedents for others to follow.

We'll be covering a lot of ground in this lesson, so my comments will be brief. My main goals here is to help you to understand what is going on and the implications for David's life – and our lives.

Amnon Lusts after His Half-Sister Tamar (13:1-14)

"¹ In the course of time, Amnon son of David fell in love with Tamar, the beautiful sister of Absalom son of David. ² Amnon became frustrated to the point of illness on account of his sister Tamar, for she was a virgin, and it seemed impossible for him to do anything to her." (13:1-2)

Amnon (whose name means "faithful") and Tamar (whose name seems to mean "date palm") are half-brother and half-sister. Amnon's mother is Ahinoam of Jezreel, while Absalom's and Tamar's mother is Maacah, daughter of Talmai, king of Geshur (2 Samuel 3:3).[1]

The text says that Amnon "fell in love" (NIV, NRSV), "loved" (KJV) Tamar. Like our English word "love," the Hebrew verb 'āhab can cover a wide variety of intents and emotions.[2] Probably Amnon's love could best be described as infatuation mixed with strong lust. Amnon doesn't care about his half-sister's welfare, but about fulfilling his own sexual obsessions.

Amnon doesn't have any way to spend time with Tamar. The king's grown sons live in their own homes rather than in the palace. However, Tamar, as the king's virgin daughter, would live in the palace, probably confined to the women's quarters and carefully guarded.[3] Amnon probably sees her at family gatherings, but otherwise has no access to her whatsoever.

Amnon's close friend and cousin Jonadab (whose name means "Yahweh is noble, liberal"), discerns something wrong with Amnon. The narrator refers to Jonadab as "crafty" (NRSV).[4] Here, Jonadab – who later in this chapter seems to be an advisor in the king's court (13:32-35) – is wise, but not very ethical. Though I'm not sure Jonadab anticipated Amnon raping Tamar, he certainly gives advice that helps Amnon get Tamar alone.

Jonadab suggests that Amnon pretend to be ill and ask David, when he visits his sick son, "I would like my sister Tamar to come and make some special bread in my sight, so I may eat from her hand" (13:6).

---

[1] David apparently married Maacah while he was king in Hebron as a way to cement a treaty with Geshur, a small Aramean kingdom in Ish-Bosheth's rear, a few miles north of his capital in Mahanaim.

[2] 'Āhab can be used of God's infinite affection for his people, of a parent's love for a child, even of illicit lovers and love for objects such as meat, oil, silver, and gifts (Robert L. Alden, 'āhab, TWOT #29).

[3] Anderson, 2 Samuel, p. 174.

[4] "Shrewd" (NIV), "crafty" (NRSV), "subtle" (KJV) is ḥākām, from ḥākam, "to be wise, act wisely." The adjective occurs widely in Proverbs, and is used to describe Solomon as well as the wise woman of Tekoa who handles a delicate matter before David at Joab's behest later in this lesson (14:2) (Louis Goldberg, TWOT #647b).

There have been all sorts of speculations about why having Tamar prepare food for Amnon was a believable ruse. Perhaps the food was thought to have some kind of special curative quality. We don't know. The Hebrew word translated "special food" (NIV), "cakes" (NRSV, KJV) may be "some kind of dumplings or puddings," since they were apparently boiled, perhaps heart-shaped. They may have been made from dough laced with healing herbs.[5]

As Jonadab anticipates, David comes, grants Amnon's request, and directs Tamar to go to her brother's house to make him the cakes. While she prepares the food, Amnon watches her through the open door from his bedroom. Then he demands that everyone leave the room – his own servants, as well as the handmaid who probably serves as chaperone for Tamar.

When she hands him the food at his bedside, he grabs her, commands her to have sex with him, and tries to rape her. She resists. She tries to argue that raping her:

1. Is an outrageous breach of the law of Israel.

2. Will disgrace her publicly,

3. Will hurt Amnon's reputation – he will be regarded as "one of the wicked fools in Israel," and

4. Is not necessary, since if he asks the king, David could grant Amnon's request to marry her legally.

Amnon doesn't listen to reason. He is stronger, overpowers her, and rapes her.[6]

Whether this would be considered incest in David's time, we're not sure. To marry a half-sister is forbidden in the Torah (Leviticus 18:9), but there is the precedent of Abraham and Sarah. At least Tamar tells Amnon that marriage would be possible. She is doing everything she can to avoid being raped!

For the crown prince to rape his sister will certainly be considered an outrageous breach of Israel's law![7] Tamar's words – "Such a thing should not be done in Israel!"– are a deliberate echo from the story of the rape of Jacob's daughter Dinah by Shechem,

---

[5] Anderson, *2 Samuel*, p. 174; Holladay, p. 172; Bergen, *1 and 2 Samuel*, pp. 380-381.

[6] "Rape" (NIV), "force" (NRSV, KJV) is 'ānâ, "afflict, oppress, humble." "The primary meaning of 'ānâ is 'to force,' or 'to try to force submission,' and 'to punish or inflict pain upon'" (Leonard J. Coppes, 'ānâ, TWOT #1652, 'ānâ III).

[7] "Wicked thing" (NIV), "vile" (NRSV), "folly" (KJV) in 13:12 is *nebālâ*, "folly, villainy, vile." The word implies a sinful "disregard for moral and spiritual claims." The word describes a request for homosexual sex (Judges 19:23-24; 20:6) and the rape of Jacob's Dinah by Shechem (Genesis 34:7).

who "had committed an outrage in Israel by lying with Jacob's daughter, for such a thing ought not to be done" (Genesis 34:7).

Amnon Rejects Tamar (8:15-20)

Now that Amnon has raped Tamar, his "love" turns to intense hatred. Why did Amnon now hate the sister whom he once "loved"?

First, because he never truly loved her. Rather he was infatuated, fed by obsessive lust.

Second, he was probably transferring to her the loathing he felt for himself for such a despicable act as rape, especially incestuous rape. This hatred is a form of projection. Amnon subconsciously denies his own sin and projects it on his half-sister. We saw projection at work with David's judgment on the man in Nathan's parable in Lesson 10 above.

Absalom commands Tamar, "Get up and get out!" She protests that sending her away is worse yet. The law requires the rapist of an unbetrothed virgin to marry her. By sending her away, Amnon is putting her in a position in this culture that no decent man will ever marry her – and indeed that is the case!

Tamar rips her beautiful royal robe and puts ashes on her head – marks of deep mourning – and goes away weeping loudly. She leaves with her hand on her head, apparently another sign of grief (Jeremiah 2:37).[8] She is not slinking away, hiding her shame. She is shattered, unable to contain her grief!

When her brother Absalom hears of it, he realizes what has happened. He says, "Be quiet now, my sister; he is your brother. Don't take this thing to heart" (13:20a). This sounds like little comfort to me. However, it also seems that Absalom is saying, "Don't worry about it. I'll deal with him." The narrator concludes this sordid business with the statement: "Tamar lived in her brother Absalom's house, a desolate woman" (13:20b). How sad!

David Does Nothing (13:21-22)

Now we read of David's reaction:

---

[8] In reliefs and tomb paintings in the ancient Near East, putting one's hand on one's head seems to symbolize captivity, or perhaps the mourning of being taken captive. Baldwin (1 and 2 Samuel, p. 249), cites pictures in J.B. Pritchard, *The Ancient Near East in Pictures Relating to the Old Testament* (ANEP; Princeton University Press, 1954, 1969), illustrations 634, 640.

"[21] When King David heard all this, he was furious. [22] Absalom never said a word to Amnon, either good or bad; he hated Amnon because he had disgraced his sister Tamar." (13:21-22)

David's reaction is anger – but he takes no action to punish a criminal act. Indeed, some early versions of the text add a sentence to verse 21 that could well have been in the original, but was omitted by a copyist from the Masoretic text:

"But he did not curb the excesses (literally, 'spirit') of his son Amnon; he favored him because he was his firstborn."[9]

The king's son, the heir to the throne, can get away with rape and incest.

Here is another hint of a flaw in David's leadership that we first noticed in Lesson 7, when Joab murders Amasa and David takes no action to bring justice (3:39).

Perhaps the very reason that Amnon rapes his sister is because he is sure that his father won't do anything to him. If this were judged to be incest according to Leviticus 18.9, 29, the exact punishment seems vague,[10] but we are not sure this is the issue here.

For raping an unbetrothed virgin, Amnon could be forced to pay a bride price and marry Tamar (Exodus 22:16-17).[11] However, within the king's own household, payment of a bride price would mean nothing. In addition David doesn't want to cloud the crown prince's status by a marriage that neither he nor Tamar really wanted – and a marriage which would be unacceptable to the people.

What David *could* have done – and probably *should* have done – would have been to formally remove Amnon from succession to the kingship for such a despicable act. However, beyond being angry, David doesn't do anything. Sadly, he has lost the moral authority he had as the righteous king who loves Yahweh. How can he judge his own son for sexual sins and not judge himself?

Where parents lose the moral leadership of their families, their children have neither a consistent role model nor an authority figure by which to guide their own actions. Dear friends, Satan would have us believe that illicit sex between "consenting adults" is no one's business but their own. That is a lie. Our sins have consequences beyond

[9] Found in the Septuagint and the Samuel manuscript from Qumran Cave IV, quoted by Anderson, 2 *Samuel*, p. 176

[10] G.J. Wenham (*The Book of Leviticus* (Eerdmans, 1979), pp. 241-242) discusses the various interpretations of "being cut off from one's people": (1) be punished by God directly, (2) to receive the death penalty, (3) to be exiled, or perhaps even (4) a hint of judgment in the life to come. BDB takes "be cut off from his people" in the sense of the death penalty (*kārat*, BDB, Niphal, 504). However, only for some instances of incest is the death penalty specified in Leviticus 20:11-21, and incest with one's sister isn't mentioned there.

[11] The Torah apparently doesn't consider this a capital offence, as it would have been if she had been betrothed (Deuteronomy 22:23-29).

ourselves, and can damage anyone within our sphere of influence. At the political level, sexual misdeeds have toppled governments, made it difficult for presidents to lead, and kept people from running for high office. In churches, we have seen congregations devastated and parishioners disillusioned, their faith destroyed. On the home front, sexual misdeeds destroy families, create poverty, and mess up the lives of children. God help us and have mercy on us!

Absalom, who appears to be in second position to assume the kingship on David's death, does not do anything either – for now. He makes no public statements. He waits.

Q1. (2 Samuel 13:21-22) Why do you think David doesn't discipline his son Amnon for his sexual assault on his half-sister? What are the consequences of David's inaction?
http://www.joyfulheart.com/forums/index.php?showtopic=1195

Absalom Murders Amnon, then Flees (13:23-39)

Absalom's hatred simmers for two years. Then he makes his move. Spring sheep shearing is often celebrated with festive meals and a spirit of generosity as the wool is harvested (1 Samuel 25:8). Absalom arranges a huge party at his ranch located in Baal Hazor, on a hill identified with Jebel ʿAsûr, 4 to 5 miles northeast of Bethel,[12] and about 17 to 18 miles north of Jerusalem.

Absalom makes a big point of trying to get his father and his court to come – knowing that they will not attend. When David makes his excuses, Absalom moves to his real purpose: to request that his father send Amnon, the crown prince, to represent him and convey his blessings on this occasion. David questions this, but then agrees to send all his sons to the festivities. Now Absalom can get to Amnon unguarded.

Absalom orders his men to kill Amnon when he becomes drunk and they do. The crown prince is assassinated by the second in line to the throne – who now is in line for the throne himself! Absalom's primary motive is to avenge his sister's rape and rejection. However, this is aligned with another strong ambition – to be king himself someday!

[12] "Baal-Hazor," ISBE 1:380.

With the crown prince dead on the ground, the other princes flee to Jerusalem while Absalom flees in the opposite direction, north to the Aramean kingdom of Geshur, northeast of the Sea of Galilee, his mother's birthplace. Absalom seeks asylum with his mother's relatives – a powerful royal family. True, at some point David had conquered the Aramean kingdoms and made them his vassals (8:3-8; 10:6-19), but it would be embarrassing –

James J. Tissot, "David Mourns His Son Amnon" (1896-1902), gouache on board, The Jewish Museum, New York

and potentially expensive – to force Geshur to extradite Absalom. David doesn't try. The narrator says, "King David mourned for his son every day" (13:37b). His firstborn is dead.

Joab Conspires to Bring Absalom Home (13:39-14:24)

Absalom's exile is now in its third year.

> "The spirit of the king longed to go to Absalom, for he was consoled concerning Amnon's death." (13:39)

David's nephew Joab has known him for a long time – ever since the fugitive days in the Judean desert. Occasionally, Joab acts purely in his own self-interest, as he did when he murdered Abner. However, Joab is loyal to David. He knows David longs to see Absalom again (14:1). In addition, he realizes the importance for a succession plan to be in place, so when David dies there won't be a bloody civil war. Absalom is next in line for the throne and is the logical choice. He is headstrong, perhaps, but he is handsome. He looks like a king. So Joab devises a way to get David to reconcile with Absalom.

Now we might look down proudly on all this petty court intrigue. But consider the manipulations that take place in households or workplaces to get the father or the boss to do something. Palaces are pretty human places after all – only richer.

The problem with kings (and bosses and fathers) is that you cannot tell them what to do – directly. So Joab comes up with a "judicial parable," something like Nathan had used to help David understand his sin with Bathsheba (12:1-4).

He sends for a wise old woman from Tekoa, a town about 10 miles south of Jerusalem, which would be known centuries later as the birthplace of the prophet Amos.[13] This is a woman who is a good enough actress that she can pull off Joab's ruse, sharp enough to think on her feet, and wise enough to keep from offending the king while still pressing her point home. Not an easy task.

Joab tells the woman to dress as if she were a widow who has been mourning for a long time. Then she is to ask for an audience before the king to plead for justice.

She is to explain that her sons got in a fight and one killed the

David's Family Troubles
2 Samuel 13-15

other. Her clan demands that the murderer be put to death for the crime. The result would be that neither son would be alive to take care of his mother, and since women didn't normally inherit, her husband's property would go to another. She would be destitute, and her husband's name and descendants would be cut off.

The story is carefully devised to gain David's sympathy. She is mourning for a son; so is he. The murderer may be cut off, but that would leave her fully bereaved. David feels

[13] Tekoa is near the present Khirbet Tequ´.

her hopelessness. He wants to help. "Go home, and I will issue an order in your behalf," he says (14:8).

The woman gets David to affirm it twice. Moreover, David swears that he will protect the son from anyone seeking blood vengeance. "As surely as the LORD lives," he said, "not one hair of your son's head will fall to the ground" (14:11b).

She has the king firmly on her side. Now is the time to spring the trap. She asks permission to speak freely – and then she confronts the king directly regarding Absalom:

> "¹³ Why then have you devised a thing like this against the people of God? When the king says this, does he not convict himself, for the king has not brought back his banished son? ¹⁴ Like water spilled on the ground, which cannot be recovered, so we must die. But God does not take away life; instead, he devises ways so that a banished person may not remain estranged from him." (14:13-14)

David isn't stupid. He begins to see that this is a ruse propagated by Joab. He demands of her: "Isn't the hand of Joab with you in all this?" (14:19).

She admits that this is so, concluding with sweet words designed to turn away any anger: "My lord has wisdom like that of an angel of God – he knows everything that happens in the land" (14:20).

It works. David sees the logic in it and tells Joab to bring Absalom back to Jerusalem – on one condition.

> "He must go to his own house; he must not see my face." (14:24a)

Perhaps you have heard the expression in the Aaronic blessing:

> "The LORD make his face to shine upon you,
> and be gracious to you;
> the LORD lift up his countenance [face] upon you,
> and give you peace." (Numbers 6:25-26)

To "make his face to shine upon you" is another way of saying "to smile at you." To "lift up his countenance" means to look at you. David neither admits Absalom into his presence nor smiles upon him.

Absalom comes home a free man – essentially pardoned for murdering Amnon the crown prince. But since the king refuses to readmit him to court, it is clear to everyone in the kingdom that Absalom is out of favor with the king. No one wants to associate with a person under this kind of cloud. Absalom is home from exile, but the stalemate continues for another two years (14:28).

Q2. (2 Samuel 13:39-14:24) Why do you think Joab conspires to get David to bring Absalom home? Why do you think David does not immediately show Absalom his favor?
http://www.joyfulheart.com/forums/index.php?showtopic=1196

Absalom Is Restored to David (14:25-33)

The narrator paints an appealing picture of Absalom so that we will understand why so many people began to like Absalom and shift their loyalty from the father to the son.

"25 In all Israel there was not a man so highly praised for his handsome appearance as Absalom. From the top of his head to the sole of his foot there was no blemish in him. 26 Whenever he cut the hair of his head – he used to cut his hair from time to time when it became too heavy for him – he would weigh it, and its weight was two hundred shekels by the royal standard. 27 Three sons and a daughter were born to Absalom." (14:25-27a)

The king's son is extremely handsome and has three sons who could succeed him.[14] Future succession won't be a problem. Absalom is seen be a perfect choice as David's successor. But Absalom is still out of favor with the king.

Joab helped Absalom be recalled from exile. Now Absalom needs Joab to help him be restored to the king's favor. But Joab refuses to see him. He won't return his calls.

Absalom is frustrated. Finally, he has Joab's barley field set on fire. Immediately, Joab comes to Absalom's house. If I were trying to gain Joab's favor, I don't think I would fire his crops. But Absalom is bold and direct:

"Look, I sent word to you and said, 'Come here so I can send you to the king to ask, "Why have I come from Geshur? It would be better for me if I were still there!"' Now then, I want to see the king's face, and if I am guilty of anything, let him put me to death." (14:32-33)

Absalom's demand has the desired effect. Perhaps Joab realizes that David wants to reconcile with his son and that it will be good for the kingdom. He can't foresee that Absalom will try to usurp the kingdom from his father. So he relays Absalom's message to David – and apparently tells the king what he wants to hear:

[14] Perhaps his sons subsequently died, for later he complains that he has no sons (18:18).

"Then the king summoned Absalom, and he came in and bowed down with his face to the ground before the king. And the king kissed Absalom." (14:33)

The kiss is the sign of David's restored favor. David loves Absalom – even after what he has done. It is good to have Absalom home again. David feels like the father in Jesus' Parable of the Prodigal Son (Luke 15:11-32). He is ready to celebrate!

David's Gradual Decline

Let's step back for a moment to look at the bigger picture. In his early years, David was strong in faith – the ultimate warrior, full of a holy boldness. He moves from Hebron to Jerusalem and builds an empire that extends from Egypt to Mesopotamia.

Now we are witnessing a David who is corrupt and soft because of his wealth, his victories over all his enemies, his absolute power – and from his lack of purpose. The once-righteous king has been compromised. Though his relationship with God has been restored, David's weaknesses are beginning to take their toll.

He has been coasting on the achievements and the faith of his vital years. He has become a victim of court intrigue and the accommodations he has made to stay in power and to reward his supporters. Instead of being a player, David is being played by Joab, by Amnon, and by Absalom.

One of the most serious problems is David's inability – or unwillingness – to discipline his family and his officers. Joab, it seems, can get away with murder, even if it works directly against his king's interest in uniting the kingdom. Amnon gets away with rape. Absalom gets away with murder. David seems incapable of restoring order to his family or to his kingdom. David's subjects aren't stupid. They see the decline – and, no doubt, they begin to comment about it to one another.

Absalom's Public Relations Campaign (15:1)

The kingdom is ripe for overthrow and Absalom realizes it. He begins to take steps to endear himself to the people. Absalom becomes the consummate politician. The narrator informs us of his strategies.

Absalom begins to take full advantage of the perks of the crown prince to advance himself in the eyes of the people.

"In the course of time, Absalom provided himself with a chariot and horses and with fifty men to run ahead of him." (15:1)

Chariots are effective for making an impression. When Absalom goes anywhere, he doesn't walk. He rides in a chariot hitched to fine horses, and has a 50-man bodyguard jogging ahead of him wherever he goes. His retinue projects the intended message: Absalom is a very great and important man!

David had been born a shepherd and had spent years as a warrior and a fugitive. He doesn't mind walking barefoot (15:30) or riding on a donkey (16:2). He is used to hardship. However, Absalom has been born a prince and the trappings of power feel natural to him. They reinforce his position in the eyes of people.

Why does David allow such extravagance? Can't he see what is going on? David seems out of touch. As an indulgent father, he allows Absalom to satisfy his whims, even if they are overblown. What's the harm? he thinks.

Absalom Undermines the King's Justice (15:2-4)

Absalom is not just exalting himself. He also begins to undermine his father's reputation and point out his father's weaknesses.

> "2 He would get up early and stand by the side of the road leading to the city gate. Whenever anyone came with a complaint to be placed before the king for a decision, Absalom would call out to him, 'What town are you from?' He would answer, 'Your servant is from one of the tribes of Israel.'
>
> 3 Then Absalom would say to him, 'Look, your claims are valid and proper, but there is no representative of the king to hear you.'
>
> 4 And Absalom would add, 'If only I were appointed judge in the land! Then everyone who has a complaint or case could come to me and I would see that he gets justice.'" (15:2-4)

Personal injury attorneys are sometimes criticized as "ambulance chasers," because some of them will stop at nothing to sign up newly injured clients for expensive lawsuits. In a way, that's what Absalom is doing.

Israel had a judicial system where most disputes were settled at the local level by tribal elders or Levites. But if a person didn't get the justice he desired, he or she had a right to appeal directly to the king – as had the wise woman from Tekoa (14:1-20). We see two prostitutes appearing before Solomon to determine a baby's true mother (1 Kings 3:16-28). In Near Eastern countries that have monarchs, such as Saudi Arabia and Jordan, common people have such a right even today.

Absalom now stands outside the city gate to spot people coming to Jerusalem to appeal to the king for justice. He inquires about them, listens to their case, and tells them that they should be entitled to win a verdict in their favor. But then he bemoans the weaknesses of the king's judicial system and promises that if he were appointed judge, he would bring justice.

He does this consistently for four years. His subtle disloyalty to his father is somehow overlooked. David probably chooses to interpret Absalom's interest in justice as good training for a future king. He has no clue that his son is seeking to undermine him with the people.

Absalom, Man of the People (15:5-6)

The third piece of Absalom's public relations campaign is a kind of baby-kissing politician role that we in the twenty-first century understand well.

> "5 Also, whenever anyone approached him to bow down before him, Absalom would reach out his hand, take hold of him and kiss him. 6 Absalom behaved in this way toward all the Israelites who came to the king asking for justice, and so he stole the hearts of the men of Israel." (15:5-6)

Absalom is campaigning to be the people's king who loves the common man. But it's obvious that this is all a sham of image building, empty promises, and flattery. While David is the man for all seasons, his handsome son is merely an actor. Yet, for the moment, this hypocrisy is enough to help him achieve his objective – the kingship.

Q3. (2 Samuel 15:1-6) What are the elements of Absalom's public relations campaign to win over the people to his side? How effective is it? What should David have done differently? Which of David's weaknesses does Absalom exploit?
http://www.joyfulheart.com/forums/index.php?showtopic=1197

Absalom Conspires in Hebron against David (15:7-13)

After four years of this campaign, Absalom receives permission of the king to return to his birthplace, Hebron, an ancient Yahweh sanctuary (Genesis 13:18), to fulfill some supposed vow made to Yahweh while he was in exile. Absalom needs a ruse so David won't suspect anything when 200 admirers accompany him out of the capital.

If Absalom were to stage a palace coup in Jerusalem, David's mercenary army would immediately crush him. But Hebron is far enough away to give his claim to the throne enough space to be accepted and time to draw followers to his cause. Hebron also has the honor of once being David's royal capital (2:1-4), a history that lends credence to Absalom's claim to the throne.

The 200 invited guests are not part of his secret conspiracy, but have been hand-picked because of their influence in Israel – and because Absalom knows they are likely to follow him when the secret plot is revealed. They are needed to lend credibility and acceptance to the new kingdom, since they will be named as supporters.

Once in Hebron, Absalom hatches his plan for the announcement of his rise to the throne to be made simultaneously throughout Israel.

> "Then Absalom sent secret messengers throughout the tribes of Israel to say, "As soon as you hear the sound of the trumpets, then say, 'Absalom is king in Hebron.'" (15:11)

Absalom is successful. The coup is announced as if it were already complete, discouraging any resistance. The 200 guests are caught in the middle. They are naturally inclined towards Absalom, but now will be perceived by all as on Absalom's side, whether or not they would have chosen this allegiance on their own. Perception becomes reality.

As the news of Absalom's ascension to the throne spreads, it gains momentum; more and more people back him. The report comes to David, "The hearts of the men of Israel are with Absalom" (15:13). Perhaps the most prominent of these new followers is Ahithophel the Gilonite, David's revered advisor. To have Ahithophel on Absalom's side is considered decisive.

Factors in Absalom's Favor

Christians who have been raised on stories of David's faith and valor find it difficult to understand how the people of Israel could so quickly reject a truly great king in place of his upstart son. Let's consider ten factors (not necessarily in this particular order) that lead to Absalom's accession:

1. **David's Age**. David is now over 60,[15] old by standards of the time. People know he isn't likely to live much longer, whereas Absalom is probably a bit less than 30 years old and in the prime of life. Who wants to fight to retain a king who won't reign much longer anyway? David's most ardent supporters are now old men. He is the hero of a previous generation. Most alive now only remember stories of David's exploits. They weren't even born when he was at his prime. David is an honored "has-been," while Absalom is the up-and-coming king for the new generation.

---

[15] See Appendix 4. A Chronology of David's Life.

2. **David's Corruption.** We get the perception in 2 Samuel 11 that David has slowed down. He is rich. He is arrogant enough to feel he can take any woman he wants and kill even a faithful and loyal comrade-in-arms who keeps him from covering it up. David's spiritual influence has been diminished, as well. Though he has repented from his affair with Bathsheba and Uriah, he is no longer perceived by the people to be the righteous king. David's actions have weakened the throne and "made the enemies of the Lord show utter contempt" (12:14). His image has been severely tarnished.

3. **Absalom's Title.** Absalom is the crown prince. For nearly a decade, Absalom has been the heir apparent – even though he had killed the previous crown prince. People have short memories. They have gotten used to the idea that Absalom will be their next king.

4. **Absalom's Beauty.** Absalom is a handsome man – and studies show that handsome men and beautiful women succeed in life more easily than others, all things being equal. Absalom looks kingly!

5. **Absalom's Perceived Power.** Absalom has been effective in projecting an image of power and glory with his chariot, horses, and 50-man escort. Since the people perceive him as powerful already, they are much less likely to oppose him when the coup is announced.

6. **Absalom's Populism.** Absalom has positioned himself as a man of the people. His followers hope that he will be a king who will help them more than David has. Of course, David had delivered Israel from the Philistine threat, but that is now decades past. People forget what it was like. On the other hand, by this time in his long reign, David is more comfortable in the luxury of his palace than with the struggles of the average citizen. He is out-of-touch (see 19:5-7), while Absalom promises hope and change.

7. **Tribal Resentment of David.** Anyone who rises to power makes enemies, if for no other reason than jealousy. In particular, David is resented by elements of Saul's tribe of Benjamin, who believe that Saul's house should still be on the throne (2 Samuel 16:5-13; 20:1-2). There is also tension between the 10 northern tribes and David's tribe of Judah (19:41-43).

8. **David's Taxation and Conscription.** Though not in the forefront, because most of the national expenses are paid from tribute by vassal nations, we see hints of

taxation and compulsory military service in chapter 24 and 1 Samuel 8:11-18. Growing an empire through taxation and the draft are never popular.

9. **Absalom's Brilliant Execution of a Coup**. Absalom has brilliantly executed a coup d'état. By the time the coup is known, Absalom has gathered wide support and continuing momentum. Absalom has won the throne through a clever plan and consistent follow-through.

10. **Yahweh's Judgment**. Last, but most important, Nathan had prophesied: "the sword will never depart from your house" (12:10). Now this prophecy is coming to pass. David is experiencing the Lord's discipline: "When he does wrong, I will punish him with the rod of men, with floggings inflicted by men" (7:14).

We are inclined to see David's monarchy as absolute and totalitarian. But that isn't quite the case. Though David is *anointed* king by Samuel under the Lord's direction, he doesn't actually *become* king until made so by the elders of Judah (2:4) and the elders of Israel (5:1-3). Even after David's troops overthrow Absalom, there is a lot of popular discussion and political string-pulling before an official decision is made to bring David back as king (9:8-15). Even then, he has to deal with Sheba the Benjamite, who leads a rebellion against the newly reestablished kingdom that is serious enough for troops to be sent to put it down (20:1-22).

I conclude that in David's time, even though the king's word is law, in a strong sense, the king rules only by the consent of the governed – and with the permission of God himself.

Q4. (2 Samuel 13-15:13) It's difficult to find positive spiritual lessons in these sad and grim chapters. What negative spiritual lessons do you find?
http://www.joyfulheart.com/forums/index.php?showtopic=1198

Disciple Lessons

Four lessons are hard to miss – most of them negative examples to avoid:

1. **Prophecy**. Nathan's prophecy (12:10-11) comes to pass – with terrible results. God's judgment is inevitable.

2. **Learned Behaviors**. The sins of the father often become the sins of the son. We don't sin in isolation. Our children see us and emulate our behavior. Parents, your most important ministry is to raise your children in the Lord by your godly example.

3. **Discipline**. We must discipline our children so long as they are under our authority. In many cultures, children are considered adults in their late teens. In other cultures, children are under their parents' authority far longer. We must do what we can. To neglect our responsibility to discipline shows a lack of love for our children (Proverbs 3:12; 13:24; 19:18; 22:15; 23:13; 29:15; 29:17). Showing favoritism to your own children rather than disciplining them lowers you in others' minds. When the king excuses his children for blatant crimes, he rapidly loses any credibility for righteousness and justice.

4. **Situational Awareness**. Pay attention to what is going on around you! Take action early, if you need to. David should have been aware of Absalom's attempts to undermine him, and taken steps to protect himself and his kingdom. In this case, neglect is extremely costly. Leaders in churches and other organizations need to know who is conspiring against them. We serve Christ in a fallen world.

We have traced the sad pattern of David's decline and fall. In the next lesson, we'll see how David handles defeat and rises again to rule Israel.

Prayer

Father, when we see David's decline from his greatness as a man of God, we are sad. How much it must have pained your heart! We pray with David: "Keep your servant also from willful sins; may they not rule over me. Then will I be blameless, innocent of great transgression" (Psalm 19:13). Where we have fallen, have mercy on us and on our children. Renew your Holy Spirit's freedom within our spirits. In Jesus' name, we pray. Amen.

Key Verses

"In all Israel there was not a man so highly praised for his handsome appearance as Absalom. From the top of his head to the sole of his foot there was no blemish in him." (2 Samuel 14:25)

12. David's Exile from Jerusalem (2 Samuel 15:14-20:26)

"A messenger came and told David, 'The hearts of the men of Israel are with Absalom.'" (15:13)

Absalom's coup in Hebron has been a success, and his support has spread up and down Israel "from Dan to Beersheba." The momentum has definitely shifted in Absalom's favor. David still has many supporters all over the land, but he can no longer rely on key elements of his strength outside Jerusalem.

This is a long lesson, but rich in learnings for us to ponder.

James J. Tissot, "David Praying in the Night" (1896-1902), gouache on board, The Jewish Museum, New York.

David Flees Jerusalem (15:14-17)

David's reaction to this news, however, seems strange.

"Come! We must flee, or none of us will escape from Absalom. We must leave immediately, or he will move quickly to overtake us and bring ruin upon us and put the city to the sword." (15:14)

David has just heard the report, but now calls for urgent evacuation. He doesn't have time to make preparations to hold Jerusalem. As it turns out, Absalom's forces seem to be entering the city from the south about the time the last of David's supporters are leaving to the east (15:37; 16:16). There is no time to waste.

Jerusalem was one of the strongest fortresses in the ancient Near East. It was designed to hold out against an army for many months or even years. Why would David be so quick to leave? David's immediate challenges are two-fold:

1. **Food and supplies.** To survive a siege, a city must stock up with food and military supplies to last for many months. If they don't, they'll be starved out. David

has had no advance notice of Absalom's coup. There is no stock of food, which means that it is inevitable that Jerusalem will fall to Absalom – and soon! This assumes that Jerusalem's fortifications are not under construction or in disrepair. There hasn't been a military threat to the city in more than twenty years.

2. **Military weakness.** David's professional mercenary troops – Kerethites, Pelethites, and Gittites – are with him in Jerusalem. And they are a fierce fighting force! But their numbers are very small compared to the national militia Absalom has access to, which can draw on tens of thousands of Israelites from all over the kingdom.

David is a military strategist of the first order. From his fugitive days he knows the value of a strategic retreat. That's what's called for here. If David stays to fight, he will inevitably lose and bloodshed will be great, since Absalom will "put the city to the sword" (15:14b). David has been self-absorbed for years, but suddenly this crisis forces him to look to the welfare of his people. David calls for an evacuation.

> " ¹⁶ The king set out, with his entire household following him; but he left ten concubines to take care of the palace. ¹⁷ So the king set out, with all the people following him." (15:16-17a)

Why does he leave ten concubines? These aren't his official wives, but his harem, wives of secondary status. Absalom doesn't bring an invading foreign army; they are Israelites, after all, so rape isn't a danger. David expects to be back eventually. The palace needs looking after in his absence. He fully expects his concubines to be safe when his son's forces enter the city. As we'll see, David is wrong.

Ittai the Gittite Pledges David Loyalty (15:18-22)

Once outside the city, David stops by the side of the road to review his troops and others who are fleeing the city.

> "The whole countryside wept aloud as all the people passed by." (15:23)

When Ittai the Gittite marches by with his army of 600 Gittite mercenaries, David gives him an opportunity to return to the city without any blame. "You've only joined me recently," says David. "You're a foreigner; this isn't your fight." But Ittai's reply probably reflects the sentiments of many of David's followers that day:

> "As surely as the LORD lives, and as my lord the king lives, wherever my lord the king may be, whether it means life or death, there will your servant be." (15:21)

The Gittites and their families and hundreds of others march by on their way to exile and a very uncertain future.

The Ark and High Priests Remain in Jerusalem (15:23-29)

The priests, Zadok and Abiathar, come out of the city carrying the ark of the covenant. They pause where David is standing and are making sacrifices to Yahweh outside the city until all the people have evacuated the city. The company of exiles is headed toward the dry and foreboding Wilderness of Judea, towards the Jordan River and relative safety.

The ark represents the presence and blessing of God. We know how much David loves God and loves to worship in the tent that had enclosed the ark (Psalm 62:2). We also know how important it was to have Abiathar and the ephod with him on his previous wilderness exile so that he could inquire of the Lord for guidance. So we're very surprised when we hear David tell Zadok:

> "25 Take the ark of God back into the city. If I find favor in the LORD's eyes, he will bring me back and let me see it and his dwelling place again. 26 But if he says, 'I am not pleased with you,' then I am ready; let him do to me whatever seems good to him." (15:25-26)

If we didn't know David better, we'd hear this as a kind of resigned fatalism. But it's not. David realizes that the current threat is the Lord's discipline for his sins, prophesied by Nathan some years before. David is in deep repentance mode, for shortly we read:

> "David continued up the Mount of Olives, weeping as he went; his head was covered and he was barefoot." (15:30a)

Covering one's head is a sign of dismay and despair (Jeremiah 14:3-4; Esther 6:12; cf. Ezekiel 24:17, 23; Leviticus 10:6; 21:10), as is going barefoot (Micah 1:8). Is David just feeling sorry for himself? I don't think so. His attitude is clearly one of submission to Yahweh (15:25-26; 16:10-12). David knows that God is a merciful God, and if he humbles himself, God may change his mind and bring mercy instead of judgment. That's what motivated him to fast while his son by Bathsheba was dying (12:22), and that's what motivates him now. Just because God didn't answer his prayer on that occasion is no reason to doubt that God will hear his prayer now.

So when David says, "let him do to me whatever seems good to him," he means it. This is not weakness we're seeing, but strength. Faith! David knows that the Lord is with him, whether or not he has the ark of the covenant in his procession. It belongs, he believes, in the capital city. Yahweh is Israel's God. The ark is not David's personal shrine to take with him wherever he goes.

Through his tears and his mourning and his repentance, this is the faith-filled, obedient David we see.

But we also see David the consummate strategist, who is going to use the priests to set up an intelligence network inside of occupied Jerusalem. David asks Zadok to use his eyes[1] to observe what Absalom is doing, and then send a report to David via his son Ahimaaz and Abiathar's son Jonathan. David will wait at the west side of the ford over the Jordan near Gilgal until he receives word what to do next.

Q1. (2 Samuel 15:14-30) Why does David flee Jerusalem rather than stay and fight? What are David's emotions during this retreat? Why doesn't he take the ark with him into exile? Does this exhibit faith, fatalism, or submission? What does this tell us about his faith?
http://www.joyfulheart.com/forums/index.php?showtopic=1199

Hushai Remains to Oppose Ahithophel's Counsel (15:30-37)

Now David follows his people up the grade of the Mount of Olives to the summit east of Jerusalem where there is a final view of Zion. Then he is ready to begin the long trek down the mountains to the Jordan plain, well below sea level.

David has been seeking God to intervene. He is constantly in prayer now. When he hears that his wisest counselor Ahithophel had joined Absalom, he prays:

"O LORD, turn Ahithophel's counsel into foolishness." (15:31)

David is encouraged to see God answering already. As he comes to the summit he is met by Hushai the Arkite, in mourning, with "his robe torn and dust on his head". Elsewhere Hushai is known as "David's friend" (15:37; 16:16). It appears that "friend" (rē'eh) is probably used here in a technical sense as a "royal office of high standing,"[2] as it is in Solomon's court, where the NIV translates the word as "personal advisor to the king" (1 Kings 4:5).

---

[1] "Aren't you a seer?" (NIV, KJV, NASB) is the verb rā'â, "see look at, inspect" with an interrogative particle to indicate a question. Anderson notes that "Aren't you a seer?" is only stating the obvious. He translates it, "Are you not an observant man?" (Anderson, 2 Samuel, p. 204). A couple of other possible translations are "Look," (NRSV), "Can you make good use of your eyes?" (New English Bible).

[2] Anderson, 2 Samuel, p. 205. "Friend" (NIV, NRSV), "companion" (KJV) in 1 Chronicles 27:33 is rēa', "friend, neighbor, associate." A closely related word rē'eh sometimes seems to be used in a technical sense of an office: "Friend of the King" (R. Laird Harris, rēa', TWOT #2186a).

Hushai is probably an old man like David. On the long road to exile, he would be a burden, but David has a sensitive job for him. He wants him to offer to be an advisor to Absalom – and be the head of his palace intelligence network. He tells Hushai to say to Absalom:

> "I will be your servant, O king; I was your father's servant in the past, but now I will be your servant." (15:34a)

Ziba Claims Mephibosheth Is Disloyal to David (16:1-4)

David is trying to get out of town, but there's another person who wants to see him –

Ziba, the steward of Mephibosheth, Jonathan's sole surviving son, to whom David had granted a permanent place at his table – and all of Saul's property. Mephibosheth isn't present, but Ziba has come with "a string of donkeys saddled and loaded with two hundred loaves of bread, a hundred cakes of raisins, a hundred cakes of figs and a skin of wine" (16:1b). That's pretty welcome when you're fleeing unprepared into the wilderness. Ziba has been busy, probably putting together supplies from the harvest of Mephibosheth's lands that Ziba manages.

When David asks where Mephibosheth is, Ziba claims that he is disloyal, staying in Jerusalem in hopes of regaining his throne. David doesn't question further; he grants all of Mephibosheth's lands to Ziba and continues on his journey. As we'll see later, David may have acted prematurely; Ziba may well have slandered Mephibosheth for personal gain (19:24-30).

James J. Tissot, "David Quits Jerusalem" (1898-1902), gouache on board, The Jewish Museum, New York.

Shimei Curses David (16:5-14)

Now, as David reaches the village of Bahurim on the outskirts of Jerusalem, he is suddenly assaulted by stones, dirt clods, and curses being thrown from a distance. It is Shimei, a Benjamite relative of Saul's, who blames David for the fall of Saul's dynasty. He shouts:

"Get out, get out, you man of blood, you scoundrel! [8] The LORD has repaid you for all the blood you shed in the household of Saul, in whose place you have reigned. The LORD has handed the kingdom over to your son Absalom. You have come to ruin because you are a man of blood!" (16:7-8)

Perhaps he is blaming David for aiding the Philistines in the battle in which Saul was killed (1 Samuel 27, 29) or for delivering some of Saul's sons and grandsons to settle a demand of the Gibeonites (21:1-14). Or for the murder of Abner (3:27) or Ish-Bosheth (4:7). We're not sure. David's hands are clean here, but Shimei can't be reasoned with and won't be silenced.

Abishai, Joab's brother and a mighty warrior in his own right, wants permission to "cut off his head," since it is a crime to curse the ruler of God's people (Exodus 22:28). But the king won't let him. David believes that perhaps the Lord has told Shimei to curse him as part of the Lord's judgment. In that case, David doesn't want to put himself in the place of opposing God. Notice again David's trust in God's mercy:

"It may be that the LORD will see my distress and repay me with good for the cursing I am receiving today." (16:12)

So Shimei keeps cursing and pelting him with rocks and dirt until David is too far away – and David takes it with humility. He is in repentance; his arrogance is gone.

Finally, we read that,

"The king and all the people with him arrived at their destination exhausted. And there he refreshed himself." (16:14)

The exiles have pushed hard and reached the fords of the Jordan near Gilgal (15:28; 17:16), a descent of about 3,700 feet from Jerusalem to the Jordan River. It is a journey of 20 miles on foot (for most of the party) – an exhausting trip, since all you could expect from such a travelling caravan of women and children, plus soldiers and courtiers and the old king might normally be ten miles a day. But they are running for their lives. They constitute the government in exile. If captured, most of them will be killed. They have pushed very hard, and now feel they can relax a bit.

Q2. (2 Samuel 16:5-14) Why doesn't David silence Shimei son of Gera from cursing him? Is this a political decision or a spiritual decision? What does it tell us about David's faith?

http://www.joyfulheart.com/forums/index.php?showtopic=1200

Hushai Offers His Services to Absalom (16:15-19)

While David's loyalists are leaving the city, Absalom and his army ("all the men of Israel") are entering it. Hushai, the "Friend of the King," is there to greet Absalom with the words, "Long live the king! Long live the king!" (though he neglects to clarify to which king he is wishing long life).

Absalom questions Hushai's quick turn-around. Hushai replies,

"No, the one chosen by the LORD, by these people, and by all the men of Israel – his I will be, and I will remain with him. [19] Furthermore, whom should I serve? Should I not serve the son? Just as I served your father, so I will serve you." (16:18-19)

He serves the reigning, God-appointed king, that's Hushai's answer. Absalom isn't so sure. He is happy for the support, but he doesn't include Hushai in his war-council, and Hushai leaves the king's chambers.

Absalom Sleeps with David's Concubines (16:20-23)

Now that he is in the city, Absalom turns to Ahithophel for advice. The narrator explains,

"Now in those days the advice Ahithophel gave was like that of one who inquires of God. That was how both David and Absalom regarded all of Ahithophel's advice." (16:23)

Ahithophel's first piece of advice is designed to secure the unwavering commitment of his followers. They need to know, if they are to put their lives on the line for him, that Absalom is committed to his course with no turning back. So Ahithophel advises:

"Lie with your father's concubines whom he left to take care of the palace. Then all Israel will hear that you have made yourself a stench in your father's nostrils, and the hands of everyone with you will be strengthened." (16:21)

To us this sounds perverse! And it was, according to the Torah:

"If a man sleeps with his father's wife, he has dishonored his father. Both the man and the woman must be put to death; their blood will be on their own heads." (Leviticus 20:11; cf. 18:8)

Of course, the point *is* to dishonor the father! But this isn't just a gross violation of the Torah. It is a symbol that Absalom is asserting one of the prerogatives of kingship, that is, taking possession of everything belonging to the previous king – including his harem. David had taken possession of the previous king's harem (12:8). Later, when a pretender to the throne seeks to marry the previous king's concubine it is interpreted as treason (1 Kings 2:22). It's one thing to possess the concubines of a previous dynasty, but to lie with your own father's concubines is over the top. It puts everyone on notice that Absalom will resist David to the death, and that's what it takes to get the support he needs.

> "So they pitched a tent for Absalom on the roof, and he lay with his father's concubines in the sight of all Israel." (16:22)

I doubt that Absalom had time to have sex with all 10 concubines before pursuing David, but the tent was pitched publicly – probably on the same rooftop from which David had ogled Bathsheba – and word was spread as to its significance.

Of course, this is a direct fulfillment of Nathan's prophecy of judgment upon David:

> "I will take your wives and give them to one who is close to you, and he will lie with your wives in broad daylight. You did it in secret, but I will do this thing in broad daylight before all Israel." (12:11b-12)

Hushai Frustrates Ahithophel's Counsel (17:1-14, 23)

The next order of business is to pursue David. Ahithophel advises immediate pursuit with the army of 12,000 men of Israel who had gathered to Absalom already.

> "I would attack him while he is weary and weak. I would strike him with terror, and then all the people with him will flee. I would strike down only the king and bring all the people back to you. The death of the man you seek will mean the return of all; all the people will be unharmed." (17:2-3)

It is good advice – and accepted as such by Absalom and his counselors. David and his band have traveled 20 miles and are exhausted. David is exposed and has no shelter or defensive position. Waiting to attack will allow David to find a fortified city where it will be much more difficult to attack him by himself. If David holes up in a fortress, there will be great bloodshed among his followers.

But now we see the hand of God at work. The narrator tells us:

> "The LORD had determined to frustrate the good advice of Ahithophel in order to bring disaster on Absalom." (17:14b)

Absalom is new to governing. He isn't sure enough of himself to take Ahithophel's word only. To reassure himself, he wants to hear Hushai's opinion, so he sends for him. They tell Hushai what Ahithophel has advised and ask him to comment. He replies: "The advice Ahithophel has given is not good this time" (17: 7) and proceeds to critique it:

1. **Fanatic defense**. David's men are fierce fighters and will defend David like "a wild bear robbed of her cubs."

2. **Inaccessibility**. David won't be found with his troops, but will be hidden in some other place.
3. **Danger of ambush**. If David attacks your troops on his terms it could result in a slaughter, your support will evaporate, "melt with fear."

You can say this for Hushai: he knows how to think on his feet! With each point, he introduces fear. He recites the legendary reputation of David and his mighty men as insurmountable fighters. If you don't win the first battle, Hushai warns, you'll lose all your support!

Now he offers an alternate plan – one that will give David a chance to escape. Don't attack until you can gain huge superiority in numbers. That way you'll have the manpower to defeat him wherever you find him. Even if he finds refuge in some walled city, this many troops are enough to utterly destroy the city. David won't have a chance. And he says it with such striking visual images that his hearers can almost see their victory!

Ahithophel's counsel is straightforward. Hushai's counsel is laced with powerful images and emotive phrases.

- "Fierce as a wild bear robbed of her cubs."
- Brave soldiers with a "the heart of a lion, will melt with fear."
- Troops "as numerous as the sand on the seashore."
- Fall on David's troops "as dew settles on the ground."
- Destroy any city by dragging it with ropes "down to the valley until not even a piece of it can be found."

Hushai creates a fear of attacking too soon and then inspires overconfidence in the value of waiting until they can vastly outnumber David's forces. It is a masterful speech.

Absalom and his men believe Hushai! His course seems safer to a new, unsure king. But the real reason is because "the LORD had determined to frustrate the good advice of Ahithophel" (17:14b). Hushai's presentation is flawless – because the Lord is with him. He is an instrument in God's hands.

The result is also to deprive Absalom of any further wise counsel:

> "When Ahithophel saw that his advice had not been followed, he saddled his donkey and set out for his house in his hometown. He put his house in order and then hanged himself." (17:23)

This isn't just "sour grapes." Ahithophel is wise enough to know that he will be executed as a traitor; it's just a matter of time. He knows David, the master strategist, well enough to know that with time to organize his army, there's no way Absalom can defeat him – especially since Absalom can't recognize good advice when he hears it.

Hushai Warns David via the Priests' Sons (17:15-22)

Ahithophel's suicide takes place later. But now that Hushai knows the advice Ahithophel has given – even before he knows what course Absalom will take – he hurries to send word through his spy network:

> "Do not spend the night at the fords[3] in the desert; cross over without fail, or the king and all the people with him will be swallowed up." (17:17)

What follows is an explanation of the intrigue that takes place to get the message out of Jerusalem and to David as

The Rebellion of Absalom
2 Samuel 15-19

Copyright 2012, Ralph F. Wilson.
<pastor@joyfulheart.com>
All rights reserved.

quickly as possible. A servant girl goes to the spring at En Rogel, ostensibly to fetch water. But the priests' sons are seen there and are successfully hidden in a well by a loyalist in nearby Bahurim.

---

[3] "Fords" (NIV, NRSV), "plain" (KJV) here is 'arābâ, "desert plain, steppe." It is probably referring to the Jordan-valley west of the river and adjacent plain, near ford (opposite Jericho). BDB 787. This is likely the same ford (ma'bārâ, "ford, pass, passage") that the two spies crossed near Jericho prior to Joshua's attack on the city (Joshua 2:7), and the ford near Gilgal (1 Samuel 13:7) across from Moab (Judges 3:28).

When the searchers are gone, the two young men climb out of the well, and run twenty miles to warn David, who takes immediate action to undertake a dangerous night crossing of the Jordan.

> "So David and all the people with him set out and crossed the Jordan. By daybreak,[4] no one was left who had not crossed the Jordan." (17:22)

As it turns out, the precaution isn't needed. Absalom has taken Hushai's advice to wait to attack until he can muster a large enough army. It marks the beginning of Absalom's downfall.

David Flees to Mahanaim (17:24-29)

The next day, David and his band march north along the Arabah on the east side of the Jordan, then go up to Mahanaim,[5] near the Jabbok River (now known as the Zarqa River). They probably go there for the same reasons that Abner had taken Ish-Bosheth to Mahanaim after the devastating defeat of Saul's army to the Philistines a generation previously. It is somewhat remote, and difficult for a large army to reach quickly because of the deep canyon of the Jabbok.

Once he is relatively safe within the fortress city of Mahanaim, David can relax a bit. And here, some of his supporters from east of the Jordan come to his material aid:

> "[They] brought bedding and bowls and articles of pottery. They also brought wheat and barley, flour and roasted grain, beans and lentils, honey and curds, sheep, and cheese from cows' milk for David and his people to eat. For they said, 'The people have become hungry and tired and thirsty in the desert.'" (17:28-29)

What a blessing! What welcome provisions in a time of need! One of these men is Shobi, an Ammonite vassal who remains true to his suzerain even when David can't enforce his obedience. The second is Makir from Lo Debar, who had previously hosted Mephibosheth, Jonathan's surviving son (2 Samuel 9:4-5). The third is Barzillai, a wealthy, 80-year-old friend from Rogelim in Gilead. Barzillai loves David so much that

---

[4] No doubt the spies began their twenty mile run before David and his slower band had even reached the Jordan. They left just as soon as Hushai knew of the danger. That's the only way David could get across before daybreak.

[5] Mahanaim is a city in Gilead that lies somewhat east of the Jordan, perhaps on the north bank of the Jabbok River, in the territory of Gad, a city assigned to the Merarite clan of the Levites (Joshua 21:38). Two possible suggestions for its location are Tell edh-Dhahab el Gharbi or Tell Hajjaj, but we just don't know (W.D. Mounce, "Mahanaim," ISBE 3:222-223; Anderson, 2 Samuel, p. 33). For a discussion of pros and cons of various locations in William Paul Griffin, "Mahanaim Reconsidered," March 15, 1991, unpublished. http://www.drbill.net/eu_website/otlit1/othandou/MAHANAIM.HTM Dr. Griffin is Professor of Old Testament at Evangel University, Springfield, MO.

he makes the journey with David to cross the Jordan on his return to Jerusalem (19:30-39).

These men show their true character. Many people desire to ingratiate themselves to a powerful man on his way up, who can, hopefully, use his power to help their cause in the future. But these same self-serving people are quick to desert a person who has lost power. Indeed, the men who provisioned David in Mahanaim expose themselves to retaliation by Absalom if he should ultimately be victorious. True, they all live east of the Jordan and less vulnerable to attack. But in them we see David's real friends.

The Psalm of a Pursued King at Peace with His God (Psalm 3)

Psalm 3 bears the following ascription: "A psalm of David. When he fled from his son Absalom." Here we get a window into the faith of King David at this time in his life. *Note: If your group or class is short of time, you might decide to skip Psalm 3.*

David has been pursued by armies before. Thirty years earlier, Saul had led an army of 3,000 to capture him. Now Absalom's much larger army is seeking to hunt him down.

> "O LORD, how many are my foes!
> How many rise up against me!" (verse 1)

David's star had risen high, but has fallen. Many conclude that it is just a matter of time until David is captured. It is over for him.

> "Many are saying of me,
> 'God will not deliver him.' *Selah*" [6] (verse 2)

David knows what people are saying, but the truth lies elsewhere. David knows his God. Yes, David has failed him, but at age sixty, David finds a wonderful peace in following his Lord on this journey into exile.

> "But you are a shield around me, O LORD." (verse 3a)

David is being chased by armies, but Yahweh is his Shield (*sinnâ*), a "large shield (covering the whole body)."[7] But Yahweh's shield is not just in front of him, but "around me." Hallelujah.

> "You bestow glory on me and lift up my head." (verse 3b)

---

[6] "Selah" seems to be a signal for an interlude or change of musical accompaniment, probably from the Hebrew root *sll*, "to lift up" or perhaps an Aramaic verb "to bend" (Derek Kidner, *Psalms 1-72* (Tyndale Old Testament Commentaries; InterVarsity Press/Tyndale Press, 1973). pp. 36-37).

[7] *Ṣinnâ*, BDB 857. A shield is used as a metaphor of God's protection a number of times in Scripture. For example, see Genesis 15:1; Deuteronomy 33:29; Psalm 28:7; 84:11; 91:4; 115:9-11; 119:14.

Men say that David's glory is past, but God is the One who will bestow glory on those whom he chooses. And Yahweh hasn't given up on David! The phrase "lift up my head" pictures a head bowed in humility and perhaps shame, but with God's encouragement and refreshing, he perks up and God exalts him.[8]

> "To the LORD I cry aloud,
> and he answers me from his holy hill. *Selah*" (verse 4)

There are times when David calls out to God in fear, but the Lord answers him immediately. David pictures God on "his holy hill," over the Ark of the Covenant in the tent David had pitched for it in Jerusalem (6:17).

Look at the peace this pursued warrior-king experiences. He was once young and strong. Now he is old and weak, but he is at peace.

> "I lie down and sleep;
> I wake again, because the LORD sustains me.
> I will not fear the tens of thousands
>   drawn up against me on every side." (verses 5-6)

Dear friend, what are you going through right now? Do you have a huge army pursuing you with the sole purpose of taking your life? David did, but he was able to find peace.

Now he calls on Yahweh to fight the battle for him. David has known for many, many years that "the battle is the Lord's" (1 Samuel 17:47). Just as it was in the field facing Goliath, so it is now. Yahweh has not changed!

> "Arise, O LORD! Deliver me, O my God!
> Strike all my enemies on the jaw;
> break the teeth of the wicked." (verse 7)

Now he concludes with a statement of the faith that has carried through this season of exile. When he left Jerusalem in haste to begin his exile, you can see this simple submission to God's will:

> "If he says, 'I am not pleased with you,' then I am ready;
> let him do to me whatever seems good to him." (15:26)

God's will is sufficient for David. His future is God's hands. The psalm concludes with this assurance.

> "From the LORD comes deliverance.
> May your blessing be on your people. *Selah*. " (verse 8)

---

[8] See Psalm 27:6; 110:7; Genesis 40:13; 2 Kings 25:27 KJV.

Absalom's Reign (17:24-26)

Back in Jerusalem, Absalom follows Hushai's counsel to gather all Israel before attempting to go after his father. Several events take place.

1. Hushai becomes Absalom's chief counselor in place of Ahithophel, who has gone home and committed suicide. But Hushai, we know, is secretly loyal to David.
2. Absalom is anointed king by all Israel in some kind of coronation ceremony (19:10), though perhaps this took place earlier in Hebron.
3. Absalom erects a pillar as a monument to himself in the King's Valley,[9] an indication of his arrogance as well as his low self-confidence. By this time, his three sons have presumably died (14:27; 18:18).
4. Absalom assembles a large army from all the tribes of Israel to confront David. The army is commanded by Amasa, who is a cousin of Joab and a nephew of David.[10] We know little about him, except that David admires him enough to make him commander of his army to replace Joab (19:13) – who soon murders Amasa (20:8-10).

Absalom joins the army as they advance on David's position, moving his troops across the Jordan and camping in Gilead, east of the Jordan.

The Battle of the Forest of Ephraim (18:1-8)

But Amasa is relatively untried as a commander, compared to David's long experience and the expertise of his veteran generals – Joab, Abishai, and Ittai the Gittite. David forms his army into three divisions, each under one of these commanders.

David wants to lead his troops into battle personally as Absalom is doing, but his men dissuade him.

> "[3] The men said, 'You shall not go out. For if we flee, they will not care about us. If half of us die, they will not care about us. But you are worth ten thousand of us; therefore it is better that you send us help from the city.' [4] The king said to them, 'Whatever seems best to you I will do.' So the king stood at the side of the gate, while all the army marched out by hundreds and by thousands[11]." (18:3-4)

[9] The exact location of the King's Valley is unknown, though it is near Jerusalem, where Melchizedek met with Abraham (while still known as Abram) after the defeat of the Mesopotamian kings (Genesis 14:17) (Gary A. Lee, "King's Valley," ISBE 2:40).

[10] See Appendix 3. Genealogy of the House of David.

[11] "'Thousands' and 'hundreds' were military units, not necessarily indicative of their numerical strength" (Anderson, *2 Samuel*, p. 224).

Apparently, while David has been in exile, many fighting men have come over to him, ready to join their old commander against Absalom's challenge. David is fielding a mighty army, but David gives a troubling command to his generals, in the hearing of all his troops:

> "Be gentle with the young man Absalom for my sake." (18:5a)

Just as David is the target of Absalom's army, so Absalom should be the target of David's army. This command to spare Absalom makes the task much more difficult. To obey the king's command, now they must take care to capture Absalom alive – a much riskier proposition.

The battle takes place on ground of David's own choosing, in the forest of Ephraim, in the mountainous country in Gilead, east of the Jordan, thickly wooded with oak, pine, cypress, and arbutus.[12] A large army has an advantage in the open, but heavily wooded terrain gives the advantage to the smaller force. David's experienced warriors, skilled in guerilla warfare, take full advantage. The narrator tells us,

> "There the army of Israel was defeated by David's men, and the casualties that day were great – twenty thousand men. The battle spread out over the whole countryside, and the forest claimed more lives that day than the sword." (18:7-8)

In the thick woods, Absalom's soldiers tend to lose all sense of direction, wander aimlessly, and get hopelessly lost. Separated from the main force, they are extremely vulnerable to David's warriors hiding in the forest awaiting them.

Joab Slays Absalom (18:9-18)

Chief among those claimed by the forest is Absalom himself.

> "He was riding his mule, and as the mule went under the thick branches of a large oak, Absalom's head got caught in the tree.[13] He was left hanging in midair, while the mule he was riding kept on going." (18:9b)

Josephus says, "He entangled his hair greatly in the large boughs of a knotty tree that spread a great way, and there he hung." It's probably ironic that Absalom's pride and

---

[12] The exact location of the Forest of Ephraim isn't certain. It is in the mountainous country in Gilead, east of the Jordan – either north or south of the river Jabbok. Ya`ar can also mean open woodland or even scrub, the area was probably thickly wooded, with oak, pine, cypress, arbutus, etc., since there is rich soil from the Cenomanian limestone and plentiful winter rainfall (A. Denis Baly, "Ephraim, Forest of," ISBE 2:119-120). The Bible mentions the "oaks of Bashan" (Isaiah 2:13; Zechariah 11:2).

[13] Josephus (*Antiquities* 7.10.2).

glory, namely, his hair, brought about his humiliation and death.[14] The narrator hints at another irony: the Torah specifies that for capital offences, the body is to be hung on a tree (Deuteronomy 21:22; cf. Galatians 3:13).

The man who first sees Absalom reports at once to Joab, who asks: "If you saw him, why didn't you kill him already" (18:11). But the man had heard David's command, and wisely wouldn't think of disobeying it. Joab has no such scruples. Immediately, he goes to where Absalom is hanging and stabs him with three javelins, and has ten of his armor-bearers finish him off. Then Joab sounds the trumpet to stop pursuing Israel's army. Without Absalom, they are no longer a threat to David. They flee to their homes.

> "They took Absalom, threw him into a big pit in the forest and piled up a large heap of rocks over him." (18:17)

This cairn of stones is Absalom's final monument,[15] not the pillar he erected for himself near Jerusalem (18:18).

Why would Joab so blatantly disobey King David's explicit command? It comes down to character. Let's consider the characters of Absalom, David, and Joab.

- **Absalom** will do whatever is necessary to get his own way. He has demonstrated it by killing his brother, torching Joab's field, and defiling his father's concubines. If he is allowed to continue, he will do anything to usurp David's throne.

- **David** has many strong character qualities. He is a man of honor. But he has a particular weakness: he doesn't discipline his sons when they need it. Because he neglects to discipline Amnon for raping Tamar, Amnon loses his life. Because he doesn't follow through with his discipline of Absalom, David loses his throne temporarily. Joab knows that David will be soft on Absalom.

- **Joab** is loyal to David – usually. He has performed several sensitive tasks for David, including facilitating the death of Uriah, Bathsheba's husband. As a general, he has been consistently successful. But on occasion, he acts in his own interests. In the case of killing Absalom, I believe that Joab does what needs to be done to counteract David's own weakness for his sons. Shortly, he will save David's throne by rebuking David for not thanking his army (19:5-7). When Joab is

---

[14] Anderson, 2 Samuel, p. 225, citing the Talmud, "Absalom gloried in his hair; therefore he was hanged by his hair" (*Sotah* 9b).

[15] He was given "the burial of an accursed man" (P.K. McCarter, *2 Samuel* (Anchor Bible; Doubleday, 1984), p. 407, cited by Anderson, 2 Samuel, p. 225). The pile of stones was reminiscent of the burial of Achan (Joshua 7:26) and defeated kings during the Conquest (Joshua 8:29; 10:27).

finally executed by Solomon, it is not for killing Absalom, the king's son, but for murdering Abner and Amasa in cold blood (1 Kings 2:5, 28-33).

Joab, I believe, is right in killing David's enemy – even against orders. Absalom has sought to kill the Lord's anointed – his father – and deserves to die, though David can't accept this. God's plan is for David's young son Solomon to succeed him.

News of Absalom's Death Reaches David (18:19-32)

Following Absalom's death, there's an argument about who should bring the news to David. Joab knows that David won't take the news well and may "shoot the messenger," so he tells a foreigner from Cush, south of Egypt, to be the messenger. But one of the spy couriers, Ahimaaz the priest's son, insists on carrying the message anyway.

It turns out that Ahimaaz takes the direct route and outruns the Cushite, but allows the Cushite to bring the crucial news that Absalom has been slain. It is anything but "good news" to David.

David Mourns for Absalom (18:33-19:8a)

David is devastated! He goes to his chamber and weeps.

"O my son Absalom! My son, my son Absalom! If only I had died instead of you – O Absalom, my son, my son!" (18:33)

His mourning can be heard all over the city and puts a damper on what would normally be rejoicing over a great victory.

Joab realizes the danger, and rushes to David with a stern rebuke – the kind of rebuke that only a loyal friend can give:

"5 Today you have humiliated all your men, who have just saved your life and the lives of your sons and daughters and the lives of your wives and concubines. 6 You love those who hate you and hate those who love you. You have made it clear today that the commanders and their men mean nothing to you. I see that you would be pleased if Absalom were alive today and all of us were dead.

7 Now go out and encourage your men. I swear by the LORD that if you don't go out, not a man will be left with you by nightfall. This will be worse for you than all the calamities that have come upon you from your youth till now." (19:5-7)

At this point, David's hold on the throne is tenuous at best. His core supporters are these men who have fought for him. He must keep his core and build upon it if he is to reestablish his throne.

The narrator records that David follows Joab's strong counsel. He goes and sits in the gateway to the city where the city elders would discuss civic matters. And while David doesn't show much enthusiasm, his men now come before their king and receive his thanks. By his quick action and courageous rebuke, Joab has saved David's kingdom.

Q3. (2 Samuel 18:1-19:8) Why does David command mercy for Absalom in the battle? Why does Joab kill him against David's orders? How does David's loud mourning threaten his kingdom? What does this say about his followers' loyalty? What does it say about David's faith? About his weaknesses?
http://www.joyfulheart.com/forums/index.php?showtopic=1201

Judah Recalls David to Be Its King (19:8b-15)

The huge Israelite militia called up by Absalom has been soundly defeated in the Forest of Ephraim and have fled for their homes. Absalom is dead. Now in villages, towns, and cities all over the country, they debate who should be king now? David?

> "The king delivered us from the hand of our enemies; he is the one who rescued us from the hand of the Philistines. But now he has fled the country because of Absalom; and Absalom, whom we anointed to rule over us, has died in battle. So why do you say nothing about bringing the king back?" (19:9-10)

The nation seems paralyzed. They realize that they need a strong national leader. But, as yet, they don't seem to be of a common mind. Unity is coming gradually as people remember how David has delivered them from the Philistines – and there aren't really any other options available.

David can't just march into Jerusalem proclaiming himself to be king, however. Judah and Israel had rejected him when they had anointed Absalom king. Of course, David has the military *power* to return to Jerusalem, but power is different from recognized *authority*. For David to regain his authority as king, Judah and Israel need to reaffirm David as their monarch.

Such a unified action is slow to materialize. People are talking about it, but no one is taking action to organize a formal recall of the king. Logically, support should begin with David's own tribe of Judah. To help jump-start the process, David undertakes a two-prong political strategy:

1. **David appeals to Judah's pride.** David asks his supporters, the priests, to speak to the leaders of Judah in such a way as to appeal to their tribal pride and sense of shame at the same time:

   "Why should you be the last to bring the king back to his palace, since what is being said throughout Israel has reached the king at his quarters? You are my brothers, my own flesh and blood. So why should you be the last to bring back the king?" (19:11-12)

2. **David appoints a popular Judean commander.** David's nephew Amasa had been the military commander under Absalom. To offer a concession to his fellow Judeans, David asks Amasa to be his military commander in place of Joab. David is angry at Joab for killing Absalom against his explicit orders. But, no doubt, Joab is furious over being demoted in favor of the defeated general, even though it was his actions that won the day. I have supported David all my life, he thinks. I've done what needs to be done to keep him in power. And now he rewards me like this? As we'll see, Joab refuses to tolerate David's slight and murders Amasa as soon as he gets the opportunity (20:10).

Nevertheless, the narrator records the success of David's strategies.

"He won over the hearts of all the men of Judah as though they were one man. They sent word to the king, 'Return, you and all your men.'" (19:14)

David Deals with Those Disloyal to Him (19:15-30)

Once David has received an official invitation to return as king – if only from the tribe of Judah – he leaves his fastness at Mahanaim and travels as far as the east bank of the Jordan River ford at Gilgal.

Now the pageantry begins. We may discard pomp and ceremony as an unworthy expression of pride, but this kind of pageantry is important to all to regain a sense of unity and national pride in their king.

"Now the men of Judah had come to Gilgal to go out and meet the king and bring him across the Jordan." (19:15)

Accompanying the tribe of Judah are 1,000 Benjamites. And with them are three Benjamites who need to "make nice" to the king – Shimei, who had cursed him; Ziba, who had deceived him; and Mephibosheth, whose loyalty is in question.

When a leader falls from power, he tends to be shunned, but when he returns to power, everyone bends over backwards to honor and flatter him. No wonder leaders can feel distrustful and isolated!

> "They crossed at the ford to take the king's household over and to do whatever he wished." (19:18a)

David Deals with Shimei (19:18-23)

Shimei, the Benjamite who had cursed and thrown stones at David a few months before, is now penitent. He falls prostrate before David, confesses his sin, and asks for mercy. Abishai wants to kill him for cursing the Lord's anointed, but David rebukes him. We see again the old David who is great enough to offer mercy, rather than exact strict retribution. That's one sterling quality that differentiates him from the brothers Joab and Abishai.

David Deals with Mephibosheth and Ziba (19:24-30)

Mephibosheth, Jonathan's son, whom David had honored by making him a permanent guest at the royal table, hadn't come with David when he fled Jerusalem. Ziba had told David that Mephibosheth had stayed in Jerusalem because he hoped to be set on the throne himself, as a grandson of Saul. Now David confronts him: "Why didn't you go with me, Mephibosheth?" (19:25). Mephibosheth replies that his servant Ziba had betrayed him by not preparing transportation for the invalid and by slandering him to the king. Mephibosheth appeals to David's mercy.

David can't be sure who is telling the truth, Ziba or Mephibosheth, so he orders the lands to be divided between them. Was this fair? We don't know – any more than David knew – who was telling the truth here, the opportunist Ziba or Saul's grandson Mephibosheth.

David Says Farewell to Barzillai (19:31-39)

Eighty-year-old Barzillai has made the long trek with David to the Jordan. He has provided for David in exile and now he has come to see him off. Barzillai, whose name means "iron-hearted," is a good friend!

David asks him to come to Jerusalem with him, but Barzillai demurs. He would rather spend his final days in his own home near the graves of his parents. However, Barzillai asks the king to show favor to his son[16] Kimham (Chimham) on his behalf,

---

[16] 1 Kings 2:7 suggests that Kimham was Barzillai's actual son.

which David is pleased to do. From a reference in Jeremiah, it seems possible that David gave Kimham a land grant near Bethlehem (Jeremiah 41:17).

Israel and Judah Dispute Who Is Most Loyal to David (19:40-43)

David needs to catalyze the movement to have him return as king, but his overtures to Judah result in intertribal squabbles. The other tribes are jealous because troops from the tribe of Judah brought the king across Jordan, with only some of the troops of the rest of the tribes.

> "All the troops of Judah and half the troops of Israel had taken the king over" (19:40b).

The men of Israel protest against the Judeans:

> "We have ten shares in the king; and besides, we have a greater claim on David than you have. So why do you treat us with contempt? Were we not the first to speak of bringing back our king?" (19:43)

The 10 tribes are saying that they should have 10 times the opportunity to favor the king. Then they point out they were the first to mention the possibility of bringing back David. Of course, they didn't act on it, only talked about it. But hurt feelings are powerful motivators.

The rhetoric is ratcheting up. The northern tribes accuse Judah of treating them as if they were nothing.[17] The Judeans respond with their own accusations, as the situation spirals out of control.

> "The men of Judah responded even more harshly[18] than the men of Israel." (19:43b)

The result is a fresh rebellion that begins to spread throughout the northern tribes. Baldwin faults David for this.

> "By taunting Judah with the readiness of the other eleven tribes to receive him, David is driving a wedge between Judah and the rest, whereas he would have been wise to unify the kingdom by rising above tribal factions and loyalties."[19]

I think this is an example of "armchair quarterbacking." David did what he could to get the process of recalling the king started – and succeeded. He couldn't have foreseen how poorly the elders of Judah would handle diplomacy with the northern tribes. Sometimes

---

[17] "Treat with contempt" (NIV), "despise" (NRSV, KJV) is *qālal*, "be slight, swift, trifling, of little account," or "curse." Here in the Hiphil stem it carries the idea "treat with contempt, bring contempt, dishonor" (BDB 886).

[18] "Harshly" (NIV), "fiercer" (NRSV, KJV) is *qāshâ*, "be hard, severe." The root apparently arose from an agricultural milieu, emphasizing the subjective effect exerted by an overly heavy yoke, which is hard to bear (Leonard J. Coppes, *qāshâ*, TWOT #2085).

[19] Baldwin, *1 and 2 Samuel*, p. 275.

our leadership actions succeed completely, sometimes partially, and sometimes not at all. Leaders do the very best they can, knowing that the outcome is uncertain – and that there will always be critics!

The Rebellion of Sheba the Benjamite (20:1-7)

The squabble between the elders of Israel and the leaders of the other tribes is interrupted by Sheba, a Benjamite, a man of action but also a scoundrel.[20] He sounds a trumpet to get people's attention and then shouts inflammatory words:

> "We have no share in David, no part in Jesse's son! Every man to his tent, O Israel!" (20:1)

"Every man to his tent," means, "let's all go home."

> "So all the men of Israel deserted David to follow Sheba son of Bicri. But the men of Judah stayed by their king all the way from the Jordan to Jerusalem." (20:2)

David's escort from the northern tribes of Israel evaporates and David has no choice but to return to Jerusalem escorted by his own tribe only. As you can imagine, the unity of his kingdom is in serious doubt.

Once in Jerusalem, David confines the ten concubines who remained behind for the rest of their lives, but no longer sleeps with them.

Then he moves quickly to put down Sheba's rebellion. He tells his new commander Amasa to "summon the men of Judah," that is, the militia from Judah, within three days. Given the slowness of communication in those days, that is asking for a "lightning response."

This is David's first assignment for Amasa, but Amasa doesn't meet the deadline with the troops from the tribe of Judah. David can't wait. The situation is dire. He turns to Abishai, another general, Joab's brother.

> "Now Sheba son of Bicri will do us more harm than Absalom did. Take your master's men and pursue him, or he will find fortified cities and escape from us." (20:6)

So David's personal army and the Philistine mercenary troops march north from Jerusalem to put down the rebellion under Abishai. Joab goes along, but apparently under Abishai's command.

---

[20] The narrator refers to him as a "troublemaker" (NIV), "scoundrel" (NRSV), literally, "a man of Belial (KJV). *Belîya'al* means "worthlessness," from the verb *bālâ*, "become old, worn out" (Walter C. Kaiser, *bālâ*, TWOT #246g). "Belial" is rendered as a proper name by the KJV, because "in Jewish apocalyptic writing (*Book of Jubilees, Ascension of Isaiah, Sibylline Oracles*) the name was used to describe Satan or the antichrist," as in 2 Corinthians 6:15 (R.K. Harrison, "Belial," ISBE 1:454). However, that usage occurs nearly 1,000 years after the time 1 and 2 Samuel were written.

Joab Murders Amasa (20:8-10a)

By the time Abishai's troops get as far as Gibeon, about seven miles north of Jerusalem, Amasa's forces from Judah join them.

As soon as Joab sees Amasa, he greets him as might a friend. Amasa is his cousin, after all. But as he embraces him to give him the customary kiss of greeting, Joab grabs Amasa's beard with his right hand and stabs him in the belly with a dagger in his left hand, spilling his intestines upon the ground. Amasa dies on the spot!

Without missing a beat, "Joab and his brother Abishai" lead the army north after Sheba. The chief commander lies wallowing in his blood and Abishai gives way to his impetuous brother's leadership. David's attempt to restructure the military is over.

Joab Pursues Sheba to Abel Beth Maacah (20:10b-26)

One of Joab's men shouts to the troops from Judah:

> "Whoever favors Joab, and whoever is for David, let him follow Joab!" (20:11b)

Once Amasa's body is removed from the center of the road, the Judeans follow Joab north on the mission.

In the meantime, Sheba is travelling through all the tribal areas on his way, trying to gain support. He has no organization, so he is ineffective, but he does his best to turn people away from David to his own leadership.

Sheba has had a three- to four-day head start, but Joab's troops are hot on his trail.[21] Finally, Sheba finds shelter in the walled city of Abel Beth Maacah in the far north of Israel's territory.

What David had feared, that Sheba would find refuge in a fortified city, has come to pass.

But Joab doesn't admit defeat. He begins a siege of the city, building a siege ramp so that he can bring a battering ram up to the walls and create a breach.

It is just a matter of time until the city is taken. If the city doesn't find a way to resolve the situation, they'll likely all be slain for harboring a traitor against the king.

The negotiator for the city of Abel Beth Maacah turns out to be a "wise woman." This gives us some indication of how women were sometimes able to function at a high level within the culture of the time.

The woman asks for Joab, and when he appears she appeals to him on behalf of the city:

> "We are the peaceful and faithful in Israel. You are trying to destroy a city that is a mother in Israel. Why do you want to swallow up the LORD's inheritance?" (20:19)

Negotiations begin. Joab explains that they have nothing against the citizens of the city. It is Sheba only that they are seeking. If he is turned over to them, they will lift the siege and leave. The woman responds:

> "His head will be thrown to you from the wall." (20:21c)

Within a short time the head is thrown out, the troops disperse, and Joab – in full command of the army once again, returns to Jerusalem in victory. To regain the full loyalty of the 12 tribes will take years of careful diplomacy to accomplish, but for now, the rebellion is over. David is in charge once again in his capital city.

Q4. (2 Samuel 16-20) What does this passage teach us about David's character and faith? What does it reveal about Joab's character? What kind of faith do you see in Joab? What does this passage teach us about the importance of friends? Is Joab really David's friend?
http://www.joyfulheart.com/forums/index.php?showtopic=1202

---

[21] Berites (NIV, KJV), Bichrites (NRSV) is *bērîm*. Bichri is the father of Sheba, a Benjamite. The word probably means "descendant of Becher" or "Beker", who was the second son of Benjamin (Genesis 46:21, 1 Chronicles 7:6, 8) (ISBE 1:509).

Lessons for Disciples

The full-of-faith David is most visible when times are tough – fighting Goliath, escaping Saul's army, recovering his family from the Amalekites, and fleeing from Absalom. But when David is rich, powerful, and successful, he tends to coast, to rely on his own achievements and less on God.

The Apostle Paul learned a valuable spiritual insight when he was struggling with a difficult "thorn in the flesh, a messenger from Satan." He entreats God three times to remove it, but God finally says to him:

> "My grace is sufficient for you, for **power is made perfect in weakness**." (2 Corinthians 12:9)

And Paul concludes:

> "Therefore I am content with weaknesses, insults, hardships, persecutions, and calamities for the sake of Christ; for **whenever I am weak, then I am strong.**" (2 Corinthians 12:10)

We hate suffering, but suffering while trusting in the Lord brings out our best, since hardship stimulates our faith much more than does comfort. God's goal is not our continued happiness, but our growth into maturity, "to the measure of the full stature of Christ" (Ephesians 4:13). Christ is being formed in us, and in that we can rejoice.

As I consider some of the disciple learnings from this lesson, I see:

1. **Weakness and strength**. When we are weak and struggling, we often turn afresh to the Lord and become stronger in him.
2. **Friends**. Our true friends are those who rally around us when we're down and they have nothing to gain by the friendship. Friends show generosity in our times of trouble. Which friend of yours does God want to bless through you this week?
3. **Submission**. In defeat, we can learn submission to the Lord's will, much better than when we're fresh from victory.
4. **Sovereignty of God**. The battle is in the hands of the Lord.
5. **Emotions**. If we're not careful, our emotions can sabotage God's will for our lives. David's love for his son and his grief at Absalom's death almost ruined what God intended – victory and return. Sometimes, when we are overwrought, we need to listen to our friends' counsel and follow it.

Prayer

Father, thank you for strengthening us when we are weak and struggling. Teach us well to follow you in the difficult times, so that we may also follow you in times of abundance and blessing. Give us hearts submitted to your will, so we can say, like David: "let Him do to me whatever seems good to Him." In Jesus' name, we pray. Amen.

Key Verses

"Take the ark of God back into the city. If I find favor in the LORD's eyes, he will bring me back and let me see it and his dwelling place again. But if he says, 'I am not pleased with you,' then I am ready; let him do to me whatever seems good to him." (2 Samuel 15:25-26)

"Let him alone, and let him curse; for the LORD has bidden him. It may be that the LORD will look on my distress, and the LORD will repay me with good for this cursing of me today." (2 Samuel 16:11b-12)

"For the LORD had ordained to defeat the good counsel of Ahithophel, so that the LORD might bring ruin on Absalom." (2 Samuel 17:16)

"When David came to Mahanaim, Shobi son of Nahash from Rabbah of the Ammonites, and Machir son of Ammiel from Lo-debar, and Barzillai the Gileadite from Rogelim, brought beds, basins, and earthen vessels, wheat, barley, meal, parched grain, beans and lentils, honey and curds, sheep, and cheese from the herd, for David and the people with him to eat; for they said, 'The troops are hungry and weary and thirsty in the wilderness.'" (2 Samuel 17:1-29)

"The king ordered Joab and Abishai and Ittai, saying, 'Deal gently for my sake with the young man Absalom.' And all the people heard when the king gave orders to all the commanders concerning Absalom." (2 Samuel 18:5)

"The king was deeply moved, and went up to the chamber over the gate, and wept; and as he went, he said, 'O my son Absalom, my son, my son Absalom! Would I had died instead of you, O Absalom, my son, my son!'" (2 Samuel 18:33)

"Shall anyone be put to death in Israel this day? For do I not know that I am this day king over Israel?" (2 Samuel 19:22)

13. The Legacy of David (2 Samuel 21-1 Kings 2)

The final four chapters of 2 Samuel form a kind of appendix to Samuel – but since 1 and 2 Samuel and 1 and 2 Kings probably once formed a single work, they are more likely an "aside" or "excursus" within the flow of the narrative.

2 Samuel 21-24 includes six elements, none of which can be easily dated within David's story. That's why they're probably grouped together here towards the end of David's life.

1. Vengeance for the Gibeonites (21:1-14)

2. Exploits of David's Mighty Men against the Philistines (21:15-22)

3. David's Song of Praise (chapter 22 = Psalm 18)

4. The Last Words of David (23:1-7)

5. David's Mighty Men (23:8-39, already treated in Lesson 4)

6. David's Census of Israel (2 Samuel 24:1-9)

James J. Tissot, "David Singing" (1896-1902), gouache on board, The Jewish Museum, New York.

We conclude with David's death and Solomon's accession to the throne in 1 Kings 1-2.

Note: This is a long lesson. If your group or class are short on time, you might want to treat David's Song of Praise (2 Samuel 22 = Psalm 18) as a separate lesson.

Vengeance for the Gibeonites (2 Samuel 21:1-14)

The first of these elements, bringing justice for the Gibeonites, probably occurred between the time David had brought Mephibosheth to his table (9:1-3) and Absalom's rebellion, since that's the point when Shimei accuses David of the blood of Saul's household (16:7-8).

What precipitates the crisis is a prolonged drought. The greatest rainfall in Israel typically occurs between November and March, with a long dry summer. Fall rains were referred to as the "early or former rain"; spring rains were referred to as the "latter rain."[1] The Israelites were used to erratic rainfall, often with a year or two of drought. But when the crops failed for three years in a row, the people were desperate.

The narrator tells us that in the third year of famine, "David sought the face of the Lord" (21:1a). God spoke to him either through his own prophetic gift, or through his court prophet (Gad or Nathan), or through the Urim and Thummim cast by the high priest. In any case, the word of the Lord was clear concerning the cause of the drought:

> "It is on account of Saul and his blood-stained house; it is because he put the Gibeonites to death." (21:1b)

Gibeon is a city about five miles northwest of Jerusalem , identified as the present-day el-Jîb.[2] "You may recall that during the Conquest centuries earlier, the Gibeonites had tricked Joshua into thinking that they were from far away.

> "Then Joshua made a treaty of peace with them to let them live, and the leaders of the assembly ratified it by oath." (Joshua 9:15)

Throughout the intervening years, the Gibeonites had continued as an ethnic enclave within Israel. By now they seem to be worshippers of Yahweh with the rest of Israel.

We aren't told elsewhere of the incident where Saul, "in his zeal for Israel and Judah had tried to annihilate[3] them." Verse 5 indicates that this is a deliberate plan to exterminate the entire people group.[4] Hundreds of Gibeonites have been killed despite promised protection under the ancient treaty. Because of this broken covenant, God has withheld the rain. He expects Israel to take seriously what they have pledged.

---

[1] Deuteronomy 11:14; Job 29:23; Psalm 84:6; Proverbs 16:15; Jeremiah 3:3; 5:24; Hosea 6:3; Joel 2:23; Zechariah 10:1; James 5:7.

[2] Keith N. Schoville, "Gibeon," ISBE 2:462.

[3] "Annihilate" (NIV), "wipe them out" (NRSV), "slay" (KJV) is *nākâ*, "smite, strike, hit, beat, slay, kill." Here, since a people group is in mind, it carries the idea of "attack" and/or "destroy" (Marvin R. Wilson, *nākâ*, TWOT #1364).

[4] In 21:5 two words describe this well-planned campaign. "Destroyed" (NIV), "consumed" (NRSV, KJV) is *kālâ*, which has the basic idea, "to bring a process to completion." Here it refers to violent destruction during war, in the Piel stem, "put an end to, destroy" (cf. 1 Samuel 15:18) (TWOT #982). The second word, "decimated" (NIV), "destroyed" (NRSV, KJV) is *shāmad*, in the Piel stem, "to destroy" or "annihilate." (Herman J. Austel, "*shāmad*, TWOT #2406).

So David asks the Gibeonites how Israel might make amends and treats them with great deference. Since Saul is dead and cannot be judged for his bloodguilt, they tell David:

> "Let seven of his male descendants be given to us to be killed and exposed before the LORD at Gibeah of Saul – the Lord's chosen one." (21:6)

Their request seems just as a retribution-in-kind according to the Torah (Exodus 21:23; Leviticus 24:21; Deuteronomy 19:21).

> "You must purge from Israel the guilt of shedding innocent blood, so that it may go well with you." (Deuteronomy 19:13b)

> "Atonement cannot be made for the land on which blood has been shed, except by the blood of the one who shed it." (Numbers 35:33)

True, the Torah specifies that the children should not be punished for the deeds of their fathers (Deuteronomy 24:16; Ezekiel 18:4, 20), but in a kind of corporate identity sense, Saul's descendants bare his guilt (Exodus 34:7; Numbers 14:18). This is a difficult case, but David is eager to remove the curse of famine from upon his people (Leviticus 26:20; Deuteronomy 28:18). Saul's seven male descendants are symbolic, seven representing the totality,[5] though hundreds of Gibeonites had actually been slaughtered.[6]

As chief judge in Israel, David has to walk carefully because of other covenants and oaths. David's covenant with Jonathan precludes any of his descendants being given over (1 Samuel 18:3; 20:42; 23:18). David had also made a pledge to Saul. Saul had asked David:

> "'Now swear to me by the LORD that you will not cut off my descendants or wipe out my name from my father's family.' So David gave his oath to Saul." (1 Samuel 24:21-22a)

The operative verbs are "cut off" (*kārat*, figuratively, "root out, eliminate, remove, excommunicate, or destroy by a violent act"[7]) and "wipe out" (NIV, NRSV), "destroy" (KJV, *shāmad*, "destroy, annihilate"[8]).

The seven descendants that the Gibeonites ask for aren't an exact retribution, and David decides to spare Mephibosheth and his descendants – thus keeping his covenant to Jonathan and his oath to Saul, since by sparing Mephibosheth, he maintains Saul's

---

[5] Seven is the most significant symbolic number in the Bible, appearing in nearly 600 passages. Seven is especially prominent in passages dealing with ritual observance and oath taking. Indeed, the Hebrew number seven (*šeba*) and the verb "swear, take an oath" (*šāba*) are etymologically related (Bruce C. Birch, "Number," ISBE 3:563). It seems to have some sense of totality or completeness.

[6] Anderson, *2 Samuel*, pp. 249-250.

[7] Elmer B. Smick, *kārat*, TWOT #1048.

[8] Herman J. Austel, *"shāmad*, TWOT #2406.

line from being completely eliminated. However, David designates two sons of Rizpah, Saul's concubine, and five of Saul's grandsons and turns them over to the Gibeonites to expiate for Saul's attempted genocide that breached the covenant.

The form of execution is not specified.[9] Whatever the method, afterward their bodies are left exposed on the hillside rather than buried as a sign of dishonor and punishment (1 Samuel 17:44; Psalm 79:2; Jeremiah 16:4). But to prevent jackals and vultures from tearing their corpses, Rizpah, mother of two of the men, protects them day and night until the longed-for rain finally comes down. When David hears of Rizpah's valiant act, he takes their bones and buries them with the bones of Saul and Jonathan, which were reburied with honor at this time.[10]

"After that," the narrator records, "God answered prayer in behalf of the land." (21:14b).

David Is Too Weak to Go to War (2 Samuel 21:15-17)

Now we come to the second element in this "aside" or "appendix." Though this incident is not set chronologically, I imagine that David is in his mid-60s by now (though some see this taking place earlier).[11] All his life, the Philistines have been a threat, except for a period when David's forces had utterly subdued them. Now they are probably beginning to raid the cities of Judah in the Shepelah or low hills to the west.

During Absalom's ascension to the throne and civil war, it is likely that vassals on the edges of the empire took advantage of Israel preoccupation with civil war. "The natives are restless." To maintain an empire of this type takes constant diplomacy as well as military vigilance.

Once David is firmly in control of Jerusalem again, his army is called out to meet them. Joab is commander, but David, who has been a warrior from his youth, doesn't want to miss the excitement of battle.

[9] "Killed" (NIV), "impaled" (NRSV), "hanged" (KJV) translate a rare Hebrew word, *yāqa'* (Paul R. Gilchrist, TWOT #903).

[10] We're not sure where Zela is located. It is one of 14 cities of Benjamin listed in Joshua 18:28, probably northwest of Jerusalem, perhaps at Khirbet Salah – we just don't know (William S. LaSor, "Zela," ISBE 4:1187).

[11] In my view, the incident of David being too weak to go to battle must have taken place after the Battle of the Forest of Ephraim when David's forces conquered Absalom's. In that case, when David wanted to go out with the men to battle, they tell him not to because he is the target of his opponents and is too vulnerable – not that he was too old. However, some commentators see the incident in 21:15-17 coming much earlier in David's life (Bergen, *1 and 2 Samuel*, pp. 448-449).

The forces come together in close combat. David's opponent is Ishbi-Benob, apparently a huge warrior descended from Rapha, part of a family of giants mentioned in 21:18-22, perhaps the Rephaim that had lived east of the Jordan (Deuteronomy 2:10, 20-21; 3:11).[12] Ishbi-Benob's bronze spearhead is massive – 7½ pounds! – but only half the weight of Goliath's iron spearhead (1 Samuel 17:7). David thinks he can defeat him, but he becomes exhausted during combat at close quarters with this formidable foe. The fatal blow is near. Just then, Abishai, Joab's brother, sees what is going on, steps in, and strikes down the giant. David is shaken, but untouched.

It is a wake-up call for both David and his men. After that, David's men swear a binding oath[13] to David:

> "Never again will you go out with us to battle, so that the lamp of Israel will not be extinguished." (21:17c)

David is more valuable to them as a living king, than as an aged but decapitated warrior. Emotionally, this is like forced retirement, like a person's children taking away their father's car because he can't drive safely any longer. Elderly people all over the world face this time of their lives. David was no exception.

The image of the "lamp of Israel" perhaps draws on the lampstand in the tabernacle (Exodus 27:20-21). We see the image later in the Bible with regard to David's descendants (1 Kings 11:36; 15:4; Psalm 132:17). The burning lamp also may be an image of life (Job 21:17; Proverbs 13:19; 20:20; 24:20).

Victories Over Renowned Philistine Warriors (2 Samuel 21:18-22)

The narrator takes this opportunity to recount other exploits of David's men over Philistine giants.

1. **Abishai** kills Ishbi-Benob (21:17), recounted above.

2. **Sibbecai the Hushathite** kills Saph (21:18).

3. **Elhanan** [perhaps a personal name for David] son of Jaare-Oregim the Bethlehemite kills Goliath the Gittite (21:19; cf. 1 Samuel 17).[14]

---

[12] P. K. McCarter, Jr., "Rephaim," ISBE 4:137; R.K. Harrison, "Giants," ISBE 2:460. McCarter suggests that this group could be a corps of elite warriors who are devotees of the Philistine god Rapha, or even "the corps of the scimitar" tracing its ancestry to the ancient Sea Peoples. We just don't know – but we do know that these warriors were of immense physical stature!

[13] "Swear" is *shāba'*, "swear, adjure, (Niphal stem) bind oneself by an oath," related closely to the Hebrew word for the number seven (TWOT #2319).

[14] Anderson (*2 Samuel*, p. 255, citing A.M. Honeyman, "The Evidence for Regnal Names among the Hebrews," JBL 67 (1948), pp. 23-24) suggests that Elhanan may be a personal name, while David is his

4. **Jonathan son of Shimeah**, David's brother, kills "a huge man with six fingers on each hand and six toes on each foot." R.K. Harrison notes:

> "People who exhibit gigantic stature usually have either genetic abnormalities or some disease. That 2 Samuel 21:20 mentions a giant who had six fingers on each hand and six toes on each foot seems to indicate that the individual concerned was the product of genetic mutation."[15]

We're not sure about the location of Gob, since there is an uncertainty concerning the original text.

David's Song of Praise (2 Samuel 22 = Psalm 18)

Next in our "appendix" or "aside" is a representative psalm from David, the premier songwriter of all time. The psalm is a relatively long song, nearly identical with Psalm 18 in the Psalter. Note the ascription:

> "David sang to the LORD the words of this song when the LORD delivered him from the hand of all his enemies and from the hand of Saul." (22:1)

David writes this psalm to commemorate the end of the constant stress and conflict that characterize his life for the five or six years he is a fugitive from Saul. Before you read it, let me explain a bit about Hebrew poetry. In English, we expect both rhyme and rhythm in song lyrics and poems – or did before the days of free verse. But Hebrew poetry is different; it has several distinctive features:

1. **Imagery**. Hebrew poetry often uses vivid images. In this psalm we see rock, fortress, stronghold, "waves of death" swirling, "cords of the grave" entangling one's feet, and so on. Don't expect to take this imagery literally. These images are figurative, used to bring thoughts and feelings to the fore. Psalms are designed to be read aloud and experienced, not just studied and analyzed.

2. **Parallelism**. We normally see two types of parallelism. Occasionally, we'll see antithetic parallelism, where the first line says the positive, while the second line says the same thing in a negative way (e.g. Psalm 1:6; 34:10; Proverbs 3:33). But much more common is so-called synonymous or synthetic parallelism, where the first line says it one way, and the second (and occasionally third line) says the same thing with a bit of variation, moving the idea forward slightly.

---

throne name. 1 Chronicles 20:5 names the victim as Lahmi, brother of Goliath the Gittite, perhaps harmonizing the two accounts.

[15] R.K. Harrison, "Giants," ISBE 2:460.

3. **Beat**. There are many theories about how the beat of a line worked, but Hebrew scholars don't really understand it very well.

4. **Acrostic**. Nine psalms in the Psalter (but neither of the two we examine in this lesson) are acrostic in nature, that is, each verse or section begins with a successive letter of the Hebrew alphabet (Psalms 9, 10, 25, 34, 37, 111, 112, 119, and 145).

Notice that in the psalm in our passage, "LORD" is prominent (16 times), rather than the generic word "God" (*el*, 10 times), usually as "my God" – the God he relates to personally. "LORD" (often expressed in small caps in our English Bibles) represents the Hebrew word *Adonai* that was substituted for the divine name when pious Jews read the Hebrew Scriptures, to keep them from breaking the Third Commandment and misusing God's revealed name: Yahweh (Exodus 20:7).

As you examine the following psalm, look for both the imagery and parallelism that are characteristic of Hebrew poetry. I've included some section titles to help you see the flow of David's thought. Now read it aloud, section by section. Hear your own voice say these mighty words of faith!

Praise to Yahweh My Rock (22:2-4)

David uses the language of natural rocky fastnesses, like those he inhabited in the Judean wilderness when Saul was chasing him.

> "2 The LORD is my rock,
> my fortress and my deliverer;
> 3 my God is my rock, in whom I take refuge,
> my shield and the horn of my salvation.
> He is my stronghold, my refuge and my savior –
> from violent men you save me.
> 4 I call to the LORD, who is worthy of praise,
> and I am saved from my enemies." (22:2-4)

My Desperate Need (22:5-6)

> "5 The waves of death swirled about me;
> the torrents of destruction overwhelmed me.
> 6 The cords of the grave coiled around me;
> the snares of death confronted me." (22:5-6)

What a wonderful description of the terrors of death! David uses the imagery of waves and waterfalls, of ropes and snares like those you'd use to trap a bird or animal.

My Prayer to Yahweh (22:7)

In his terror, David calls upon Yahweh, and from his Holy Place God hears.

"In my distress I called to the LORD;
I called out to my God.
From his temple he heard my voice;
my cry came to his ears." (22:7)

Yahweh's Awesome Response to My Prayer (22:8-12)

David's description of Yahweh's response to his prayer is graphic and filled with power. Whoever his opponents were, they didn't plan on confronting the Almighty God himself!

"8 The earth trembled and quaked,
the foundations of the heavens shook;
they trembled because he was angry.
9 Smoke rose from his nostrils;
consuming fire came from his mountain,
burning coals blazed out of it.
10 He parted the heavens and came down;
dark clouds were under his feet.
11 He mounted the cherubim and flew;
he soared on the wings of the wind.
12 He made darkness his canopy around him –
the dark rain clouds of the sky." (22:8-12)

Yahweh Confronts my Enemies (22:13-16)

Now these enemies are directly attacked by Yahweh's weapons – bolts of lightning, deafening thunder, and mighty wind.

"13 Out of the brightness of his presence bolts of lightning blazed forth.
14 The LORD thundered from heaven;
the voice of the Most High resounded.
15 He shot arrows and scattered [the enemies],
bolts of lightning and routed them.
16 The valleys of the sea were exposed
and the foundations of the earth laid bare
 at the rebuke of the LORD,
at the blast of breath from his nostrils." (22:13-16)

Yahweh Rescues Me (22:17-20)

Now David moves from the dramatic and poetic to the personal and intimate. He knows what it is to be rescued by Yahweh. He has faced Saul's 3,000-man army. He says that God personally reached down, took hold of him, and set him down in a "spacious place" that is free of danger. The reason? God's pure grace: "He delighted[16] in me." David is a man after God's own heart (1 Samuel 13:14; Acts 13:22). David has seen the awesome deliverance of Almighty God.

> "[17] He reached down from on high and took hold of me;
> he drew me out of deep waters.
> [18] He rescued[17] me from my powerful enemy,
> from my foes, who were too strong for me.
> [19] They confronted me in the day of my disaster,
> but the LORD was my support.
> [20] He brought me out into a spacious place;
> he rescued[18] me because he delighted in me." (22:17-20)

My Righteous Path before Yahweh (22:21-25)

This psalm is written before David's grievous sin in the matter of Bathsheba and Uriah. At this point, David understands that Yahweh has delivered him because of his care to live a righteous life. But, later, when David is blood-guilty, it is different. Then he had to rely solely on the mercy of God, just as we trust in the grace of God in the cross of Christ.[19] In Psalm 32 he understands this better:

> "Blessed is he whose transgressions are forgiven,
> whose sins are covered.
> Blessed is the man whose sin the LORD does not count against him
> and in whose spirit is no deceit." (Psalm 32:1-2)

Our psalm – written before David's great sin – continues:

---

[16] "Delighted" is *ḥāpēs*, "take delight in, be pleased with, desire." The basic meaning is to feel great favor towards something. Its meaning differs from the parallel roots, *ḥāmad*, *ḥāshaq*, and *rāṣâ*, in that they connote less emotional involvement (Leon J. Wood, *ḥāpēs*, TWOT #712).

[17] "Rescued" (NIV), "delivered" (NRSV, KJV) in verse 18 is *nāṣal*, "deliver, rescue, save." An Arabic cognate confirms the judgment that its basic physical sense is one of drawing out or pulling out. The Hiphil as here has the causative idea of "make separate," a physical snatching away or separating (Milton C. Fisher, *nāṣal*, TWOT #1404).

[18] "Rescued" (NIV), "delivered" (NRSV, KJV) in verse 20 is *ḥālaṣ*, in the Piel stem, "to rescue," found only in OT poetic material in Job, Psalms (16x), and Proverbs (Elmer B. Smick, *ḥālaṣ*, TWOT #667).

[19] Of course, David's definition of sin isn't nearly so inward and of the heart as Jesus taught. We know better the full infection of sin.

> "²¹ The LORD has dealt with me according to my righteousness;
> according to the cleanness of my hands he has rewarded me.
> ²² For I have kept the ways of the LORD;
> I have not done evil by turning from my God.
> ²³ All his laws are before me;
> I have not turned away from his decrees.
> ²⁴ I have been blameless before him
> and have kept myself from sin.
> ²⁵ The LORD has rewarded me according to my righteousness,
> according to my cleanness in his sight." (22:21-25)

Yahweh's Salvation for Those Who Trust Him (22:26-28)

> "²⁶ To the faithful you show yourself faithful,
> to the blameless you show yourself blameless,
> ²⁷ to the pure you show yourself pure,
> but to the crooked you show yourself shrewd.
> ²⁸ You save the humble,
> but your eyes are on the haughty to bring them low." (22:26-28)

To David's credit, when he does confess his sins, he seeks God from a "broken and contrite heart" (Psalm 51:17). His heart, once crooked, has been cleansed. He humbles himself, and so is saved.

With Yahweh I Can Do Anything (22:29-37)

Because David has experienced the God of miracle deliverance, he realizes that through Yahweh he can do anything. His trust in the Lord soars. His confidence isn't in himself, but in the Lord.

> "²⁹ You are my lamp, O LORD;
> the LORD turns my darkness into light.
> ³⁰ With your help I can advance against a troop;
> with my God I can scale a wall.
> ³¹ As for God, his way is perfect;
> the word of the LORD is flawless.
> He is a shield for all who take refuge in him.
> ³² For who is God besides the LORD?
> And who is the Rock except our God?
> ³³ It is God who arms me with strength
> and makes my way perfect.
> ³⁴ He makes my feet like the feet of a deer;
> he enables me to stand on the heights.

³⁵ He trains my hands for battle;
my arms can bend a bow of bronze.
³⁶ You give me your shield of victory;
you stoop down to make me great.
³⁷ You broaden the path beneath me,
so that my ankles do not turn." (22:29-37)

I Have Vanquished My Enemies (22:38-43)

After he praises the God who enables him, David explains how thoroughly he has vanquished his enemies. He probably isn't thinking of Saul here, but of the Amalekites and perhaps the Philistines.

"³⁸ I pursued my enemies and crushed them;
I did not turn back till they were destroyed.
³⁹ I crushed them completely,
and they could not rise;
they fell beneath my feet.
⁴⁰ You armed me with strength for battle;
you made my adversaries bow at my feet.
⁴¹ You made my enemies turn their backs in flight,
and I destroyed my foes.
⁴² They cried for help, but there was no one to save them –
to the LORD, but he did not answer.
⁴³ I beat them as fine as the dust of the earth;
I pounded and trampled them like mud in the streets. " (22:38-43)

Now I Rule over Nations (22:44-46)

David, who began as a humble shepherd, has become – through Yahweh's working – an emperor and "head of nations," with vassals subject to him, obeying his commands. He marvels at God's amazing power.

"⁴⁴ You have delivered me from the attacks of my people;
you have preserved me as the head of nations.
People I did not know are subject to me,
⁴⁵ and foreigners come cringing to me;
as soon as they hear me, they obey me.
⁴⁶ They all lose heart;
they come trembling from their strongholds." (22:44-46)

Praise Be to Yahweh Who Lives! (22:47-51)

David concludes the psalm with a personal note, with thanks to the God who has anointed him king and bestowed upon him an eternal dynasty, which, we know, culminates in Jesus the Messiah, the Son of God.

> "[47] The LORD lives! Praise be to my Rock!
> Exalted be God, the Rock, my Savior!
> [48] He is the God who avenges me,
> who puts the nations under me,
> [49] who sets me free from my enemies.
> You exalted me above my foes;
> from violent men you rescued me.
> [50] Therefore I will praise you,
> O LORD, among the nations;
> I will sing praises to your name.
> [51] He gives his king great victories;
> he shows unfailing kindness to his anointed,
> to David and his descendants forever." (22:47-51)

The psalm ends with praise for Yahweh who lives! I think of the gospel chorus that goes:

> "He lives, he lives!
> Christ Jesus lives today!"[20]

The Prophet Jeremiah writes,

> "The LORD is the true God;
> he is the living God,
> the eternal King." (Jeremiah 10:10)

Jesus said:

> "I am the Living One;
> I was dead,
> and behold I am alive for ever and ever!" (Revelation 1:18)

Hallelujah!

Q1. (2 Samuel 22 = Psalm 18) What do you find the most inspiring in the language of this psalm? What encourages you the most? Write down all the various titles and metaphors used of God in this psalm.
http://www.joyfulheart.com/forums/index.php?showtopic=1203

---

[20] "He Lives," words by Eleanor A. Schroll (1916), music by James H. Fillmore, Sr.

Last Words of David – a Psalm (2 Samuel 23:1-7)

The narrator and editor decides to place a short prophetic psalm here to sum up David's life and his role as the ideal king that successive kings should follow. It begins with a statement of the different roles God has assigned to David:

> "These are the last words of David:
> The oracle of David son of Jesse,
> the oracle of the man exalted by the Most High,
> the man anointed by the God of Jacob,
> Israel's singer of songs." (23:1)

David is represented here as:

1. **Prophet**. "Oracle," which appears twice in verse 1, is *ne'um*, "utterance, oracle," a root that is used exclusively of divine speaking.[21] He is also recognized elsewhere in the Bible as a prophet (1 Chronicles 28:19; Matthew 22:43; Acts 2:30; 4:25).

2. **Israelite**. He is the "son of Jesse." As a true Israelite, he is qualified to be king (Deuteronomy 17:15).

3. **Appointed**. He is a humble shepherd who has been "raised up" or "appointed" to this role[22] by God himself. David is "the king the LORD your God chooses" (Deuteronomy 17:15).

4. **Anointed**. He was anointed by Samuel, of course, but at the direction of "the God of Jacob." The Holy Spirit who comes upon him at his anointing is to change the course of his life. He is the ancestor of the Anointed One, the Messiah (Hebrew *māshîah*).

5. **Sweet Psalmist** (KJV). This phrase is made up of two words in Hebrew: *zāmîr*, "song"[23] and *nā'îm*, "pleasant, sweet, lovely, agreeable."[24] I prefer "Israel's beloved singer" (NIV margin) or "the sweet psalmist of Israel" (KJV).[25]

---

[21] Leonard J. Coppes, *ne'um*, TWOT #1272a.

[22] The NASB is to be preferred over the NIV here: "the man who was raised on high" "Exalted" (NIV, NRSV), "raised on high" (KJV) is two words. The first is the verb *qûm*, a root involved with the physical action of rising up. In the Hofal stem, it has a kind of passive, causative idea, "raised up." The verb has an official usage, applying to the assumption of a particular office, e.g. religious head of a clan, prophet, judge, etc. (Leonard J. Coppes, TWOT #1999). Here it carries this sense of "be appointed" (Holladay, p. 316). The second is the adverb *'al*, "above," so that it reads, "the oracle of the young man who was raised up highly" (G. Lloyd Carr, *'ālâ*, TWOT 1624p). The NIV's "the Most High" is unlikely, though possible (Anderson, *2 Samuel*, p. 268).

Now David almost marvels at the prophetic gift he has been given:

> "² The Spirit of the LORD spoke through me;
> his word was on my tongue.
> ³ The God of Israel spoke,
> the Rock of Israel said to me...." (23:2-3a)

To be used by the Great God of the Universe to fulfill His purposes is such a great and undeserved honor!

Now David comes to the main message of this prophetic word: the importance of ruling righteously, with respect to God and his will:

> "³ᵇ When one rules over men in righteousness,
> when he rules in the fear of God,
> ⁴ he is like the light of morning at sunrise on a cloudless morning,
> like the brightness after rain that brings the grass from the earth.'" (23:3b-4)

The leader who rules righteously and fears God will be like:

1. Light of morning at sunrise on a cloudless morning.

2. Brightness after rain that brings the grass from the earth.

The psalmist uses imagery and parallelism to paint a picture of the brightness and refreshing glory for a people that righteous government brings.

The center of this short psalm shows David's wonder at God's grace towards him and his descendants. God has justified David and made with him and his offspring a secure and everlasting covenant. God's promises are great! David is assured of God's blessing to fulfill those promises:

> "Will he not bring to fruition my salvation
> and grant me my every desire?" (23:5d)

In verses 6-7 he contrasts the righteous with evil men and unrighteous rulers, who, like thorns, are gathered and burned.

> "⁶ But evil men are all to be cast aside like thorns,
> which are not gathered with the hand.

---

[23] *Zāmîr*, "song," from the verb *zāmar*, "sing, sing praise, make music." It is cognate to Akkadian *zamāru* "to sing, play an instrument." It is used only in poetry, almost exclusively in Psalms. (Herbert Wolf, *zāmar*, TWOT #558b).

[24] Marvin R. Wilson, *nāʿîm*, TWOT #1384b.

[25] The NRSV's "the favorite of the Strong One of Israel" takes *zmr* as "strength" or "protection" (Anderson, *2 Samuel*, p. 268). I think this is a stretch!

> [7] Whoever touches thorns uses a tool of iron
> or the shaft of a spear;
> they are burned up where they lie." (23:6-7)

In this short psalm, we see in David a faith and wonder that characterizes his reign as well as his body of work in the Psalter. He praises God for His gracious prophetic Spirit, Yahweh's choice and anointing of him as king, for God's own righteousness, the God-given Davidic Covenant, and all that this Covenant will mean over the centuries to David and his descendants, and ultimately to the Son of David – and all whose lives the Messiah touches.

Q2. (2 Samuel 23:1-7) How does David describe himself in verse 1? In what sense was David a prophet? What is the main message of verses 3-7? How can this psalm guide government officials and elected leaders in our day?
http://www.joyfulheart.com/forums/index.php?showtopic=1204

Exploits of David's Mighty Men (2 Samuel 23:8-39)

We looked at some of David's mighty men in Lesson 4 above, in the context of him gathering his army of 600 men.

David's Census of Israel (2 Samuel 24:1-9)

The final element in this "appendix" or set of "asides" concerns an incident that probably took place during the mid-portion of David's reign, perhaps in the phase when David is sending troops to conquer enemies and put down threats to Israel's security by its neighbors. Ultimately, as we saw in Lesson 10, David's troops subdue a huge empire at the east end of the Mediterranean. But not without cost.

Notice how this account begins: with God's anger against Israel, and desire to punish them for their sins. Specifically what these sins these are, we aren't told.

> "The anger of the LORD burned against Israel, and he incited David against them, saying, 'Go and take a census of Israel and Judah.'" (24:1)

Curiously, the Chronicler attributes this provocation to Satan, not Yahweh (1 Chronicles 21:1). Perhaps these two authors are looking at two sides of the same coin, where God uses Satan's temptations to work his will.[26] Just as earlier, where "an evil spirit from the LORD tormented him" (1 Samuel 16:14-16), we know that sometimes God uses evil and evil people to bring about his own righteous ends – even if we can't understand it (e.g., 2 Corinthians 12:7; Isaiah 10:5). After all, we see this principle in the Davidic Covenant itself:

> "I will be his father,
> and he will be my son.
> When he does wrong, I will punish him with the rod of men,
> with floggings inflicted by men." (7:14)

The purpose of the census, David says, is to "enroll the fighting men, so that I may know how many there are" (24:2b). It seems to be a survey of potential military manpower available prior to a draft or conscription. Israel is expanding. It needs troops. What's wrong with that?

Strangely, impetuous Joab, who never lets rules get in his way when he wants to do something, is the one who warns the king against such an action:

> "May the LORD your God multiply the troops a hundred times over, and may the eyes of my lord the king see it. But why does my lord the king want to do such a thing?" (24:4)[27]

Joab knows the reason for the enrollment, but he is concerned about the result if they go through with it. However, David overrules Joab as well as his other generals, and orders the census.

The census took nearly ten months to complete. The result is 800,000 potential soldiers among the ten tribes of Israel, and an additional 500,000 in the tribe of Judah.[28]

---

[26] Davis observes (*Birth of a Kingdom*, p. 164), "Satan was the immediate cause of David's action, but, theologically speaking, God was the ultimate cause in that he did not prevent the incident from occurring."

[27] The Chronicler adds a theological element to Joab's appeal: "Why does my lord want to do this? Why should he bring guilt on Israel?" (1 Chronicles 21:3b).

[28] The Chronicler notes that Joab's men didn't number either the Levites or the Benjamites, and came up with a figure of 1.1 million total (1 Chronicles 21:5-7). Baldwin (*1 and 2 Samuel*, p. 296) comments, "The word 'thousand' is likely to be used here in its military sense, 'contingent' (cf. 1 Samuel 4:2). If this is so, the figure cannot be used with any accuracy as a basis for estimating Israel's population at the time of David."

What's Wrong with a Census?

We wonder what is wrong with taking this census. There are three basic explanations of what was sinful about conducting such a census. These are fairly complex, so bear with me.

1. Failure to collect the half-shekel tax. The traditional interpretation, beginning with Josephus,[29] is that the plague is a direct result of David's neglect to collect the appropriate half-shekel tax prescribed in the Torah, just as he had neglected to find out how the ark should be carried (6:7-8).[30] We read in Exodus:

> "Then the LORD said to Moses, 'When you take a census of the Israelites to count them, each one must pay the LORD **a ransom**[31] **for his life** at the time he is counted. Then no plague will come on them when you number them.'" (Exodus 30:11-12)

Then in Numbers 1:2-3, God tells Moses to undertake just such a permitted census for military purposes, with no adverse effect.

The idea behind the half-shekel ransom is redemption.[32] To use or possess something or someone that belongs to God, you must pay a redemption fee. We see this in the redemption of the firstborn son who belongs to the Lord (Exodus 13:2; 18:15-16). Some persons cannot be redeemed from their punishment at any price, such as a manslayer (Numbers 35:31-32).

Here, I think the sense is that every Israelite belongs to God. For the leader to number them in order to use them for the leader's purpose – especially to put their lives in possible jeopardy in military service – requires a redemption-fee from the owner.[33]

This redemption fee theory explains why David sins in not conducting the census properly (24:10) and why the punishment falls upon the people, who fail (unwittingly) to render the half-shekel when they are listed in the census (24:17).

---

[29] Josephus, *Antiquities*, 7.13.1.

[30] On this passage, E.A. Speiser comments: "Since nothing is said there about a *kofer*, one is justified in assuming that the omission of that precautionary measure was somehow linked with the subsequent plague" (E.A. Speiser, "Census and ritual expiation in Mari and Israel," BASOR 149 (1958), pp. 17-25, quote from p. 22).

[31] "Ransom" is *kōper*, "ransom, gift to secure favor," from *kāpar*, "make an atonement, make reconciliation" (R. Laird Harris, TWOT #1023a). Morris defines it as "ransom price ... the sum paid to redeem a forfeited life" (Leon Morris, *The Apostolic Preaching of the Cross* (Eerdmans, 1955), p. 17). Ultimately, the concept of redemption finds its fulfillment in Jesus who "gave his life a ransom for many" (Mark 10:45).

[32] Later this half-shekel temple tax was collected annually (Matthew 17:24).

[33] E.A. Speiser, who compared ancient cuneiform tablets from Mari with the Old Testament, observed: "Military conscription was an ominous process because it might place the life of the enrolled in jeopardy. The connection with the cosmic 'books' of life and death must have been much too close for one's peace of mind" ("Census and ritual," p. 24).

What it doesn't explain is Joab's strong opposition to the census. If he had opposed it because he knew from the Torah it would bring a plague, certainly David would have listened to him and collected the half-shekel during the census. But Joab isn't the spiritual man vs. David the practical man. It's the other way around.[34] Something else is involved as well.

2. Placing excessive burdens on the people. Some wonder whether the sin is that David is over-expanding the tribal militia in order to gain greater territory, and in the process, placing excessive burdens upon the people. We know that this was an unpopular practice of Solomon's, continued by his son Rehoboam with disastrous results (1 Kings 12:4, 10-11).

You'd think that Joab would be in favor of increasing the military, since it would increase his power. Perhaps "Joab and the army commanders" (24:4) oppose increasing the size of the tribal militia of volunteers at the expense of paying for regular troops. We don't know. However, Joab is a better judge of popular sentiment than David. He has saved David more than once (2 Samuel 19:7). The Chronicler includes one interesting detail that isn't found in 2 Samuel:

> "But Joab did not include Levi and Benjamin in the numbering, because the king's command was repulsive to him." (1 Chronicles 21:6)

It makes sense for the tribe of Levi to be excluded from combat because of their religious separation to Yahweh (Numbers 1:49; 2:33). But I expect that Joab is sensitive to Benjamin's simmering tribal resentments against David, because David had displaced Saul, the Benjamite king (2:15; 6:21; 16:5-11; 20:1; 21:1-14). That is why he disobeys David's orders and doesn't do the census in Benjamin. If people believe the king has placed excessive burdens on them, it will weaken David's hold on the kingdom.

This reason, however, doesn't explain why the plague comes upon Israel.

3. An attitude of pride and lack of trust. A final explanation – not found in the text – is that David's true sin is pride and lack of trust in Yahweh. Anderson comments:

> "The military nature of the census may, perhaps, imply that the reason for Yahweh's anger was David's lack of trust. The king and the people should not rely on their own

---

[34] On the other hand, the Chronicler tells us that Joab opposed the census on spiritual grounds: "Why should he bring guilt on Israel?" (1 Chronicles 21:3b). "Guilt" (NIV, NRSV), "cause of trespass" (KJV) is 'ashmâ, "be desolate, be guilty, to offend, to acknowledge offense, to trespass.... The primary meaning of the word 'āsham seems to center on guilt, but moves from the act which brings guilt to the condition of guilt to the act of punishment" (G. Herbert Livingston, 'ashmâ, TWOT #180).

strength, but they should depend upon Yahweh (1 Samuel 14:6; Isaiah 31:1). Yahweh can deliver his people and give them victory 'by many or by few' (1 Samuel 14:6)."[35]

This makes sense. We get the feeling that David has been corrupted by his power and luxury, and is increasingly out-of-touch with the common people. This leads to the arrogance of his seduction of Bathsheba and his murder of Uriah (11:1-27), and to Absalom being able to drive a wedge between him and his people (15:2-6).

The problem is that the text doesn't blame David for pride or lack of trust. This may be true, but it is our speculation. Nor does it explain why the plague fell on the people.

When it comes down to it, we in the twenty-first century have trouble making sense of this incident that took place 3,000 years ago. My own conclusion is:

1. The sin is taking the census without collecting the tax required by Torah. David's pride may have contributed to his blindness.
2. Joab resists the command to take the military census for military and political reasons, not because the plan doesn't conform to the Torah.
3. The bottom line is that Yahweh was angry with Israel's sins and seeks this cause to punish them.

Punishment for David's Sin (2 Samuel 24:10-15)

Whatever the reasons for the sin, after the census is complete, David realizes his sin. Perhaps the Lord speaks to him directly or through one of his court prophets.

> "David was conscience-stricken after he had counted the fighting men, and he said to the LORD, 'I have sinned greatly in what I have done. Now, O LORD, I beg you, take away the guilt of your servant. I have done a very foolish thing.'" (24:10)

David may have been blinded by his pride, but when God speaks to him he has a tender and repentant heart before the Lord.

Gad the prophet, David's seer, brings David a three-way choice from Yahweh concerning Israel's (not David's) punishment for this sin:

1. Three years of famine.
2. Three months of being pursued by their enemies.
3. Three days of plague.

David is ambivalent about the decision, but he chooses the third choice ultimately because he believes strongly in the mercy of his God.

---

[35] Anderson, *2 Samuel*, p. 284. So Baldwin, *1 and 2 Samuel*, pp. 294-295.

"'¹⁴ Let us fall into the hands of the LORD, for his mercy is great; but do not let me fall into the hands of men.' ¹⁵ So the LORD sent a plague on Israel from that morning until the end of the time designated, and seventy thousand of the people from Dan to Beersheba died." (24:14-15)

David Builds an Altar at the Threshing Floor of Araunah (2 Samuel 24:16-25)

Sometimes parents grieve over the punishment they must give to discipline their children. The plague ravages the entire land of Israel. Now it comes to the City of David itself.

> "When the angel stretched out his hand to destroy Jerusalem, the LORD was grieved because of the calamity and said to the angel who was afflicting the people, 'Enough! Withdraw your hand.' The angel of the LORD was then at the threshing floor of Araunah the Jebusite." (24:16)

David, too, is in deep grief over the suffering and death. He holds himself personally responsible!

> "When David saw the angel who was striking down the people, he said to the LORD, 'I am the one who has sinned and done wrong. These are but sheep. What have they done? Let your hand fall upon me and my family.'" (24:17)

One of the struggles of leadership is the knowledge that your decisions affect the destinies of all those under your care. And one of the facts of life is that leaders make mistakes and sin. Fallibility goes hand-in-hand with responsibility. There is no way out; being leaderless is usually worse!

God answers David's anguished prayer. He sends Gad and tells him:

> "Go up and build an altar to the LORD on the threshing floor of Araunah the Jebusite." (24:18)

Threshing was the process of removing the chaff and straw from the kernels of grain. The sheaves of grain would be brought to the threshing floor – a round, flat, hard-packed place where there were prevailing breezes. It was usually bordered by stones to keep in the grain. A heavy, animal-drawn sledge would be dragged round and round over the sheaves to physically separate the grain kernels from the husks that surround them. Then this mixture of wheat, chaff, and straw is winnowed, tossed in the air with a kind of pitchfork or winnowing fork, and later with a shovel.[36] Patch explains:

> "The light husks from the wheat and fine particles of straw are dispersed by the wind in the form of a fine dust; the heavier straw, which has been broken into short pieces by the threshing process, falls near at hand on the edge of the threshing floor, while the grain falls back upon the pile."[37]

Araunah is a Jebusite[38] farmer whose threshing floor is outside the walls of Jerusalem (at least at that point in history), on high ground where there would be a breeze. The Chronicler refers to this hill as Mount Moriah (2 Chronicles 3:1), apparently identifying it with the "the land of Moriah," where centuries before, Abraham had built an altar to sacrifice Isaac and Yahweh had provided a substitute (Genesis 22:2).

> "So Abraham called that place The LORD Will Provide [Jehovah-Jireh or Yahweh Yireh]. And to this day it is said, 'On the mountain of the LORD it will be provided.'" (Genesis 22:14)

(Interestingly, Yahweh provides a sacrifice again on Mount Moriah in the form of Araunah's oxen—though this time David pays for it.) We're also told that this is the location where Solomon's temple was later built (2 Chronicles 3:1).

When David climbs the hill, he sees Araunah there, who prostrates himself before the king. Then David explains his errand:

> "'21b To buy your threshing floor,' David answered, 'so I can build an altar to the LORD, that the plague on the people may be stopped.' 22 Araunah said to David, 'Let my lord the king take whatever pleases him and offer it up. Here are oxen for the burnt offering, and here are threshing sledges and ox yokes for the wood. 23a O king, Araunah gives all this to the king.'" (24:21b-23)

When the king who has conquered your city asks for something, you give it to him without question, if you want to stay alive – or so Araunah probably thinks. Araunah voices his own desire that David's sacrifice will be successful in stopping the plague: "May the LORD your God accept you" (24:23b). The wording suggests that Yahweh is David's God, but perhaps not yet Araunah's.

---

[36] L.G. Herr, "Winnowing," ISBE 4:1073; L.G. Herr, "Thresh, Threshing," ISBE 4:844.

[37] James A. Patch, "Chaff," ISBE 1:629.

[38] As we discussed in Lesson 7, the Jebusites who had previously controlled Jerusalem were not destroyed, but continued to live in the area around the city.

David explains that he didn't come to take the site by royal edit or eminent domain.

> "'24 No, I insist on paying you for it. I will not sacrifice to the LORD my God burnt offerings that cost me nothing.' So David bought the threshing floor and the oxen and paid fifty shekels of silver for them. David built an altar to the LORD there and sacrificed burnt offerings and fellowship offerings. Then the LORD answered prayer in behalf of the land, and the plague on Israel was stopped."(2 Samuel 24:24-25)

I've often reflected on David's reason for paying for the sacrifice – even though it was offered free.

> "I will not sacrifice to the LORD my God burnt offerings that cost me nothing." (24:24a)

When we give our tithes and offerings to the Lord, do we bring just a pittance. Or do we bring enough to actually cost us something? Is our tithe a mere token or a true piece of us?

It's interesting to see David here not only as king but as priest. It's possible, of course, that the priests actually offered the sacrifices at David's command, but they're not mentioned. Rather, like his ancestor Abraham on Mount Moriah, it's possible that David personally builds the altar, prepares the sacrifice, and intercedes for his nation.

> "David built an altar to the LORD there and sacrificed burnt offerings and fellowship offerings. Then the LORD answered prayer in behalf of the land, and the plague on Israel was stopped." (24:25)

In 2 Samuel, David is seen as prophet (23:1-2), a priest,[39] and a king – roles which the Son of David will bring to glorious completion in the cross and at his coming!

This incident teaches us several things about God and about David. God must punish his people when they sin, but desires to show mercy. Anderson says,

> "David is portrayed as a man who is capable of making mistakes and who sins greatly, yet, at the same time, he is concerned for the welfare of his people and knows how to repent."[40]

This is how 2 Samuel concludes, with David the repentant king offering sacrifices to the Lord on what will become the temple mount.

---

[39] When the ark was brought to Jerusalem, David, dressed in a priest's ephod (6:14), offered burnt offerings and fellowship offerings, and blessed the people in the name of the Lord (6:17-18). However, Saul was reprimanded for not waiting for Samuel, but going ahead and offering burnt offerings and fellowship offerings himself (1 Samuel 13:9-10).

[40] Anderson, 2 Samuel, p. 287.

Q3. (2 Samuel 24:14-25) Why does David choose the punishment of a plague on the people rather than his other choices? David insists on paying Araunah for the threshing floor and the sacrifices. What principle drives this decision? How should this principle guide our own giving to God?

http://www.joyfulheart.com/forums/index.php?showtopic=1205

David's Longing to Build the Temple

It seems, however, that following David's purchase of the threshing floor of Araunah, his passion to build the temple begins to increase. The Chronicler tells us that at this time David announces:

> "The house of the LORD God is to be here, and also the altar of burnt offering for Israel." (1 Chronicles 22:1)

Even though David knows that God doesn't want *him* to build the temple, he starts making preparations. It is also at this time that David begins to focus on his son Solomon to succeed him as king, even though Adonijah is the next oldest son (after the death of Absalom) in line to be king. Apparently, David makes no secret of which son he desires to succeed him. He announces:

> "Of all my sons – and the LORD has given me many – he has chosen my son Solomon to sit on the throne of the kingdom of the LORD over Israel." (1 Chronicles 28:5)

Chronicles records a conversation David had with his son Solomon regarding the temple:

> "7 My son, I had it in my heart to build a house for the Name of the LORD my God. 8 But this word of the LORD came to me: 'You have shed much blood and have fought many wars. You are not to build a house for my Name, because **you have shed much blood on the earth in my sight**. 9 But you will have a son who will be a man of peace and rest, and I will give him rest from all his enemies on every side. His name will be Solomon, and I will grant Israel peace and quiet during his reign. 10 He is the one who will build a house for my Name....'
>
> 11 Now, my son, the LORD be with you, and may you have success and build the house of the LORD your God, as he said you would.... 14 I have taken great pains to provide for the temple of the LORD a hundred thousand talents of gold, a million talents of silver, quantities of bronze and iron too great to be weighed, and wood and stone...."

¹⁹ Now devote your heart and soul to seeking the LORD your God. Begin to build the sanctuary of the LORD God, so that you may bring the ark of the covenant of the LORD and the sacred articles belonging to God into the temple that will be built for the Name of the LORD." (1 Chronicles 22:7-10, 11, 14, 19)

David also conducts a fundraising program among the leaders. First, he sets the example by generous giving. Then he calls on leaders of families, officers of the tribes, military commanders, and members of his court to give. He asks,

"Now, who is willing to consecrate himself today to the LORD?" (1 Chronicles 29:5b)

The Chronicler records that they give huge amounts of gold, silver, bronze, and iron for the project, as well as precious stones. The generous example of the leaders, in turn, encourages the people of Israel.

"The people rejoiced at the willing response of their leaders, for they had given freely and wholeheartedly to the LORD. David the king also rejoiced greatly." (1 Chronicles 29: 9)

Under the guidance of the Holy Spirit, David also prepares architectural drawings for the entire temple complex.

"¹¹ Then David gave his son Solomon the **plans** for the portico of the temple, its buildings, its storerooms, its upper parts, its inner rooms and the place of atonement. ¹² He gave him the **plans of all that the Spirit had put in his mind** for the courts of the temple of the LORD and all the surrounding rooms, for the treasuries of the temple of God and for the treasuries for the dedicated things."

¹⁹ "All this," David said, **"I have in writing from the hand of the LORD upon me, and he gave me understanding in all the details of the plan."** 1 Chronicles 28:11-12, 19)

David purchased the temple site (2 Chronicles 22:1) and stockpiled a huge supply of expensive raw materials – as well as cut and dressed stones (1 Chronicles 22:2) – so that Solomon would have it when he began to build, rather than have to take the time and money to assemble all this later.

In addition, David develops the "order of worship" for the temple. In the Torah, the Levites' main duties were for setting up, taking down, and moving the tabernacle. But with a sedentary tabernacle or temple, they didn't have much to do. David reorganized the Levites to supervise the construction of the temple, to be officials and judges in the kingdom, gatekeepers, temple treasurers, singers, and musicians (2 Chronicles 23:2-5 and chapters 24-26).

In addition, he writes psalms that make up much of the music that is sung and played during worship, first in the tent he pitched for the ark, and later for use in the temple itself.

All this probably took place while David is strong and healthy enough to get around and supervise the preparations.

We call the resulting structure "Solomon's Temple," but in large part it is David's pet project that Solomon constructed after David's death. It could well be called "David's Temple."

Q4. (1 Chronicles 22-29) Why do you think David prepares for the temple, even after the Lord refuses to let him build it? How did David cooperate with the Holy Spirit in designing the temple and its worship? How did David's example in giving motivate others to give?
http://www.joyfulheart.com/forums/index.php?showtopic=1206

Abishag the Shunammite (1 Kings 1:1-4)

We turn now to the first two chapters of 1 Kings to complete David's story. In the original Hebrew Bible, 1 and 2 Samuel were considered to be a part of 1 and 2 Kings, so our continuation of David's story is appropriate here.

The narrator moves from a series of appendices or asides that aren't dated back to a chronological account. We fast forward to David's last year or two of life. The picture that emerges from 1 Kings 1 is of a feeble king who has largely retreated from the power of the palace.

> "¹ When King David was old and well advanced in years, he could not keep warm even when they put covers over him. ² So his servants said to him, 'Let us look for a young virgin to attend the king and take care of him. She can lie beside him so that our lord the king may keep warm.'
>
> ³ Then they searched throughout Israel for a beautiful girl and found Abishag, a Shunammite, and brought her to the king. ⁴ The girl was very beautiful; she took care of the king and waited on him, but the king had no intimate relations with her." (1 Kings 1:1-4)

To us it seems pretty bizarre to find a young teenage girl to sleep with an old king to keep him warm. We're far removed from the world of wealthy kings and their harems; we use electric blankets! There are various speculations about the reason that a beautiful virgin is sought for David. Was this planned as a way to revive his sexual desire as well as provide a warm body next to him?[41] We don't know. However, the narrator is seeking to make the reader aware of David's declining health, as well as introduce Abishag, who plays a role early in Solomon's reign (2:13-25).

David is now old and isolated from everyday court life. The result is a power vacuum and the question of "Who will succeed David?" is on everyone's mind. They know David's preference, but he is weak and out-of-touch.

The Problem of Succession

Like many surrounding nations, Israel seemed to view the kingship as the right of the oldest son of the current king. By this time, David's oldest sons are dead. Here are David's sons:

Son	Mother	Birthplace	Status
Amnon	Ahinoam of Jezreel	Hebron	Murdered by Absalom.
Kileab / Chileab	Abigail, widow of Nabal	Hebron	No further mention, probably died young.
Absalom	Machaah of Geshur	Hebron	Rebels against David, killed in battle.
Adonijah	Haggith	Hebron	Seeks to be crowned king, executed by Solomon for treason.
Shephatiah	Abital	Hebron	No further mention in Old Testament.
Ithream	Eglah	Hebron[42]	No further mention.

---

[41] "This is usually interpreted as a medical prescription, for contact with a young, warm, and fresh body could revive the king" ... "A reasonable explanation is that Abishag was introduced to the court, not merely for medicinal purposes, but was taken into David's harem in an attempt to rejuvenate him and to test his potency. The king's authority and the well-being of his people depended on his virility (so Gray, p. 77, with reference to Ras shamra, where a king's sickness disqualified him from reigning).... It was therefore time to appoint a co-regent to exercise authority on his behalf; Adonijah took it as a sign to take the throne" (Jones, *1 and 2 Kings*, 1:89-90).

[42] 2 Samuel 3:2-5; 1 Chronicles 3:1-3.

Son	Mother	Birthplace	Status
Solomon	Bathsheba[43]	Jerusalem	Succeeds David as king
Shammua	Bathsheba	Jerusalem	No further mention.
Shobab	Bathsheba	Jerusalem	No further mention.
Nathan[44]	Bathsheba	Jerusalem	No further mention.
Ibhar, Elishua, Elpelet, Nogah, Nepheg, Japhia, Elishama, Eliada and Eliphelet[45]	unknown	Jerusalem	No further mention.

We aren't told a great deal about David's relationship with his sons – except for Solomon. Apparently, Bathsheba becomes David's favorite wife – at least his most fertile wife; she bears him four or five sons. The narrator seems to indicate that Solomon is born to Bathsheba next after her firstborn who died (12:24).

From Solomon's birth, it was obvious that he was a special child. The narrator tells us:

> "The LORD loved him; and because the LORD loved him, he sent word through Nathan the prophet to name him Jedidiah." (2 Samuel 12:24b-25)

This doesn't mean that Yahweh didn't love David's other sons, but that Solomon was the special recipient of Yahweh's favor. Solomon must have been a precocious child, as later he is known far and wide for his wisdom (1 Kings 3:7-15; 4:29-34). He is probably quite mature for his age. He also loves literature – proverbs and songs – and has a deep understanding of natural history.

As Solomon grows, David clearly views him as his successor. Though he isn't as old as David's sons born to him in Hebron, he has publicly selected Solomon (1 Chronicles 28:5) and he had sworn to Bathsheba an oath:

> "Surely Solomon your son shall be king after me, and he will sit on my throne." (1 Kings 1:13).

---

[43] 1 Chronicles 3:5.
[44] Mentioned in genealogy in Luke 3:31.
[45] 1 Chronicles 3:6-8; 14:4-7.

Adonijah Sets Himself Up as King (2 Kings 1:5-10)

David's selection of Solomon, however, must have rankled Adonijah, David's oldest living son – and he has some powerful supporters. By the last year of David's life, Adonijah is in the prime of *his* life at about 35 years of age, while Solomon is an inexperienced young man of 21 or 22.

David is near death. Though his succession plans are widely known, he has neglected to take any steps for Solomon's coronation as co-regent.

Adonijah sees David's isolation and Solomon's youth as his advantage. He makes up his mind that he will become king no matter what his father's intentions are. So he adopts some of the same pomp and glory that had helped his brother Absalom become king. He gets a chariot and horses to carry him, with a 50-man bodyguard to run ahead of him as he travels through the city.

Next, Adonijah lines up some of the most powerful people in his kingdom to support him.

Adonijah's Supporters	Solomon's Supporters
Joab, David's overall military commander, over the national militia drawn from the 12 tribes.	**Benaiah**, over the David's professional mercenaries, the Gittites, Pelethites, and Kerethites.[46]
Abiathar the high priest	**Zadok** the high priest
	Nathan the prophet
	Shimei[47] **and Rei,** royal officers otherwise unknown to us.

Just as Absalom had begun his reign by inviting leading men and the royal family to a sacrifice and feast, so does Adonijah. Though instead of travelling to Hebron like Absalom, he goes only a bit outside the city to En Rogel.

En Rogel ("spring of Rogel") is a natural spring, probably near the present-day Bîr Ayyûb ("Job's Well"), where Jerusalem's two deep valleys, the Kidron and the Hinnom come together.[48] It is outside the walls of Zion, down in the valley a few hundred feet south of the fortress, within earshot of the city.

---

[46] 2 Samuel 20:23.
[47] Josephus (*Antiquities* 14.3.4) refers to him as "David's friend." Otherwise, he and Rei are unknown to us.
[48] Paul Leslie Garber, "En Rogel," ISBE 2:104.

"⁹ Adonijah then sacrificed sheep, cattle and fattened calves at the Stone of Zoheleth⁴⁹ near En Rogel. He invited all his brothers, the king's sons, and all the men of Judah who were royal officials, ¹⁰ but he did not invite Nathan the prophet or Benaiah or the special guard or his brother Solomon." (1 Kings 1:9-10)

Adonijah's plan is to be acclaimed king so that his ascension to the throne is accepted as fact by Israel, before Solomon's supporters can stop him. There's a saying that "possession is 9/10ths of the law." If he is seen as the reigning king at the time David dies, it will be viewed as a *fait accompli*, an accomplished fact. He almost succeeds.

Bathsheba and Nathan Appeal to David for Solomon (1 Kings 1:11-28)

Nathan had always known of the Lord's special love for Solomon. Indeed, the message naming Solomon as "Jedidiah" ("loved of the Lord") had come through Nathan. So when he hears that Adonijah is making immediate plans to be crowned king, he takes action by notifying Solomon's mother, who is on good terms with the aged king.

He realizes that if Adonijah succeeds in being recognized king, that Adonijah will kill Solomon, Yahweh's choice. So he conspires with Bathsheba to bring this to the attention to the king in his bedroom. They're not even sure that David remembers his promises.

As I write this, I am ministering to a 90-year-old retired pastor who has become increasingly bed-ridden and weak as he succumbs to prostate cancer. Family decisions are being turned over to his daughter who is caring for him. But when he needs to, he can be firm and decisive. Often, however, it seems like too much trouble at this stage. He can barely speak loud enough to be heard. Perhaps David is something like this.

Bathsheba enters David's bedchamber, informs him of what Adonijah is doing, reminds him of his promise to place Solomon on the throne, and tells him that he must take action immediately, or at his death she and Solomon will be killed.

Now, according to plan, Nathan enters the dying king's bedchamber to reinforce Bathsheba's words. He concludes with a question designed to arouse the king to action:

"Is this something my lord the king has done without letting his servants know who should sit on the throne of my lord the king after him?" (1 Kings 1:27)

---

⁴⁹ The Stone of Zoheleth or Serpent's Stone probably had some kind of sacred history that made it a suitable place for a sacrifice. This stone may be ez-Zehwêleh, a rocky outcrop in the village of Siloam (Ernest W.G. Masterman, "Serpent's Stone," ISBE 4:419).

David Confirms Solomon's Succession to the Throne (1 Kings 1:28-37)

By this time, David is alert and engaged. He realizes that his plan for Solomon is about to be thwarted by Solomon's older brother Adonijah. "David the Decisive" is back! He calls Bathsheba back into his bedchamber and swears an oath.

> "As surely as the LORD lives, who has delivered me out of every trouble, I will surely carry out today what I swore to you by the LORD, the God of Israel: Solomon your son shall be king after me, and he will sit on my throne in my place." (1 Kings 1:29)

Then David calls for three key supporters who are still loyal: Zadok the priest, Nathan the prophet, and Benaiah, leader of the king's mercenary troops. When they arrive he gives the order to anoint Solomon as king at the *other* spring, closest to the city, the Gihon spring.

> "Take your lord's servants with you and set Solomon my son on my own mule and take him down to Gihon. 34 There have Zadok the priest and Nathan the prophet anoint him king over Israel. Blow the trumpet and shout, 'Long live King Solomon!' 35 Then you are to go up with him, and he is to come and sit on my throne and reign in my place. I have appointed him ruler over Israel and Judah." (1 Kings 1:34-36)

The Chronicler writes:

> "When David was old and full of years, he made his son Solomon king over Israel." (1 Chronicles 23:1)

Solomon Is Anointed King (1 Kings 1:38-40)

While Adonijah's guests are finishing their feast a short distance south of the city, Solomon is being made king by Nathan the prophet, the old and honored prophet of Yahweh. Zadok is anointing him with sacred oil. The people have followed the procession down the hill from the city and, when the trumpet is sounded to herald the event, they begin to shout, "Long live King Solomon." A great rejoicing begins among the people of the city – all while their great leaders are attending a small, elite feast nearby.

Adonijah Seeks Refuge at the Altar (1 Kings 1:41-53)

Oops. The elite gathering hears the sound and the shouting and the priest's son brings the news, "Our lord King David has made Solomon king." Solomon's public *fait accompli* trumps Adonijah's private one. Now Solomon is sitting on the royal throne receiving the congratulations from all. And David, on his bed, is bowing in worship before Yahweh:

"Praise be to the LORD, the God of Israel, who has allowed my eyes to see a successor on my throne today." (1 Kings 1:48)

Adonijah's feast becomes a rout. "At this, all Adonijah's guests rose in alarm and dispersed." They are now in danger for their lives as supporters of the wrong king. Adonijah, in mortal fear, "went and took hold of the horns of the altar."

Altars in the ancient Near East were built with horns or projections on each corner (Exodus 27:2). Archeologists have found examples of altars constructed this way at Megiddo and Gezer. Since the blood of the sacrifice was put on these horns (Exodus 29:12; Leviticus 4:25, 30; 8:15; 9:9), they were considered most sacred of all (cf. Amos 3:14). Seeking refuge from an avenger of blood at the altar was an ancient law (Exodus 21:12-14). Seeking refuge in this way protected the alleged offender from being killed until a proper trial could be held to determine his guilt or appeal his case (1 Kings 2:28).

When Solomon is told that Adonijah has sought refuge at the altar, Solomon promises not to kill him unless he shows any further evidence of rebellion. Solomon begins his reign with grace.

David's Charge to Solomon (1 Kings 2:1-4)

David is dying. When Solomon comes to his bedside, David gives him a fatherly exhortation, calling him of observe Yahweh's law, and repeating to him the word and promises that he had received in the Davidic Covenant (2 Samuel 7).

> "[2] I am about to go the way of all the earth. So be strong, show yourself a man, [3] and observe what the LORD your God requires: Walk in his ways, and keep his decrees and commands, his laws and requirements, as written in the Law of Moses, so that you may prosper in all you do and wherever you go, [4] and that the LORD may keep his promise to me: 'If your descendants watch how they live, and if they walk faithfully before me with all their heart and soul, you will never fail to have a man on the throne of Israel.'" (1 Kings 2:2-4)

David Instructs Solomon Regarding Joab, Barzillai, and Shimei (1 Kings 2:5-9)

Now David commands Solomon to do some unfinished business that David could not deal with himself for one reason or another.

1. **Joab** is to be executed for the bloodguilt of murdering Abner (2 Samuel 3:27) and Amasa (2 Samuel 20:10).

2. **Barzillai's sons**, offspring of the wealthy man who helped him during his exile in Mahanaim (2 Samuel 17:27; 19:31-39), are to be honored at Solomon's table.

3. **Shimei**, the Benjamite who had cursed him as he fled from Jerusalem (2 Samuel 16:9-13), is to be executed.

I'm not sure why Joab wasn't executed for his crimes sooner. Perhaps it was because he was David's kinsman, or perhaps because he was second in the kingdom, in charge of the army. At any rate, in backing Adonijah rather than Solomon, he has lost his position and is now vulnerable.

David's had sworn an oath not to punish Shimei when David had returned from exile (2 Samuel 19:23), but Solomon is bound by no such oath.

David Dies (2 Kings 2:10-12 and 1 Chronicles 29:26-30)

Both 1 Kings and 1 Chronicles mention David's death with a kind of epitaph. The Chronicler includes a bit fuller statement:

> "[26] David son of Jesse was king over all Israel. [27] He ruled over Israel forty years – seven in Hebron and thirty-three in Jerusalem. [28] He died at a good old age, having enjoyed long life, wealth and honor. His son Solomon succeeded him as king. [29] As for the events of King David's reign, from beginning to end, they are written in the records of Samuel the seer, the records of Nathan the prophet and the records of Gad the seer, [30] together with the details of his reign and power, and the circumstances that surrounded him and Israel and the kingdoms of all the other lands." (1 Chronicles 29:26-30)

The Chronicler explains that prophets who were close to David left records that detail the events of David's reign. Of course, these source documents are no longer extant.

Adonijah, Joab, and Shimei Are Executed (2 Kings 2:13-46)

The life of David has ended. Now Solomon acts to tie up the loose ends.

Adonijah makes a request through Bathsheba, Solomon's mother, to marry Abishag, David's concubine, who had served him in his last days and remains a virgin. Bathsheba agrees to relay the request to Solomon. She isn't advocating for Adonijah, her son's arch rival. She probably knows that when Solomon hears the request, Adonijah will be executed, and her and her son's place will finally be secure.

When Solomon hears the request, "Let Abishag the Shunammite be given in marriage to your brother Adonijah" (1 Kings 2:21), he is enraged.

> "Why do you request Abishag the Shunammite for Adonijah? You might as well request the kingdom for him – after all, he is my older brother – yes, for him and for Abiathar the priest and Joab son of Zeruiah!" (1 Kings 2:22)

Solomon knows that such a request – to marry the king's concubine – is tantamount in that culture to making a new claim to the throne. Solomon recognizes this as a plot that comes from Adonijah's supporters Joab and Abiathar. Solomon executes Adonijah for treason and orders Abiathar the priest to his home, away from the power center of Jerusalem. He has yet to deal with Joab.

When Joab hears that Adonijah has been executed, he realizes his own life is in danger too, since he is a co-conspirator. He flees to the tent and takes hold of the horns of the altar. When he refuses to leave, Solomon gives orders to have him killed on the spot.

Then Solomon officially puts Benaiah over the army in Joab's place, and replaces Abiathar with Zadok as high priest.

Finally, Solomon puts Shimei under house arrest. If he leaves Jerusalem, he will be executed. When Shimei finally ventures out of the city, Solomon gives the order for his execution too.

Solomon has now fulfilled David's final instructions. The new king's enemies are gone and Solomon has developed a reputation for dealing decisively with his enemies. The narrator says:

> "The kingdom was now firmly established in Solomon's hands." (1 Kings 2: 46b)

Discipleship Lessons

There are a several lessons in these last chapters describing David's life.

1. **Difficult Decisions**. It's hard to know what to make of the incident where the Gibeonites demand justice. David seeks the Lord, the does his best to walk a tightrope between covenants, promises, and law. Some situations that leaders face have no great solutions at all. We can't hide from making decisions, even though the decisions may leave no one happy.

2. **Time to Step Back**. David's men finally prohibited David from going out to battle with his troops, because he was too weak. Knowing when to retire or step back from active work or ministry is difficult for us. Often our friends and family know better than we. We need to listen.

3. **Praise and Faith**. There are many lessons contained within 2 Samuel 22 = Psalm 18. These are lessons of praise, of faith, of God's great power, of righteous living, and of salvation to those who trust in God. We need to learn to praise God with a vision of faith no matter what we are going though.

4. **Leading Righteously**. David's "Last Words" remind us of the importance of ruling righteously. You may not be a king, but you may be a boss, a supervisor, a church officer, or on a board or committee that makes decision affecting the lives

of others. God expects you to lead with righteousness, rather than with self-serving or partiality.

5. **Trusting in God's Grace**. In the incident of the census, David has to make a decision about which penalty God will bring on the people. Though we don't normally have a clear choice as leaders, we see that David makes his choice based on his strong trust in the mercy of God. Trusting in God's mercy when we don't deserve anything but punishment is a good example for us to follow.

6. **Sacrificial Giving**. When David is offered a ready-made sacrifice for free, he refuses to take it without paying because he understands the principle of sacrificial giving: "I will not sacrifice to the Lord my God burnt offerings that cost me nothing." If our giving is just a token or a pittance, where we could afford more, it doesn't honor God.

7. **Preparing for the Future**. David spends much of his later years in stockpiling materials for the temple that he knows won't be built in his lifetime. As Paul says,

   "So neither the one who plants nor the one who waters is anything, but only God who gives the growth. The one who plants and the one who waters have a common purpose, and each will receive wages according to the labor of each." (1 Corinthians 3:7-8)

   If we focus only on short-term goals, we short-change the future.

8. **Participants with the Sovereign God**. It is God's plan to put Solomon on the throne rather than Adonijah. To accomplish His will, God uses some leaders who believe the prophetic vision concerning Solomon's reign: Nathan, Benaiah, Zadok, Shimei, and Rei. God may well be using you to accomplish His will in your community. Will you be faithful to the vision God has given, even though it is risky?

David's Place in History

David holds a unique place in Bible history. Though he isn't the first king, he is the ideal king during the golden days of Israel's history. That alone makes him memorable.

But David leaves us a vast body of poetic literature – songs and psalms from David's heart to the heart of God – that inspire us and lift us up. He is the singer-songwriter par excellence, the "sweet psalmist of Israel."

He is the man after God's own heart, who, though he sins greatly, never leaves the God he loves. We can identify with his struggles – even with the depths of his depression. But we are encouraged in our faith as we see how he reaches out to God afresh.

The Apostle Paul sums up David's greatness in a single sentence (Acts 13:36a):

"David ... served God's purpose in his own generation." (NIV, NRSV)

"David ... served his own generation by the will of God." (KJV)

God calls on you and me to do the same!

No doubt, David is best known for his descendant, the Son of David, Jesus of Nazareth. David was the ideal king. Jesus is the Messiah who comes to set up the kingdom of God on earth.

As you've studied David's life, I hope you've observed again and again his intensely personal connection to Yahweh. He takes time to pray, to get his bearings, and to seek God's guidance instead of merely reacting to circumstances. He is close to God. Dear friend, it is my prayer that, like David, you too will reach out to God through Jesus Christ. He loves you and He died for you, to forgive you where you have sinned.

May the anointing of Spirit of God, who is the secret to David's life, be powerful in your life as well!

Prayer

Father, thank you for the example of David. As we've pondered his life these last thirteen weeks, we've grown to appreciate him more. Help us to learn from his strengths and his weaknesses. And draw us closer to David's God and our Savior, Jesus Christ the Lord. In his name, we pray. Amen.

Key Verses

"Never again will you go out with us to battle, so that the lamp of Israel will not be extinguished." (2 Samuel 21:17c)

"2 The LORD is my rock,
my fortress and my deliverer;
3 my God is my rock, in whom I take refuge,
my shield and the horn of my salvation.
He is my stronghold, my refuge and my savior –
from violent men you save me.
4 I call to the LORD, who is worthy of praise,
and I am saved from my enemies." (1 Samuel 22:2-4)

"[2] The Spirit of the LORD spoke through me;
his word was on my tongue.
[3] The God of Israel spoke,
the Rock of Israel said to me...." (2 Samuel 23:2-3a)

"Let us fall into the hands of the LORD, for his mercy is great; but do not let me fall into the hands of men." (2 Samuel 24:14)

"When David saw the angel who was striking down the people, he said to the LORD, 'I am the one who has sinned and done wrong. These are but sheep. What have they done? Let your hand fall upon me and my family.'" (2 Samuel 24:17)

"I will not sacrifice to the LORD my God burnt offerings that cost me nothing." (2 Samuel 24:24a)

"As surely as the LORD lives, who has delivered me out of every trouble, I will surely carry out today what I swore to you by the LORD, the God of Israel: Solomon your son shall be king after me, and he will sit on my throne in my place." (1 Kings 1:29-30)

"Praise be to the LORD, the God of Israel, who has allowed my eyes to see a successor on my throne today." (1 Kings 1:48)

Appendix 1. Genealogy of the Priesthood in David's Time

Genealogy of the Priests in David's Time

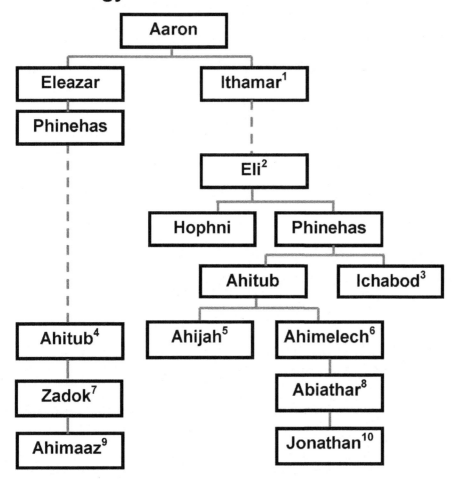

[1] Ithamar. 1 Chronicles 24:1-6

[2] Eli was high priest when Samuel was born and helped raise him (1 Samuel 1-4).

[3] Ichabod, which means, "The glory has departed from Israel" (1 Samuel 1:21).

[4] Ahitub. 1 Chronicles 6:7-8; 18:16; 2 Samuel 8:17; Ezra 7:2.

[5] Ahijah is the son of Ahitub, son of Phinehas, son of Eli (1 Samuel 14:3, 18). Perhaps he is the same person as Ahimelech.

[6] Zadok. 2 Samuel 8:17; 15:24-36; 17:15; 18:19; 1 Kings 1:8, 26-39; 2:35. According to Josephus (Antiquities 8.1.3), Eli (of the house of Ithamar) was given the high priesthood when it was removed from Abishua (of the house of Eleazer). When Abiathar was deposed by Solomon, the priesthood returned to the house of Eleazer, to Zadok, who, for a time, had been co-high priest with Abiathar (Antiquities 7.5.4). Zadok's son Shallam was the father of Hilkiah was the chief leader during the revival in 621 BC under Mosiah, who was the ancestor Ezra (Ezra 7:1-2) as well as Jehozadak (Jozadak), high priest under Zerubbabel when the Israelites returned from the exile.

[7] Abiathar. When Abiathar's family was executed by Saul, Abiathar fled to David, bringing the ephod, by which David inquired of the Lord (1 Samuel 22:20-23; 23:6). Abiathar was deposed when he supported Solomon's brother Adonijah for the kingship, when David was on his deathbed. Zadok and Nathan the prophet supported Solomon (1 Kings 2:26-27).

[8] Ahimaaz. 1 Chronicles 6:8, 53; 2 Samuel 15:27, 36; 17:17, 20; 18:19ff.

[9] Jonathan was loyal to David while Absalom reigned in Jerusalem. He carried news from his father Abiathar to David (2 Samuel 15:27, 36; 17:17, 20; 1 Kings 1:42f).

Appendix 2. Genealogy of the House of Saul

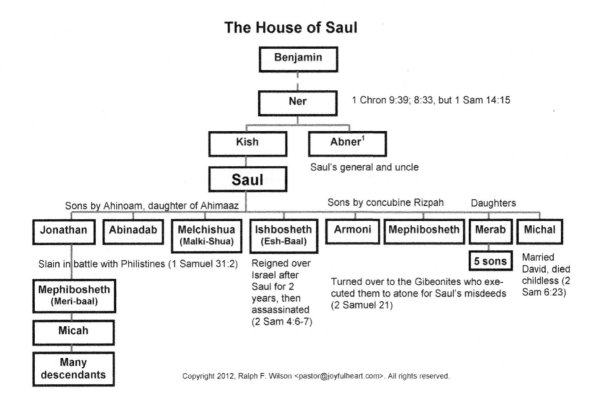

The House of Saul

Benjamin

Ner — 1 Chron 9:39; 8:33, but 1 Sam 14:15

Kish   Abner[1]

Saul's general and uncle

Saul

Sons by Ahinoam, daughter of Ahimaaz

Sons by concubine Rizpah   Daughters

Jonathan | Abinadab | Melchishua (Malki-Shua) | Ishbosheth (Esh-Baal) | Armoni | Mephibosheth | Merab | Michal

Slain in battle with Philistines (1 Samuel 31:2)

Mephibosheth (Meri-baal)

Micah

Many descendants

Reigned over Israel after Saul for 2 years, then assassinated (2 Sam 4:6-7)

Turned over to the Gibeonites who executed them to atone for Saul's misdeeds (2 Samuel 21)

5 sons

Married David, died childless (2 Sam 6:23)

Appendix 3. Genealogy of the House of David

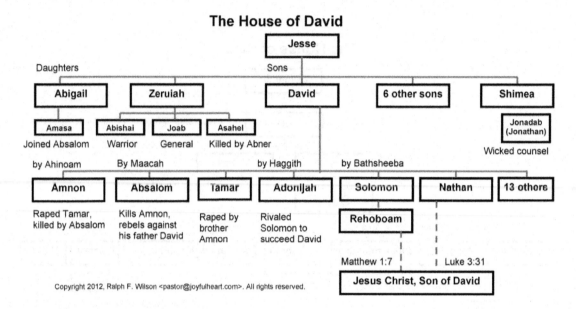

The House of David

Jesse

Daughters — Sons

Abigail | Zeruiah | David | 6 other sons | Shimea

Amasa — Joined Absalom
Abishai — Warrior
Joab — General
Asahel — Killed by Abner

Jonadab (Jonathan) — Wicked counsel

by Ahinoam | By Maacah | by Haggith | by Bathsheeba

Amnon | Absalom | Tamar | Adonijah | Solomon | Nathan | 13 others

Amnon — Raped Tamar, killed by Absalom
Absalom — Kills Amnon, rebels against his father David
Tamar — Raped by brother Amnon
Adonijah — Rivaled Solomon to succeed David

Rehoboam

Matthew 1:7 — Luke 3:31

Jesus Christ, Son of David

Appendix 4. A Chronology of David's Life

The absolute date of David's reign is based primarily on counting backwards from a fixed event, the Battle of Qarqar in 853 BC, in which Israel's King Ahab took part, as recorded on the Kurkh stela.[1] It's pretty complex when you get into it. K.A. Kitchen determines the date for David's 40-year reign to be from about 1010 to 970 BC.[2]

It is difficult to pinpoint relative dates for events in David's life. The primary scripture with relative dates of David's life follows:

> "David was thirty years old when he became king, and he reigned forty years. In Hebron he reigned over Judah seven years and six months, and in Jerusalem he reigned over all Israel and Judah thirty-three years." (2 Samuel 5:4-5; cf. 1 Kings 2:11)

Here and there the scripture tells us the number of years for some event. But the rest of the dates in David's life are only approximate, suppositions based on the amount of time something might take.

Date	David's Age	Event	Reference
1040	-	David born	2 Samuel 5:4
	~15-20	David and Goliath	
1012	~25-30	David is a fugitive from Saul[3]	
1010	30	David becomes king at Hebron	2 Samuel 5:4-5
1003	37	David becomes king over all Israel and conquers Jerusalem	2 Samuel 5:4-5
	~37-47	Palace built, Philistine and Aramean campaigns	
	~47	David's kingdom established	
	~47	David sins with Bathsheba	
	~45-50[4]	Amnon rapes Tamar	

[1] Baldwin, *1 and 2 Samuel*, p. 19.

[2] K.A. Kitchen, "Chronology," DOTHB, 183-184. K.A. Kitchen, *On the Reliability of the Old Testament* (Eerdmans, 2003), pp. 82-83. So John N. Oswalt, "Chronology of the OT," ISBE 1:673-685.

[3] Bright (*History*, p. 194, fn. 23) says, "Saul's death end came within a very few years after he had driven David from him, perhaps three or four years at the outside. David's stay in Philistia was only a bit over a year (1 Samuel 27:7) – and his outlaw days perhaps two or three years (?)"

Date	David's Age	Event	Reference
	~47-52	Absalom kills Amnon, flees to Geshur, stays 3 years	2 Samuel 13:38
	~52-57	Absalom returns to Jerusalem	2 Samuel 14:28
	~54-59	Absalom sees David's face after 2 years in Jerusalem	2 Samuel 14:28
	~56-61	Absalom wins the hearts of Israel over 4 years	2 Samuel 15:7
	~61	Absalom becomes king in Hebron, David flees Jerusalem	
	~62	Absalom killed	
	~62-63	Sheba's rebellion	
	~65-67	David becomes exhausted in Philistine battle	2 Sam 21:15
	~69	Adonijah and Solomon vie for the throne.	
970	70	David dies	2 Samuel 5:4-5; cf. 1 Kings 2:11

---

[4] If David were 45, Amnon, Absalom, and Tamar would be no older than 15. If he were 50, they wouldn't be any older than 20 (Michael A. Whitney, "Lessons from the Life of David" (Navigators of Maine, 2009)

Appendix 5. The Tabernacle of David Today (2 Samuel 6:17; Acts 15:16)

"They brought the ark of the LORD and set it in its place inside **the tent that David had pitched** for it, and David sacrificed burnt offerings and fellowship offerings before the LORD." (2 Samuel 6:17)

"After this I will return and rebuild **David's fallen tent**.
Its ruins I will rebuild, and I will restore it...." (Acts 15:16)

What is the relationship to the tent (*'ōhel*) David pitched for the ark and David's tent that will be restored?

James quotes a prophecy by Amos at the Council of Jerusalem (Acts 15:16-18).

"'In that day I will restore **David's fallen tent** (*sukkâ*).
I will repair its broken places, restore its ruins,
and build it as it used to be,
 so that they may possess the remnant of Edom
and all the nations that bear my name,'
declares the LORD, who will do these things." (Amos 9:11-12)

"'After this I will return and rebuild **David's fallen tent**.
Its ruins I will rebuild, and I will restore it,
that the remnant of men may seek the Lord,
and all the Gentiles who bear my name,'
says the Lord, who does these things,
'that have been known for ages.'"(Acts 15:16-18)

The word translated "tabernacle" or "tent" or "booth" in Amos is *sukkâ*, "covert, thicket, booth, a temporary abode." It is often used in connection with the Feast of Tabernacles or Feast of Booths. Once a year the Israelite left his home to tabernacle in a 'booth' made from tree branches.[1] However, the term used in the Pentateuch for the "tent of meeting" and our passage, "the tabernacle that David had pitched for it" (6:17) is a different word (*'ōhel*), the more common word for "dwelling, habitation, home," as

---

[1] R.D. Patterson, *sākak*, TWOT #1492d.

well as "tabernacle, tent." It is used figuratively for David's palace (1 Kings 8:66; Isaiah 16:5).[2]

In our day you'll sometimes find a teaching in Pentecostal and Charismatic circles based on these verses to this effect. David instituted singing worship and prophecy in the tabernacle he pitched in Jerusalem (spelled out in 1 Chronicles 15). Amos' prophecy, quoted in the New Testament relates to the restoration of worship that is being fulfilled in our time.

David Allan Hubbard outlines four possible interpretations for "booth of David" in the Amos passage.

1. **Judah's Davidic dynasty**, which had collapsed (fallen) at the hands of the Babylonians (which assumes a later date for Amos).

2. **Judah's Davidic dynasty's influence**, which had been diminished ever since the dividing of the kingdom under Rehoboam.

3. **The City of Jerusalem**, as depicted in Isaiah 1:8 as "a *shelter* in a vineyard, like a hut in a field of melons, like a city under siege."

4. **A return to the premonarchic period** when David championed the cause of the peasantry before capturing Jerusalem. (Hubbard favors this interpretation.)[3]

5. **The restoration of worship** conducted in "the tent David had pitched" (a view taught by some Pentecostal groups).

If you study it carefully, the Amos passage seems to require some kind of *political* interpretation, since the restoration includes possessing territory – perhaps the same territory that David had ruled over in his prime.

My own conclusion is that instead interpreting "the tabernacle of David" (in Amos and Acts) *literally* as "the tent David had pitched" for the ark – thus speaking of a restoration of Davidic worship – the Amos passage refers to a restoration of David's realm, that is the Kingdom of God that will be ushered in by the Messiah. Having said that, I *do* believe that God has been bringing a renewal of worship in the Church since the Charismatic Renewal of the 1960s and 1970s, though I don't think that's what Amos is referring to.

[2] Jack P. Lewis, *'āhal*, TWOT #32a.

[3] David Allan Hubbard, *Joel and Amos: An Introduction and Commentary* (Tyndale Old Testament Commentaries; Inter-Varsity Press, 1989), pp. 239-240.

Appendix 6. Considering David's Deceit – The Ethics of Lying

It troubles us to see David lying. Is this right? While we can't discuss all the ramifications of truth-telling here, let's look briefly at some of the issues.

Part of it depends on how you define lying. *Merriam Webster's Collegiate Dictionary* defines "lie" as "to make an untrue statement with intent to deceive." *Baker's Dictionary of Christian Ethics* is more nuanced. It defines lying as

"the intention to deceive when we are bound to speak or do the truth."[1]

This second definition makes a distinction related to the circumstances of the lie – "when we are bound to speak or do the truth."

Lying in War

When they think about it, most Christians would probably agree that, while not ideal, lying to the enemy is acceptable in war.

1. Homeowners sometimes put the lights in their houses on timers when they leave, for the purpose of deceiving burglars into believing that they might be home.

2. Dutch Christians hiding Jews from the Nazis wouldn't tell the Gestapo, when asked, if they were harboring Jews.

3. War strategy uses all sorts of methods to deceive an enemy – camouflage, misinformation, troop movements intended as feints to distract an enemy from the main attack, etc.

Maybe so. But it isn't always so clear cut. Is it acceptable for the police to use deceit when interrogating suspects in a crime? Is it acceptable to lie to deceive business competitors in order to gain greater marketshare? Is it acceptable to deceive customers by marketing copy that makes untrue or unproved claims concerning their products?

The standard in the Old Testament is stated clearly in the Ninth Commandment:

"You shall not bear false witness against your neighbor." (Exodus 20:16)

---

[1] Ralph H. Alexander, "Lying," *Baker's Dictionary of Christian Ethics* (Carl F.H. Henry, editor; Canon Press/Baker, 1973), pp. 400-401.

Clearly, in a court of law, you must not speak falsely, because the court has a right to know "the truth, the whole truth, and nothing but the truth." Otherwise, the court can't act justly for the good of society and the protection of the innocent. The ethical definition that adds, "when we are bound to speak or do the truth" is useful in helping us determine when we must always tell the truth.

Similarly, you have an obligation to be honest with your spouse – he or she has a right to know the truth because your lives are bound together. We are also bound together with Christians in God's family:

> "Therefore each of you must put off falsehood and speak truthfully to his neighbor, for we are all members of one body." (Ephesians 4:25)

We know that sometimes we shouldn't tell a person the truth when it might hurt them. However, we need to be extremely careful, since we can be very self-serving in our bending of the rules.

One side of the coin is to consider lying. The other side of the coin involves truth and faith. We serve "the God of truth" (Isaiah 65:16). We believe with Jesus, "Your word is truth" (John 17:17). If God isn't trustworthy, how can we believe on him? God is consistently true! He is our exemplar of trustworthiness and faithfulness. If we are men and women of God, then we must be men and women of truth. We must be believable.

There's quite a bit of deceit found in 1 and 2 Samuel. For example:

- Michal deceives Saul so David can escape (1 Samuel 19:17). The purpose is to protect an innocent person.
- David deceives Ahimelech the priest at Nob (1 Samuel 21:2). The purpose is to protect Ahimelech from knowingly helping a fugitive from the king. But Ahimelech ended up being killed anyway.
- David feigns madness before Achish king of Gath (1 Samuel 21:10-15). The purpose is to protect himself from being killed by his nation's enemies, the Philistines.
- David deceives Achish concerning where he had raided (1 Samuel 27:10). It isn't clear that this involves either war or protecting the innocent.
- Saul deceives the witch of Endor as to his true identity (1 Samuel 28:12).
- Amnon deceives his sister Tamar by feigning sickness in order to rape her (2 Samuel 13:6-14).
- Absalom slays Amnon to avenge his sister Tamar (2 Samuel 13:24-28).
- Absalom deceives when he begins his conspiracy to become king (2 Samuel 15:7).

- Hushai deceives Absalom (2 Samuel 16:15-19). This is deceiving an enemy in war.

- David's spy network deceives Absalom's men at En Rogel (2 Samuel 17:20). This is deceiving an enemy in war.

It seems clear that *sometimes* it is permissible to lie, such as in war, to protect innocent life, or to keep people from harm. However, since we humans find it easy to justify whatever action we desire to take, no matter how wrong it might be, we need to be extremely careful to be truth tellers.

Our standard of behavior must be Jesus, who started many of his most important sayings with, "Truly, truly, I say to you...." We serve a God of truth! Let us rise to his high standard.

Appendix 7. Locations of the Ark and the Tabernacle

	Tabernacle	Ark
Wilderness (at various encampments for about 38 years)	X	X
Shiloh (after the Conquest, Joshua 18:1; Judges 18:31). The ark was lost in a battle with the Philistines (1 Samuel 4)	X	X
Philistine cities (1 Samuel 6, 7 months)		X
Kiriath-Jearim, house of Abinadab (1 Samuel 7:1-2; many years)		X
Gibeon at the high place (unknown duration; 1 Chronicles 16:39; 2 Chronicles 1:3-6, 13)	X	
House of Obed-edom (3 months; 2 Samuel 6:10-12)		X
Jerusalem, in a tent David pitched for it (2 Samuel 6:17), while sacrifices continue at the Tabernacle at the high place of Gibeon (1 Chronicles 16:37-40)		X
Jerusalem. Solomon's Temple now replaces the ancient Tabernacle at Gibeon (1 Kings 8).		X
Babylon. The temple is destroyed and the ark was captured in 587 BC by the Babylonians, who apparently took it with other items of the temple to Babylon (2 Kings 25:9, 13-15; 2 Chronicles 36:18; 2 Esdras 10:21-23). The ark was apparently never found again (Jeremiah 3:16).		X

Appendix 8. David's Psalms of Repentance (Psalms 51 and 32)

If you have time, you might want to consider in conjunction with Lesson 10, "David's Rise, Fall, and Punishment" (2 Samuel 8-12), David's two penitential psalms – Psalm 51 and 32 give us some wonderful insights into the depth of sin and the wonder of God's grace. I've included them in this appendix to keep Lesson 10 at a manageable length. If you're studying this with a group, this appendix could serve as an additional lesson.[1]

Stained glass window, St. Wenedlin Catholic Church, St. Henry, Ohio. Photo © Russ Martin, AKA Steeple Chaser. Used by permission of the photographer. Artist is unknown.

Psalm 51 – Create in Me a Clean Heart, O Lord

How did David deal with this terrible fall from grace? The ascription to Psalm 51 reads,

> "For the director of music. A psalm of David. When the prophet Nathan came to him after David had committed adultery with Bathsheba."

This psalm provides some tremendous insights into David's spiritual recovery from a place of arrogance and callousness towards God's voice. I encourage you to read the psalm right now, then we'll look at a few verses in particular.

Pleading for God's Mercy (Psalm 51:1-2)

> "[1]Have mercy on me, O God,
> according to your unfailing love;

---

[1] This appendix is adapted from Chapter 11 of my book *Experiencing the Psalms* (JesusWalk Publications, 2007, 2010). http://www.jesuswalk.com/books/psalms.htm

according to your great compassion
blot out my transgressions.
[2]Wash away all my iniquity
and cleanse me from my sin." (Psalm 51:1-2)

David begins by calling out for mercy. Why? Because he recognizes that God's revealed character is one of love and compassion. From the time of Moses, God has revealed himself as "the compassionate and gracious God," who forgives sin (Exodus 34:6). David calls upon the God based on his known merciful character.

- **"Have mercy"** (*ḥānan*) means "be gracious, pity … a heartfelt response by some-one who has something to give to one who has a need."[2]

- **"Unfailing love"** (NIV), "lovingkindness" (KJV), and "steadfast love" (NRSV) translate the common Hebrew noun *ḥesed*, which includes the ideas love, faith-fulness, good-heartedness, kindness.[3]

- **"Compassion"** (NIV), "tender mercies" (KJV), and "mercy" (NRSV) represent the Hebrew noun *raḥămîm*, "tender mercy, compassion, deep love."[4]

David knows he doesn't deserve forgiveness, so he calls on God's character of mercy to remove his sins. He asks for renewal, purity, and pardon.

"… Blot out my transgressions.
Wash away all my iniquity
and cleanse me from my sin." (Psalm 51:1b-2)

- **"Blot out"** (*māḥā*) means "wipe, wipe out,"[5] here "removing a stain."

- **"Wash away"** (NIV, *kābas*) or "wash thoroughly" (KJV, NRSV) here and in verse 7b means "wash, be washed, perform the work of a fuller," that is "to make stuffs clean and soft by treading, kneading and beating them in cold water."[6]

- **"Cleanse"** (*ṭāhēr*) means "be pure, be clean." The word is used of wind sweeping the skies clear and the purifying of silver, of moral purity as well ritual purity.[7]

Confessing and Acknowledging Sin (Psalm 51:3-5)

Notice especially verse 4:

[2] Edwin Yamauchi, *ḥānan*, TWOT #694.
[3] R. Laird Harris, *ḥesed*, TWOT #698.
[4] Leonard J. Coppes, *rāḥam*, TWOT #2146a.
[5] Walter C. Kaiser, *māḥā*, TWOT #1178.
[6] KB, p. 422, cited in John N. Oswalt, *kābas*, TWOT #946.
[7] Edwin Yamauchi, *ṭāhēr*, TWOT #792.

"Against you, you only, have I sinned
and done what is evil in your sight."

Does this mean that David's sins against Bathsheba and her husband Uriah were meaningless, inconsequential? No, not at all. But David recognizes that the greatest sin of all is against the Lord that he purports to love. When he sins, he is flaunting his rebellion in God's face. Yes, we can sin against people and need to make these sins right (Matthew 5:23). But our sin is even more against our heavenly Father. It is *that* breach that must be healed at all costs.

Hungering for Fellowship Once More (Psalm 51:6-12)

David has painted his iniquity in clear colors. Now he begins to contrast his own sinfulness with what God desires. He looks within. Sinfulness is not primarily in one's actions, but in one's heart.

"Surely you desire truth in the inner parts; [8]
you teach me wisdom in the inmost place." (Psalm 51:6)

It is this inner person who must be converted and cleansed and discipled. Our actions (when we are not putting on an act for others) flow from this inner person, from our heart of hearts.

He offers a prayer for deep cleansing:

"Cleanse[9] me with hyssop, [10] and I will be clean;
wash me, and I will be whiter than snow." (Psalm 51:7)

If God cleanses him, if God washes him, then he will be "whiter than snow."

While he has been separated from God he has withered. Now he longs for the joy of the Lord once again:

"Let me hear joy and gladness;
let the bones you have crushed rejoice." (Psalm 51:8)

---

[8] The noun *ṭuḥōt* describes an object "covered over, hidden, or concealed," carrying the idea of the inner being of a person covered up by the body (Ralph H. Alexander, *ṭûah*, TWOT #795b). The parallel idea in 6b is of an "inmost place" (NIV), "hidden part" (KJV), "secret heart" (NRSV), from the word *sātam*, "stop up, shut up, keep close" (*sātam*, TWOT #1550). In the New Testament Paul talks about the "inner being" (Romans 7:22), the "new self" (Ephesians 4:24; Colossians 3:9). Peter uses the expression of "the inner self" (NIV, 1 Peter 3:4) or "the hidden man of the heart" (KJV).

[9] The verb *ḥāṭā'* which means "sin, miss the way" in the Qal stem, means in the Piel and Hithpael stems "to make a sin offering" or a cleansing or purifying ceremony during which sin is done away with (G. Herbert Livingston, *ḥāṭā'*, TWOT #638). See Exodus 12:22; Leviticus 14:4-6, 49-52; Numbers 19:6, 17-19; Hebrews 9:19, John 19.29.

[10] Hyssop is a small plant that grows on walls, probably marjoram in the mint family. It was used in purification ceremonies to apply blood and water (Herbert Wolf, *'ēzōb*, TWOT #55).

"Restore to me the joy of your salvation." (Psalm 51:12a)

In verse 12a, the word "restore" (*shûb*), "turn back, return," carries the idea of "give back, restore."[11] David has known the joy of God's salvation and rescue before. Now he longs for this joy in fellowship to be restored to him once more. It is his earnest prayer.

Have you lost the "joy" of your salvation? Have you become somewhat distant from God? Have you taken God for granted? Or perhaps have you never really gotten to know him. God wants to restore the joy to you that is your birthright as a Christian. Joy is a fruit of the Holy Spirit's work in your life (Galatians 5:22-23). Call out to him in repentance and receive the joy God desires for you.

Q1. (Psalm 51:1-9) It seems that in verses 1-9 David emphasizes God's mercy, his own sinfulness, and the completeness of God's hoped for cleansing. Is it healthy to dwell on your own sinfulness? Why or why not? Does a person who has sinned greatly appreciate forgiveness more than one who has not? Why or why not?
http://www.joyfulheart.com/forums/index.php?showtopic=1207

The Longing for a Pure Heart (Psalm 51:10, 12)

David also prays for a pure heart and a willing spirit.

"**Create**[12] in me a **pure**[13] heart, O God,
and renew a steadfast spirit within me." (Psalm 51:10)

"and grant me a **willing spirit**, to sustain me." (Psalm 51:12b)

But isn't he asking for too much? David has been a slave to lust, drunk with power, stained by murder. How can he now pray for a pure heart? Isn't it too late? No. Can we be pure again once we've been corrupted? Yes. God spoke to Peter, "Do not call anything impure that God has made clean" (Acts 10:15). God is in the heart purification business. The author of Hebrews wrote:

---

[11] *Shûb*, BDB 999, Hiphil 1d.

[12] "Create" (*bārā'*) in this verse carries the connotation of "to initiate something new" (Thomas E. McComiskey, TWOT #278). A different synonym for "create," is *yāsar*, which suggests "to fashion, to shape something new."

[13] "Pure" (NIV) or "clean" (KJV) comes from *ṭāhēr* which we saw in 51:2, "to cleanse," used of ritual or moral purity and of the pureness of the unalloyed gold of the temple furniture (Edwin Yamauchi, TWOT #792).

"How much more, then, will the blood of Christ, who through the eternal Spirit offered himself unblemished to God, cleanse our consciences from acts that lead to death, so that we may serve the living God!" (Hebrews 9:14)

Do you feel unforgiven? Unforgivable? Jesus died for your sins and he desires to forgive you, no matter what you have done. Pray this prayer with David:

"Create in me a pure heart, O God,
and **renew**[14] a **steadfast**[15] **spirit** within me." (Psalm 51:10)

In verse 12b he prays for a "willing spirit"[16] (NIV, NRSV) or to be upheld by God's "free spirit" (KJV). Oh, for a spirit that longs to serve God, a heart that is inclined to him!

Do Not Take Your Holy Spirit from Me (Psalm 51:11)

Now David prays against his great fear:

"Do not cast me from your presence
or take your Holy Spirit from me." (Psalm 51:11)

As we observed in Lesson 1, David received the Holy Spirit at the same time as Saul lost God's Spirit. So David is terrified that in his sin this would happen to him as well, that God's Spirit will desert him. But he repents and trusts God nevertheless.

Q2. (Psalm 51:10-11) In what way can God give us a "pure heart" after great sin? How would you define a pure heart? How does God purify our hearts? How does he purify our minds?

http://www.joyfulheart.com/forums/index.php?showtopic=1208

Resolving to Declare God's Grace (Psalm 51:13-15)

Now David looks forward to the answer to his prayer and how he will serve God.

---

[14] ḥādash, "repair, renew, rebuild" (Carl Philip Weber, TWOT #613).

[15] "Right" (KJV, NRSV) or "steadfast" (NIV) is kûn, "established, prepared, made ready, fixed, certain, right" (John N. Oswalt, TWOT #964). "The root meaning is to bring something into being with the consequence that its existence is a certainty."

[16] The adjective nādīb, "noble, willing, inclined," is from the root nādab, "make willing, incite, an uncompelled and free movement of the will unto divine service or sacrifice" (Leonard J. Coppes, nādab, TWOT #1299b).

"[13]Then I will teach transgressors your ways,
and sinners will turn back to you.
[14]Save me from **bloodguilt**,[17] O God,
the God who saves me,
and my tongue will sing of your righteousness.
[15]O Lord, open my lips,
and my mouth will declare your praise." (Psalm 51:13-15)

Offering the Sacrifice of a Contrite Heart (Psalm 51:16-17)

David compares true repentance to ritual sacrifice, but he realizes:

"The sacrifices of God are a **broken spirit**;
a broken and contrite heart,
O God, you will not despise." (Psalm 51:17)

David's pride has been broken (*shābar*). His heart is broken and contrite.[18] Until our hearts break with sorrow for our sin, we are not quite ready for forgiveness. So often, we are sad at being caught or exposed, but not sad at hurting the God who loves us or injuring his reputation by our sins (2 Samuel 12:14). Many conversions these days seem to lack the deep repentance that rends the heart (Joel 2:13). Oh, that our sins would break our hearts! The psalm concludes with a prayer for Jerusalem.

Q3. (Psalm 51:16-17) How does one achieve a truly "broken and contrite heart"? What are the earmarks of this condition? How does this differ from "being sorry" for a sin? How does humility relate to this condition?
http://www.joyfulheart.com/forums/index.php?showtopic=1209

Psalm 32 – Blessed Is the One Whose Sin Is Forgiven

Another psalm that reflects David's reflection on the agony of sin, the struggle to confess, and the blessedness of forgiveness is Psalm 32.

---

[17] Bloodguilt (*dām*, "blood") was the sin of shedding innocent blood, considered a mortal sin. In David's case, he had ordered the death of Uriah, Bathsheba's husband. TWOT #436; BDB 197, g.

[18] "Contrite" is *dākă*, a by-form of the verb *dk'*, which also means "to crush," and of *dûk*, "to pound, beat." The verb is consistently used of one who is physically and emotionally crushed because of sin or the onslaught of an enemy (Herbert Wolf, *dākă*, TWOT #428).

Blessed Is the Forgiven Person (32:1-2)

David begins his sonnet of guilt and forgiveness with a comment on how fortunate the forgiven person really is:

> "[1]Blessed is he
> whose transgressions (*pesha'*) are forgiven,
> whose sins (*hattā't*) are covered.
> [2]Blessed is the man
> whose sin (*'āwōn*) the LORD does not count against him
> and in whose spirit is no deceit." (32:1-2)

David uses several synonyms for sin and guilt in Psalms 32 and 51, each with its own flavor:

- **"Transgression"** (*pesha'*) means "rebellion, revolt," designating those who reject God's authority.[19]

- **"Sin"** (*hattā't* and *hēt'*) from the root *hātā'* that means to miss a mark or miss the way.[20]

- **"Iniquity"** (*'āwōn*), is "infraction, crooked behavior, perversion, iniquity, etc." from a root that means "to bend, twist, distort."[21]

- **"Deceit"** (NIV, NRSV) or "guile" (KJV) is *remiyyâ*, "deceit, fraud."[22]

We sometimes try to rationalize and minimize our "weaknesses" and "mistakes." But David calls them for what they are – rebellion, revolt, iniquity. David also uses a pair of synonyms for forgiveness in verse 1:

- **Forgiven** (*nāśā'*), "lift, carry, take." Here the emphasis is on "taking away, forgiveness, or pardon of sin, iniquity and transgression." Sin can be forgiven and forgotten because it is taken up and carried away.[23]

- **Covered** (*kāsā*), "cover, conceal, hide." It is probably the meaning "hide" that leads to the sense "forgive."[24]

Given how sinful we can sometimes be, David is reflecting upon God's grace, his willingness to forgive. The Apostle Paul cites these verses as speaking "of the blessed-

---

[19] G. Herbert Livingston, *pāsha'*, TWOT #1846a.

[20] G. Herbert Livingston, *hātā'*, TWOT #638e.

[21] Carl Schultz, *'āwā*, TWOT #1577a.

[22] William White, *rāmā*, TWOT #2169a. Holladay sees two derivatives and thus two meanings for this word (I) "slackness, looseness" and (II) "deceit" (340b).

[23] Walter C. Kaiser, *nāśā'*, TWOT #1421.

[24] R. Laird Harris, *kāsā*, TWOT #1008.

ness of the man to whom God credits righteousness apart from works" (Romans 4:6-8). Is there genuine grace in the Old Testament? Oh, yes!

The Agony of Guilt (32:3-4)

How miserable we are when we try to wriggle away from our sins and avoid dealing with them:

> "³When I kept silent,
> my bones wasted away
> through my groaning all day long.
> ⁴For day and night
> your hand was heavy upon me;
> my strength was sapped
> as in the heat of summer. *Selah*." (32:3-4)

Why do we do this? The clue is found in verse 2:

> "Blessed is the man ... in whose spirit is no deceit." (32:2b)

It is this self-deceit in our inner person that is so self-destructive. We might know deep down that we've done something wrong, but at the surface level we rationalize our actions, refusing to admit the depth of our guilt. The result David describes from personal experience in verses 3 and 4 – a physical and emotional drain that takes its toll on the life. The key is to apply truth to the self-deceit. That is what the Word does for us, what pastors and counselors do in public exhortation and private counsel. When we apply lies to mask our sin, the result is ultimately unsatisfying. There is no secular substitute for forgiveness. The inner soul of a human being cries out for relief from guilt at some level.

The Freedom of Confession (32:5)

If this was the incident with Bathsheba and Uriah, then Nathan the prophet was the one God used to pierce David's wall of self-deceit with the truth (2 Samuel 12:3-15), like you might lance an infected boil. Whatever sin and guilt it was that was causing David inner turmoil, he finally found release through confession.

> "Then I acknowledged my sin to you
> and did not cover up my iniquity.
> I said, 'I will confess
> my transgressions to the LORD' –
> and you forgave
> the guilt of my sin. *Selah*." (32:5)

David uses three synonyms for confession:

- **"Acknowledge"** is *yāda'*, "notice, observe." In the Hiphil stem this word has the causative connotation, "let someone know something, inform, announce, make known."[25]

- **"Not cover up,"** that is, *not* to pretend it didn't happen or wasn't important.

- **"Confess"** is *yādā*, "to acknowledge or confess sin." We've seen this verb often in our studies of praise psalms, since it is translated "praise, give thanks, thank," in the sense of to acknowledge or confess God's character and works.[26]

In a reaction to the Catholic practice of confession and absolution, many Protestants have let the pendulum swing far in the other direction, imagining that they have no need of confession or a confessor. Yes, we can and should confess our sins to God. But confessing our sins to a godly Christian leader can also help bring healing to the soul:

> "Therefore confess your sins to each other and pray for each other so that you may be healed. The prayer of a righteous man is powerful and effective." (James 5:16)

Q4. (Psalm 32:2-5) How does self-deceit operate with sin to enslave us? How does confession enable us to get free from sin? Why do we sometimes resist the truth about ourselves? What does it take to get us to see truth sometimes?
http://www.joyfulheart.com/forums/index.php?showtopic=1210

You Are My Hiding Place (32:6-7)

Now that sin is confessed and dealt with, the tenor of the psalm turns to an acknowledgement of God as Savior and Protector:

> "Therefore let everyone who is godly pray to you
> while you may be found." (32:6a)

David urges praying to the Lord "while you may be found," implying that there are definite times when God is near and accessible to us, and times when because of our sin

---

[25] *Yāda'*, Holladay 129b.
[26] Ralph H. Alexander, *yādā*, TWOT #847.

or hardness we just are unable or unwilling to come to him. We must take advantage of the opportunity to draw close to him. A few centuries later, Isaiah wrote:

> "Seek the LORD while he may be found;
> call on him while he is near.
> Let the wicked forsake his way
> and the evil man his thoughts.
> Let him turn to the LORD, and he will have mercy on him,
> and to our God, for he will freely pardon." (Isaiah 55:6-7)

When we do make peace with God, then we have his promise of protection:

> "6bSurely when the mighty waters rise,
> they will not reach him.
> 7You are my hiding place;
> you will protect me from trouble
> and surround me with songs of deliverance. *Selah.* " (Psalm 32:6b-7)

I've heard skeptics disparage the concept of God as a Protector as a crutch for the weak. But this comes from an arrogance that has never faced the "mighty waters" of life, the overwhelming enemies. In chapter 6 we examined psalms of protection, especially Psalm 91:1 that addresses, "He who dwells in the shelter of the Most High." Here "shelter, secret place" (*sēter*) is the same word as "hiding place" in 32:7, from *sātar*, "hide, conceal," with the idea of protection.[27]

The shouts or "songs of deliverance" in verse 7 that surround us are what you would expect in the camp of the victorious army, not in a fear-filled hovel. God both protects us and encourages our faith.

A Call to Teachability rather than Stubbornness (32:8-11)

We have heard the psalmist's voice. But now God speaks through David a promise and an admonition:

> "8I will instruct you and teach you in the way you should go;
> I will counsel you and watch over you.
> 9Do not be like the horse or the mule,
> which have no understanding
> but must be controlled by bit and bridle
> or they will not come to you.
> 10Many are the woes of the wicked,

---

[27] R. D. Patterson, *sātar*, TWOT #1551a.

> but the LORD's unfailing love
> surrounds the man who trusts in him." (32:8-10)

Once the Lord has cleansed us from guilt and sin, and brought us into his protective care, he wants to teach us and instruct us. He uses the metaphor of a stubborn horse or mule that will only come to their master when forced to by a bit and bridle. Don't be like that, the Lord says, let me teach you. Let my "unfailing love" (ḥesed) surround you. Don't resist me. Sin causes us to run away from God, to "kick against the goads" (Acts 26:14). Relax, let your rebellion and sin go, and hear his words of instruction in a safe place.

Q5. (Psalm 32:8-10) How does sin make us stubborn? Why is it nearly impossible to discern God's will for us when we hold on to unconfessed sin?
http://www.joyfulheart.com/forums/index.php?showtopic=1211

The psalm concludes with a call to praise:

> "Rejoice in the LORD and be glad, you righteous;
> sing, all you who are upright in heart!" (32:11)

Prayer

Father, thank you for the blessing of forgiveness that we experience by the grace of Christ our Savior. We take so much for granted! Thank you for cleansing and for a new heart. In Jesus' name, we pray. Amen.

Key Verses

> "Against you, you only, have I sinned
> and done what is evil in your sight." (Psalm 51:4)

> "Surely you desire truth in the inner parts;
> you teach me wisdom in the inmost place.
> Cleanse me with hyssop, and I will be clean;
> wash me, and I will be whiter than snow." (Psalm 51:6-7)

"Create in me a pure heart, O God,
and renew a steadfast spirit within me.
Do not cast me from your presence
or take your Holy Spirit from me." (Psalm 51:10-11)

"The sacrifices of God are a broken spirit;
a broken and contrite heart,
O God, you will not despise." (Psalm 51:17)

"[1] Blessed is he whose transgressions are forgiven,
whose sins are covered.
[2] Blessed is the man whose sin the LORD does not count against him
and in whose spirit is no deceit.
[3] When I kept silent, my bones wasted away
through my groaning all day long.
[4] For day and night your hand was heavy upon me;
my strength was sapped as in the heat of summer. *Selah*.

[5] Then I acknowledged my sin to you
and did not cover up my iniquity.
I said, 'I will confess my transgressions to the LORD' –
and you forgave the guilt of my sin." (32:1-5)

"You are my hiding place;
you will protect me from trouble
and surround me with songs of deliverance. " (Psalm 32:7)

Appendix 9. Participant Handout Guides

If you're working with a class or small group, feel free to duplicate the following handouts at no additional charge. If you'd like to print 8-1/2" x 11" or A4 size pages, you can download the free Participant Guide handout sheets at:

www.jesuswalk.com/david/david-lesson-handouts.pdf

Discussion Questions

You'll typically find 3 to 4 questions for each lesson, depending on the topics in each lesson. Each question may include several sub-questions. These are designed to get group members engaged in discussion of the key points of the passage. If you're running short of time, feel free to skip questions or portions of questions. These notes also contain key maps and charts to help your students understand David's life.

Introduction to the Life of David
1. Samuel Anoints David as King (1 Samuel 15-16)
2. David and Goliath: Bold Faith (1 Samuel 17)
3. Jonathan's Friendship, Saul's Jealousy (1 Samuel 18-20)
4. David Flees from Saul (1 Samuel 21-23)
5. David Spares the Lord's Anointed (1 Samuel 24-28)
6. David Strengthens Himself in the Lord (1 Samuel 29-2 Samuel 1)
7. David Becomes King and Conquers Jerusalem (2 Samuel 2-5)
8. David Brings the Ark to Jerusalem (2 Samuel 6)
9. The Davidic Covenant (2 Samuel 7)
10. David's Rise, Fall, and Punishment (2 Samuel 8-12)
11. Rape, Murder, and Conspiracy in David's Family (2 Samuel 13:1-15:13)
12. David's Exile from Jerusalem (15:13-20:26)
13. The Legacy of David (2 Samuel 21-1 Kings 2)
    Optional: David's Psalms of Repentance (Psalms 51 and 32)

Because of the length of the these handouts (29 pages) – and to keep down the page count so we can keep the book price lower – they are being made available at no cost online. www.jesuswalk.com/david/david-lesson-handouts.pdf

CPSIA information can be obtained
at www.ICGtesting.com
Printed in the USA
LVOW04s0901250817

546067LV00010B/380/P

9 780984 734061